# An American Sailor's Treasury

# An American Sailor's Treasury

## Sea Songs, Chanteys, Legends, and Lore

*Two Volumes in One*

By **FRANK SHAY**

*Illustrations by EDWARD A. WILSON*

SMITHMARK

THIS EDITION PUBLISHED IN 1991 BY SMITHMARK PUBLISHERS INC., 112 MADISON AVENUE, NEW YORK, NEW YORK 10016

SMITHMARK BOOKS ARE AVAILABLE FOR BULK PURCHASE FOR SALES PROMOTIONS AND PREMIUM USE. FOR DETAILS WRITE OR TELEPHONE THE MANAGER OF SPECIAL SALES, SMITHMARK PUBLISHERS INC., 112 MADISON AVENUE, NEW YORK, NEW YORK 10016. (212) 532-6600.

0-8317-0288-5

PRINTED IN THE UNITED STATES OF AMERICA

# Contents

## AMERICAN SEA SONGS AND CHANTEYS

## FORECASTLE SONGS

## WARDROOM BALLADS

## MISCELLANEOUS SONGS AND BALLADS

# Contents
## *A Sailor's Treasury*

# AMERICAN SEA SONGS

# *AND*

# CHANTEYS

*from the days of*

## Iron Men and Wooden Ships

By FRANK SHAY

*Illustrated by*
EDWARD A. WILSON

*Musical Arrangements by*
CHRISTOPHER THOMAS

IN TRIBUTE
TO
NATHANIEL BOWDITCH
MATTHEW FONTAINE MAURY
DONALD McKAY

# Introduction

IN THE DAYS of iron men and wooden ships, when the motive power was human muscle and white canvas, it was the custom of American sailors to ease their work and their leisure with song. The songs they sang were the songs of their craft, chanteys and ballads of the sea. It is conceivable that at the beginning of a voyage the tailor-made songs of the shore enjoyed some favor, but sooner or later they were forgotten and the crew returned to their own melodies.

The work song, which we spell "chantey" and pronounce "shanty," was of the sailors' own making. The rhythm was supplied by the task; the words had to fit whether they made sense or not, and only too often had meanings known only to the sailors of the day. The wording was simple, direct, and the music often had a wild, spirited quality, salty as the sea and as rough as the waves in a storm. The songs were designed to lighten certain back-breaking tasks: the chorus lines, on which action was based, became rigid and changeless, but the solo lines were always at the mercy of the chanteyman and improvisation and parody were frequent. In singing, the chanteyman, who also put his back to the task, would sound off:

CHANTEYMAN: When I come ashore and get my pay,
CREW: Walk with me, Miss Edie, *do!*
CHANTEYMAN: On that bright and always sunny day,
CREW: Oh, my Edie, walk with me, *do!*

the final word in the chorus line being the signal for the men to fall back on the rope. There was much repetition and many verses,

17

though, as a short job song, a very few verses served for a task.

The chantey, though English in origin, early became American in content. The New York packets, beginning in 1818 with the famous Black Ball Line, brought the chantey into efficient use. These ships sailed on schedule; that is, they left their ports on stated dates and tried to make the fastest passage possible. To achieve this end the ships and their crews had to be driven, full sail was carried day and night, through fair weather and foul. The old methods of securing prompt action from the crew—a foul oath, a blow of the fist, or a taste of the rope's end—could not be employed in the presence of polite passengers. The work song became the rule, and a really good chanteyman was worth four men in a watch. Dana says, in *Two Years Before the Mast:* "A song is as necessary to sailors as the drum and fife to a soldier. They must pull together as soldiers must step in time, and they can't pull in time, or pull with a will, without it. Many a time, when a thing goes heavy, one fellow yo-ho-ing a lively song, like 'Heave, to the Girls!,' 'Nancy, O!,' 'Jack Crosstree,' 'Cheer'ly man,' has put life and strength into every arm."

Roughly the chanteys may be divided into three classes: capstan and windlass chanteys, used in catting or weighing anchor or hoisting sails; the halliard or long-drag chantey, used at topsails and topgallant sails; and the sheet, tack, and bowline songs, known as short-drag chanteys. Others, such as walkaways, hand-over-hand and pumping chanteys were, as a rule, adaptations of other work songs and ballads.

It is a mistake to think that the chantey went out with the full-rigged sailing ship; the old sailors went into steam, reluctantly it is true, and they took their gear and their songs with them. The newer men heard the songs and passed them on, even if they found little practical use for them. In steam there was no heavy heaving; steam did the work, and steam sings its own song. Though most of the back-breaking tasks were gone, the singers came and passed and the songs stayed on because of their character and charm and today are sung with as great enthusiasm as in the old days.

The songs of leisure were usually the story-ballads that followed closely the pattern of shore folk song: they honored woman, home, ships and battles, sobriety and the lack of it, and they deplored hard work, poor grub, and harsh treatment. Some of these songs were tailor-made and, contrary to general opinion, were liked and sung by sailors, especially those of the Navy. In fact, most Navy songs show the hand of the scrivener in rhyme and meter. There was no chanteying it up in the service, where all work was done in silence and in response to the boatswain's pipe. But in the wardrooms and at the scuttle butt much time was given to singing.

The old merchant sailors were not all the stupid oafs or the fools they have been pictured who, once ashore, got drunk and remained that way until their money was spent. There were plenty of that type, but there were many who, like Reuben Ranzo, studied navigation and made their way to the quarter-deck and eventual command of their own vessels. Many had families and hurried home as soon as their ships made port. They took care of themselves and when the wintry winds began to blow, when going aloft meant flirting with sudden death, exerted every effort to get shore jobs for the winter. Some went into the southern cotton packets for a voyage to Mobile or New Orleans; others went into the railway construction gangs, some to northern lumber camps. All these changes influenced their songs.

Many of the sailors' songs were and still are beautiful and an experience to hear. There is no song in the world quite like "Shenandoah," a capstan chantey that was also a favorite between watches. Its haunting melody was seldom heard ashore. "The Dreadnought," "The Yankee Man-of-War," "Home, Dearie, Home," and "Rolling Home" will live as long as men have voices to sing.

For all his rowdiness, his traditional use of profanity, the old sailor's songs for the most part remained unsullied while they stayed at sea. They closely followed the pattern of the singer's own life: he was clean and sober at sea and something else ashore. Yet some of the songs, beginning with simple decent verses, eventually wound up in obscenity. Shore songs have the same tendency.

Those of us who have heard the chanteys sung in their native habitat are often distressed by the efforts of shorebirds to animate them: most sound as though they were hillbilly ballads, which they emphatically are not. There is a rollicking, exuberant quality that is found in no other music—the rhythmic straining of human muscle, of hard breathing, of work going well, measured by sea legs and emitted from lungs filled with the salt sea air. But, as has been pointed out, the tasks that brought them into being are now gone and all must be sung without the original maritime activities.

There is an old Spanish story of a man loafing on the shore who saw a ship drawing near its wharf. The old sailorman at the wheel sang a wondrous sweet song, and, going to the pier, the idler asked him to repeat it, but the old sailor replied:

"I can sing the song to no one,
Save to him who sails with me."

# Acknowledgments

I HEARD my first chantey in 1915 while serving as a foremast hand aboard the tanker *Standard*. She took fire off Yucatan and her entire power plant was burned out; all subsequent work had to be done by hand. Another ship stood by to take us in tow, and heavy hawse lines were passed, only to part, and repassed, all handled by the small crew. Work was going poorly until a shipmate sounded off with "Whiskey for My Johnny." The song brought immediate results and others were broken out, mostly in fragments. By the time the *Standard* made port I had a small collection of the old chanteys: subsequent voyages increased my repertory.

The names of those shipmates and of the sailors met in shore traps have long been forgotten, but their songs have not nor have my recollections of a fine body of men. Certain shorebirds and sailors-who-have-swallowed-the-anchor have, during the intervening years, aided in the collection of my material. Grateful acknowledgment is made to Paul Chavchavadze, C. D. Harvey, Harry Kemp, Christopher Morley, William McFee, Eugene O'Neill and Charles B. Palmer for both material help and enthusiasm.

To Miss Joanna C. Colcord for permission to include material from her admirable *Songs of American Sailormen*.

To Arch H. Ferguson, of Brown, Son & Ferguson, Ltd., Glasgow, for selections from *Sea Songs and Shanties*, by Captain W. B. Whall.

To Duncan Emrich, chief of the Folklore Section, and to the staff of the Library of Congress.

To Harvard University Library, the New York Public Library, the Public Library of the City of Boston, and to the Wellfleet Public Library.

My indebtedness to my distinguished collaborators, Mr. Edward A. Wilson and Mr. Christopher Thomas is evident on every page of this book.

And to my wife, Edith Shay, for constant and painstaking aid and encouragement.

F.S.

FIDELITY

# Chanteys

# Away, Rio!

SAILING DAY for a famous clipper was always a gala affair. All the great ships had their fans who followed their careers, cheered their speedy passages, and often welcomed them home. But sailing day attracted the greatest crowds. In New York the ships were loaded at their East River wharves and then dropped down to the Battery to await the tide, to take on tardy foremast hands, and to receive final orders.

It was the first mate's day, it was his show and he knew that his future rating would be determined by the smart manner in which he got his vessel to sea. The sailors were not insensible to the drama of the moment and, drunk or sober, wanted to make the most of it. Captain and pilot were on the quarter-deck, with the captain's eye on his chronometer; the mate was on the forecastle, with his eye on the captain. As the tide prepares to ebb, the order is passed forward and the chief officer goes into action and snaps out his order: "Now, men and sogers both, heave away at the windlass. You, chanteyman, give us 'Rye-O!' and raise the decks, aye, raise the very dead. Heave and a-way!" And the rollin' bollin' words of the best of all outward-bound chanteys rolls across the water and brings cheers from the shorebirds.

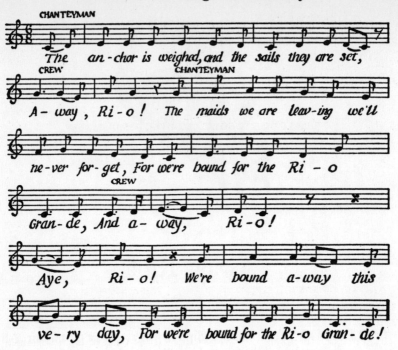

The anchor is weighed, and the sails they are set,
*Away, Rio!*
The maids we are leaving we'll never forget,
*For we're bound for the Rio Grande,*
*And away, Rio! Aye, Rio!*
*We're bound away this very day,*
*For we're bound for the Rio Grande!*

So it's pack up your donkey and get under way,
The girls we are leaving can take our half pay.

We've a jolly good ship and a jolly good crew,
A jolly good mate and a good skipper, too.

We'll sing as we heave to the maidens we leave,
And you who are listening, good-by to you.

Heave with a will and heave long and strong,
Sing the good chorus, for 'tis a good song.

Heave only one pawl, then 'vast heavin', belay!
Heave steady, because we say farewell today.

The chain's up and down, now the bosun did say,
*Away, Rio!*
Heave up to the hawsepipe, the anchor's aweigh.
*For we're bound for the Rio Grande,*
*And away, Rio! Aye, Rio!*
*We're bound away this very day,*
*We're bound for the Rio Grande!*

Once the anchor is apeak, the chief mate turns to the quarter-deck and, receiving his orders from the captain, cries: "Lay aloft there, ye walkin' corpses, and loose all sails!" The second and third mates, the bosun, and the bosun's mate rush to their stations, repeating orders and checking the progress of the work. But the first mate's men had the jump and the foremast is the first to break out white, followed quickly and in decent order by the main and mizzen masts. Other chanteys break out, and from the shore comes another great cheer that puts even more heart and brawn into the crew. The pilot goes to the helm, the ship moves, and a new voyage has begun.

# Sally Brown

THERE WERE a lot of girls in Jack's shore life, but Sally Brown was the belle of them all. To her were attributed all the virtues of a good wife and all the vices of a strumpet. Although she hailed from New York City, she was seen in almost every port and was as great a favorite with the English as with Americans. Often she was sung to more cozily and intimately than in the present version, which was used as a capstan chantey.

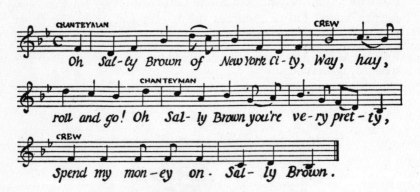

Oh, Sally Brown, of New York City,
*Way, hay, roll and go!*
Oh, Sally Brown you're very pretty,
*Spend my money on Sally Brown!*

30

Oh, Sally Brown's a bright mulatto,
   *Way, hay, roll and go!*
She drinks rum and chews tobacco,
   *Spend my money on Sally Brown!*

Oh, Sally Brown's a Creole lady,
   *Way, hay, roll and go!*
She's the mother of a yellow baby,
   *Spend my money on Sally Brown!*

Seven long years I courted Sally,
   *Way, hay, roll and go!*
Sweetest girl in all the valley,
   *Spend my money on Sally Brown!*

Seven long years and she wouldn't marry,
   *Way, hay, roll and go!*
And I no longer cared to tarry,
   *Spend my money on Sally Brown!*

So I courted Sal, her only daughter,
   *Way, hay, roll and go!*
For her I sail upon the water,
   *Spend my money on Sally Brown!*

Sally's teeth are white and pearly,
   *Way, hay, roll and go!*
Her eyes are blue, her hair is curly,
   *Spend my money on Sally Brown!*

Now my troubles are all over,
   *Way, hay, roll and go!*
Sally's married to a dirty soldier,
   *Spend my money on Sally Brown!*

# The Dead Horse

WHEN A SAILOR shipped aboard a vessel for a new voyage, he was often in debt to his boardinghouse, his tavern, or to the owners for clothing and gear. This debt, called the "horse," had to be worked out before he was again on the receiving end. When he was free and clear of the debt, his horse was said to be dead.

They say old man your horse will die,
*And they say so and they hope so.*
Oh, poor old man your horse will die,
*Oh, poor old man!*

For thirty * days I've ridden him,
*And they say so, and they hope so.*
And when he dies we'll tan his skin,
*Oh, poor old man!*

And if he lives, I'll ride him again,
*And they say so, and they hope so.*
I'll ride him with a tighter rein.
*Oh, poor old horse!*

It's up aloft the horse must go,
*They say so, and they hope so.*
We'll hoist him up and bury him low.
*Oh, poor old horse!*

* or sixty or ninety days.

# Five Short-Drag Chanteys

THE SHORT-DRAG CHANTEY is the oldest form of sailors' work songs and to modern ears probably the least entertaining. They were, as the title indicates, used in short, quick hauls, when the fore, main, or crossjack sheets were hauled aft and the bowlines tautened and made fast. "Haul on the Bowline" is reputedly the oldest of all chanteys, dating from the time of England's Henry the Eighth. Modern usage has enlivened "Haul Away, Joe!"

## Haul on the Bowline

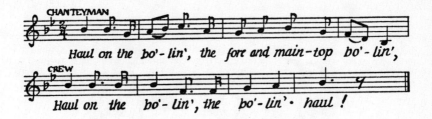

Haul on the bo'lin', the fore and maintop bo'lin',
    Haul on the bo'lin', the bo'lin' *haul!*
Haul on the bo'lin', the packet is a-rollin',
Haul on the bo'lin', the skipper he's a-growlin',
Haul on the bo'lin', to London we are goin',
Haul on the bo'lin', the good ship is a-bowlin',
Haul on the bo'lin', the main-topgallant bo'lin',
    Haul on the bo'lin', the bo'lin' *haul!*

# Johnny Boker

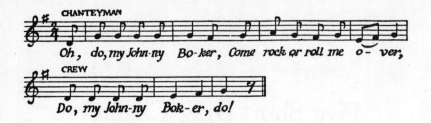

CHANTEYMAN

*Oh, do, my John-ny Bo-ker, Come rock or roll me o-ver,*

CREW

*Do, my John-ny Bok-er, do!*

Oh, do, my Johnny Boker,
Come rock or roll me over,
*Do, my Johnny Boker, do!*

Oh, do, my Johnny Boker,
They say that you're no rover,
*Do, my Johnny Boker, do!*

Oh, do, my Johnny Boker,
I'm bound away to leave you,
*Do, my Johnny Boker, do!*

# Boney

Boney was a warrior,
  *Away-ay, ah!*
A warrior, a terrier,
  *Jean Francois!*

Boney beat the Prussians,
Then he licked the Russians.

Boney went to Waterlow,
There he got his overthrow.

He went to Saint Helena,
  *Away-ay, ah!*
There he was a prisoner,
  *Jean Francois!*

# Haul Away, Joe

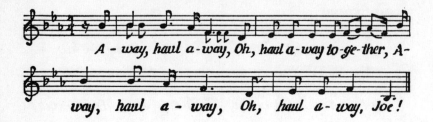

A - way, haul a-way, Oh, haul a-way to-ge-ther, A-
way, haul a - way, Oh, haul a - way, Joe!

Away, haul away, Oh, haul away together,
*Away, haul away, Oh, haul away, Joe!*

When I was a little lad, my mother told me,
*Away, haul away, Oh, haul away together,*
That if I did not kiss the girls my lips would grow moldy
*Away, haul away, Oh, haul away, Joe!*

So first I had a Spanish girl but she was fat and lazy.
*Away, haul away, Oh, haul away together,*
But now I've got an Irish girl and she nearly drives me crazy.
*Away, haul away, Oh, haul away, Joe!*

Away, haul away, Oh, haul away together,
*Away, haul away, Oh, haul away, Joe!*

Another version goes:

> King Louie was the king of France,
> Before the riv-*vi*-lution!
>
> Then he got his head cut off,
> Which spiled his cons-*ti*-tution!

# Paddy Doyle

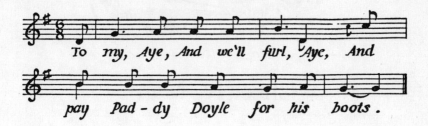

To my, Aye, And we'll furl, Aye, And
pay Pad - dy Doyle for his boots.

To my,
   Aye,
And we'll *furl*,
   Aye,
And pay Paddy Doyle for his *boots*.

We'll *sing*,
   Aye,
And we'll *heave*,
   Aye,
And we'll hang Paddy Doyle for his *boots*.

We'll *heave*,
   Aye,
With a *swing*,
   Aye,
And we'll all drink brandy and *gin*.

# Cheer'ly, Man

THIS IS a long-drag chantey and is probably another version of the chantey used in catting the anchor mentioned by Dana in *Two Years Before the Mast*. The verses heard today are a bit more intimate and reveal to a greater degree the charms of the ladies mentioned.

Oh, Nancy Dawson, hio!
  *Cheer'ly, man!*
She's got a notion, hio!
  *Cheer'ly, man!*
For our old bosun, hio!
  *Cheer'ly, man,*
  *Oh! hauley, hio!*
  *Cheer'ly, man!*

Oh, Betsy Baker, hio!
Lived in Long Acre, hio!
Married a Quaker, hio!

Oh, the ladies of the town, hio!
All as soft as down, hio!
In their best gown, hio!

Oh, haughty cocks, hio!
Oh, split the blocks, hio!
And stretch her luff, hio!

38

There is another version called *Cheer'ly, O!*

Oh, haul pulley, yoe!
  *Cheer'ly, men!*
Oh, long and strong, yoe!
  *Cheer'ly men!*
Oh, yoe, and with a will!
  *Cheer'ly, men!*
  *Cheer'ly, Cheer'ly, Cheer'ly, O!*

A long haul for Widow Skinner,
Kiss her well before dinner,
At her, boys, and win her!

A strong pull for Mrs. Bell,
Who likes a lark right well,
And, what's more, will never tell!

Oh, haul and split the blocks,
Oh, haul and stretch her luff,
Young lovelies, sweat her up!

Dana offers a revealing glimpse of the morale of the American sailor of his time. It was after the cruel floggings of the sailors, Sam and John the Swede, by Captain Thompson: "In no operation can the disposition of a crew be better discovered than in getting under way. Where things are done 'with a will,' every one is like a cat aloft; sails are loosed in an instant; each one lays out his strength on his handspike, and the windlass goes briskly round with the loud cry of 'yo heave ho! Heave and pawl! Heave hearty, ho!' and the chorus of 'Cheerily, men!' cats the anchor. But with us, at this time, it was all dragging work. No one went aloft beyond his ordinary gait, and the chain came slowly in over the windlass. The mate, between the knight-heads, exhausted all his official rhetoric in calls of 'Heave with a will!' 'Heave hearty, men! heave hearty!' 'Heave, and raise the dead!' 'Heave, and away!' etc., etc., but it would not do. Nobody broke his back or his handspike by his efforts. And when the cat-tackle-fall was strung along, and all hands, cook, steward and all, laid hold to cat the anchor, instead of the lively song of 'Cheerily, men!' in which all hands join the chorus, we pulled a long, heavy, silent pull, and, as sailors say a song is as good as ten men, the anchor came to the cat-head pretty slowly. Give us 'Cheerily!' said the mate; but there was no 'cheerily' for us and we did without it."

'TWAS A LONG TIME AGO

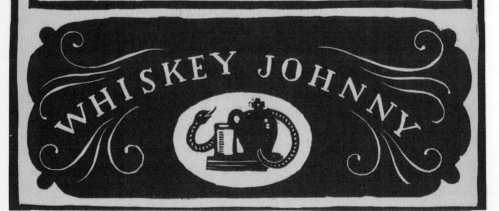

WHISKEY JOHNNY

# The Black Ball Songs

THERE ARE enough versions of this justly famous old chantey to fill a volume. It would seem to be the oldest American chantey, dating from the earliest days of the Black Ball Line. For the purpose of this work three versions are selected and divided, quite arbitrarily, as follows: the Original, known as The Black Ball Line, the Liverpool, and the Shore versions. That it was originally a long-drag chantey seems certain, but with the addition of the first two verses it became a comeallye, a sort of chantey-ballad used for many purposes, and as such it is sung today. The chantey proper began at verse three.

43

# The Black Ball Line

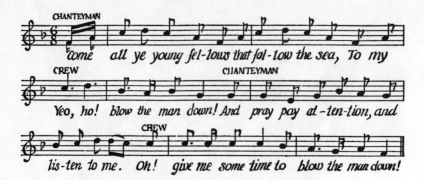

CHANTEYMAN
'Come all ye young fel-lows that fol-low the sea, To my

CREW       CHANTEYMAN
Yeo, ho! blow the man down! And pray pay at-ten-tion, and

CREW
lis-ten to me.    Oh!    give me some time to    blow the man down!

Come all ye young fellows that follow the sea,
*To my yeo, ho! blow the man down.*
And pray pay attention and listen to me.
*Oh, give me some time to blow the man down!*

I'm a deep water sailor just in from Hong Kong,
If you'll give me some whiskey I'll sing you my song.

'Twas on a Black Baller I first served my time,
And on that Black Baller I wasted my prime.

'Tis when a Black Baller's preparin' for sea,
You'd split your sides laughing at the sights you see.

With the tinkers and tailors and sogers and all,
That ship for prime seamen on board a Black Ball.

'Tis when a Black Baller is clear of the land,
Our boatswain then gives us the word of command.

"Lay aft," is the cry, "to the break of the poop!
Or I'll help you along with the toe of my boot!"

'Tis larboard and starboard on the deck you will sprawl,
For "Kicking Jack" Williams commands that Black Ball.

Pay attention to orders, now you one and all,
For right there above you flies the Black Ball.

'Tis when a Black Baller comes back to her dock,
    *To my yeo, ho! blow the man down!*
The lads and the lasses to the pierhead do flock.
    *Oh, give me some time to blow the man down!*

Robert Greenhalgh Albion in his splendid *Square Riggers on Schedule* states that the only Captain Williams in the Black Ball service was John Williams, of the *Pacific*, and that he did not have the reputation of a bucko. Captain John Williams was lost at sea in the wreck of the *Albion*, off Old Head, Kinsdale, Ireland, April 5, 1822. Many years later another Captain John H. Williams commanded the *Gladiator* and the *American Congress* in the Red Swallowtail Line to London. Captain A. H. Clark tells of a third, Captain John E. Williams, of Mystic, Connecticut, who commanded the California clipper, *Andrew Jackson*.

Some day a daring singer is going to change blow to knock and it won't hurt the old song any. No one has ever explained why the old sailorman was so happy in the contemplation of knocking people down, why he had to have time, or why he continues after all these years to sing about it. The following is the Liverpool version.

# Blow the Man Down, I

Oh, blow the man down, boys, blow the man down,
    *Way ay, blow the man down!*
Oh, blow the man down in Liverpool town,
    *Give me some time to blow the man down!*

As I was walking down Paradise Street,
A brass-bound policeman I happened to meet.

Says he, "You're a Black Baller by the cut of your hair,
I know you're a Black Baller by the clothes that you wear."

"Oh, policeman, policeman, you do me great wrong,
I'm a *Flying Fish* sailor just in from Hong Kong."

They gave me three months in Walton Gaol,
  *Way ay, blow the man down!*
For booting and kicking and blowing him down,
  *Give me some time to blow the man down!*

# Blow the Man Down, II

As I was walking down Paradise Street,
  *Way, ay,—blow the man down!*
A saucy young clipper I happened to meet,
  *Give me some time to blow the man down!*

Her flag was three colors, her masts they were low,
She was round in the counter and bluff in the bow.

I dipped her my ensign, a signal she knew,
For she backed round her mainyards and hove herself to.

I hailed her in English, she answered "Aye, aye!"
She was from the Blue Water and bound for Tiger Bay.

I passed her my hawser and took her in tow,
And yardarm to yardarm away we did go.

We tossed along gaily, both friskly and fleet,
  *Way ay, blow the man down!*
Till she dropped her bow anchor, 'twas in Avon Street,
  *Give me some time to blow the man down!*

In a waterside saloon this can be carried much farther without becoming any more interesting. There is another shore version entitled "While Strolling through Norfolk," the only one in which the traditional chorus lines are abandoned for the following:

Singing fal de eye idol, sing fal de eye idol,
Sing fal de eye idol, sing fal de eye de aye!

KEEP ON IT

# Lowlands

THE WRITER first heard this capstan chantey in a dense fog off Quarantine: our ship had come up in the night and anchored in the Narrows awaiting the clearing. Tumbling on deck at dawn, unable to see our hands before our faces, let alone the always welcome green hills of Staten Island, we tried to find our position with our ears. All we could distinguish was the clanking of an anchor chain on our starboard, the noises usual in an iron ship, more sonorous because of the fog, and then a doleful voice with a Cockney accent singing the song as a ballad. It was the perfect setting for a dirge.

49

I dreamed my love came in my sleep,
  *Lowlands, Lowlands, away, my John.*
His eyes were wet as he did weep,
  *My Lowlands, away!*

I shall never kiss you again, he said,
  *Lowlands, Lowlands, away, my John!*
For I am drowned in the Lowland seas.
  *My Lowlands, away!*

No other man shall think me fair,
  *Lowlands, Lowlands, away, my John!*
My love lies drowned in the windy Lowlands,
  *My Lowlands, away!*


That the chantey derives from an old Scottish coronach, "The Lawlands o' Holland," seems evident, and English Jack handled it with more or less reverence.

# The Lawlands o' Holland

The love that I hae chosen,
  I'll therewith be content;
The saut sea sall be frozen
  Before that I repent.
Repent it sall I never
  Until the day I dee;
But the Lawlands o' Holland
  Hae twinn'd * my love and me.

My love he built a bonny ship,
  And set her to the main,
Wi' twenty-four brave mariners
  To sail her out and hame.
But the weary wind began to rise,
  The sea began to rout,
And my love and his bonny ship
  Turned withershins † about.

There sall nae mantle cross my back,
  Nor kaim gae in my hair,
Neither sall coal nor candle light
  Shine in my bower mair;
Nor sall I choose anither love
  Until the day I dee,
Sin' the Lawlands o' Holland
  Hae twinn'd my love and me.

Noo haud your tongue, my daughter dear,
  Be still, and bide content;
There's ither lads in Galloway;
  Ye needna sair lament.

* twinn'd: parted
 † withershins: counterclockwise, the way witches dance, possibly the ship
turned turtle.

O, there is nane in Galloway,
There's nane at a' for me.
I never lo'ed a lad but ane,
And he's drown'd in the sea.

Lowlands suffered a sea change in crossing the Atlantic. The American sailor cared little enough for dirges: laments, yes, and gripes. In many versions he complained bitterly that he received but a dollar a day while the Negro roustabouts with whom he worked were paid a dollar and a half a day.

# Lowlands, II

Lowlands, lowlands, away, my John,
My old mother she wrote to me,
  *My dollar and a half a day!*
She wrote to me to come home from sea,
  *Lowlands, lowlands, away, my John!*
She wrote to me to come home from sea.
  *My dollar and a half a day!*

Lowlands, lowlands, away, my John,
Oh, were you ever in Mobile Bay?
  *My dollar and a half a day!*
A-screwing cotton by the day,
  *Lowlands, lowlands, away, my John!*
A-screwing cotton by the day,
  *My dollar and a half a day!*

Lowlands, lowlands, away, my John,
A dollar a day is a Hoosier's pay,
  *My dollar and a half a day!*
Yes, a dollar a day is a Hoosier's pay,
  *Lowlands, lowlands, away, my John!*

Yes, a dollar a day is a Hoosier's pay.
*My dollar and a half a day!*

# Lowlands, III

I wish I were in the Dutchman's Hall,
*Lowlands, lowlands, hurrah, my boys!*
A-drinking luck to the old Black Ball.
*My dollar and a half a day!*

# A Long Time Ago

*Long-drag Chantey*

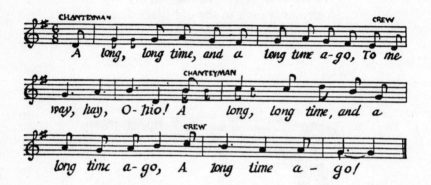

A long, long time, and a long time a-go, To me way, hay, O-hio! A long, long time, and a long time a-go, A long time a-go!

A long, long time, and a long time ago,
*To me way, hay, o-hio!*
A long, long time, and a long time ago,
*A long time ago!*


A smart Yankee packet lay out in the bay,
A-waiting for a fair wind to get under way,


With all her poor sailors all sick and all sad,
For they'd drunk all their whiskey, no more could be had,


She was waiting for a fair wind to get under way,
*To me way, hay, o-hio!*
If she hasn't had a fair wind she's lying there still.
*A long time ago!*

A more recent version using the same melody.

# Around Cape Horn

Around Cape Horn we've got to go,
*To me way, hay, o-hio!*
Around Cape Horn to Call-eao,
*A long time ago!*

'Round Cape Horn where the stiff winds blow,
'Round Cape Horn where there's sleet and snow.

I wish to God I'd never been born
*To me way, hay, o-hio!*
To drag my carcass around Cape Horn.
*A long time ago!*

# Reuben Ranzo

THIS LONG-DRAG chantey starts off on a note of disarming sympathy for poor Reuben, supposedly one Reuben Lorenzo, who was anything but a sailor. But that sympathy is short-lived and the chantey becomes a caustic comment on all foremasthands who curry favor with the captain to gain a place on the quarter-deck. Captain Whall insists he never heard any improvisations, but there are so many versions we must credit his lack of information traceable to the fact he never served on an American vessel.

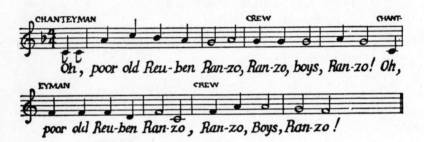

Oh, poor old Reu-ben Ran-zo, Ran-zo, boys, Ran-zo! Oh, poor old Reu-ben Ran-zo, Ran-zo, Boys, Ran-zo!

Oh, poor old Reuben Ranzo,
  *Ranzo, boys, Ranzo!*
Oh, pity poor Reuben Ranzo,
  *Ranzo, boys, Ranzo!*

Oh, Ranzo was no sai-lor,
He shipped aboard a wha-ler.

Oh, Ranzo was no beau-ty,
He could not do his du-ty.

So, they gave him nine and thir-ty,
Yes, lashes nine and thir-ty.

56

KEEP ON

THE
MAID OF
AMSTERDAM

Oh, cap'n being a good man,
He took him to the cab-an.

He gave him wine and wa-ter,
Rube kissed the cap'n's daugh-ter.

He taught him navi-gashun,
To fit him for his stay-shun.

Now, Ranzo, he's a sai-lor,
Chief mate of that wha-ler.

He married the cap'n's daugh-ter,
  *Ranzo, boys, Ranzo!*
And sails no more upon the wa-ter.
  *Ranzo, boys, Ranzo!*

In some instances the final verse goes:

Now, he's cap'n of a Black Ball li-ner,
  *Ranzo, boys, Ranzo!*
And nothing could be fi-ner.
  *Ranzo, boys, Ranzo!*

# Hanging Johnny

*Long-drag Chantey*

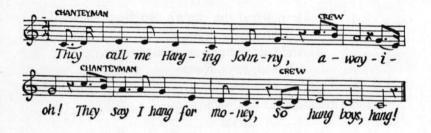

They call me Hanging Johnny,
  *A-way-i-oh!*
They say I hang for money,
  *So hang, boys, hang!*


First I hung my mother,
Then I hung my brother.


I'll hang you all together,
  *A-way-i-oh!*
We'll hang for better weather,
  *So hang, boys, hang!*


A good chanteyman could hang quite a lot if the task lasted
long enough.

# Whiskey for My Johnny

*Long-drag Chantey*

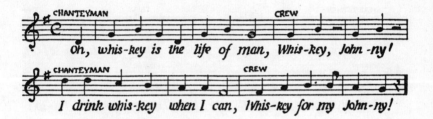

Oh, whiskey is the life of man,
*Whiskey, Johnny!*
I drink whiskey when I can
*Whiskey for my Johnny!*

Whiskey from an old tin can,
I'll drink whiskey when I can.

I drink it hot, I drink it cold,
I drink it new, I drink it old.

Whiskey makes me feel so sad,
Whiskey killed my poor old dad.

I thought I heard the old man say,
I'll treat my crew in a decent way.

A glass of grog for every man,
And a bottle full for the chanteyman.

# Tommy's Gone to Hilo

*Long-drag Chantey*

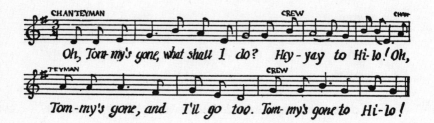

> Oh, Tommy's gone, what shall I do? Hey-yay to Hi-lo! Oh,
> Tommy's gone, and I'll go too. Tommy's gone to Hi-lo!

Oh, Tommy's gone, what shall I do?
*Hey-yay to Hi-lo!*
Oh, Tommy's gone, and I'll go too.
*Tommy's gone to Hi-lo!*

Oh, I love Tom and he loves me,
He thinks of me when out to sea.

Oh, away around to Callao,
The Spanish gels he'll see, I know.

Oh, Tommy's gone for evermore,
*Hey-yay to Hi-lo!*
I'll never see my Tom no more.
*Tommy's gone to Hi-lo!*

Hilo is Ilo, the southernmost port in Peru. For long periods Chilean ports were closed to foreign vessels and skippers coming up the West Coast from the Cape Horn passage put in at Ilo for water. It was also a guano port and something of a message center for whalers.

62

JOSIAH PERKINS CRESSY
MASTER
SHIP FLYING CLOUD

# Blow, Bullies, Blow

*Long-drag Chantey*

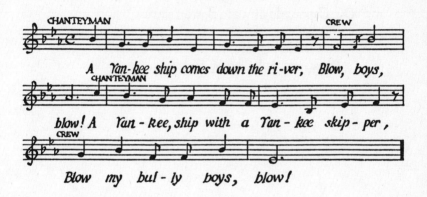

A Yankee ship comes down the river,
  *Blow, boys, blow!*
A Yankee ship with a Yankee skipper,
  *Blow, my bully boys, blow!*

How do you know she's a Yankee clipper;
Because her masts and yards shine like silver.

Who do you think is captain of her?
Old Holy Joe, the darky lover.

65

What do you think she's got for cargo?
Why, "black sheep" that have run the embargo.

What do you think they'll have for dinner?
Why, monkeys' tails and bullocks' liver.

Oh, blow today and blow tomorrow,
  *Blow, boys, blow!*
Oh, blow me down to the Congo River,
  *Blow, my bully boys, blow!*


A maverick verse that still has some currency in New England
is:


Oh, Captain Hall was a Boston slaver,
  *Blow, boys, blow!*
He traded in niggers and loved his Maker,
  *Blow, my bully boys, blow!*

# Early in the Morning

THIS SONG, capstan chantey or walkaway chorus, is heard more often ashore than afloat. The writer first heard it used as a quick-time effect in a New York National Guard drill, and it was very effective for use in training recruits, save that the stomping that went with it was not in the best military tradition. More recently it was heard used as a conga dance tune.

Way, hay, there she rises,
Way, hay, there she rises,
Way, hay, there she rises,
Early in the morning!
What will we do with a drunken sailor?
What will we do with a drunken sailor?
What will we do with a drunken sailor?
Early in the morning!

Way, hay, there she rises,
Way, hay, there she rises,
Way, hay, there she rises,
Early in the morning!
Put him in the longboat and make him bale her,
Put him in the longboat and make him bale her,
Put him in the longboat and make him bale her,
Early in the morning!

Way, hay, there she rises,
Way, hay, there she rises,
Way, hay, there she rises,
Early in the morning!
What will we do with a drunken soldier?
What will we do with a drunken soldier?
What will we do with a drunken soldier?
Early in the morning!


Way, hay, there she rises,
Way, hay, there she rises,
Way, hay, there she rises,
Early in the morning!
Put him in the guardroom till he gets sober,
Put him in the guardroom till he gets sober,
Put him in the guardroom till he gets sober,
Early in the morning!

# Stormalong

OLD STORMALONG is the only heroic character in the folklore of the sea: he was born, like the great clipper ships, in the
imaginations of men. There is a legend, told in prose, of the time
he was quartermaster of the *Courser*, the world's largest clipper.
Stormy was taking his vessel from the North Sea through the
English Channel, which was just six inches narrower than the
*Courser's* beam. He suggested that if the captain sent all hands
over to plaster the ship's side with soap he thought he could ease
her through. It was a tight passage but the ship made it, the Dover
cliffs scraping all the soap off the starboard side. Ever since, the
cliffs at that point have been pure white and recent observers say
the waves there are still foamy from the *Courser's* soap.

This version was used as a capstan chantey.

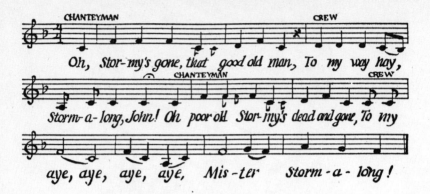

Oh, Stormy's gone, that good old man,
  *To my way hay, Stormalong, John!*
Oh, poor old Stormy's dead and gone,
  *To my aye, aye, aye, aye, Mister Stormalong!*

We dug his grave with a silver spade,
His shroud of the finest silk was made.

We lowered him with a silver chain,
Our eyes all dim with more than rain.

An able sailor, bold and true,
A good old bosun to his crew.

He's moored at last, and furled his sail,
No danger now from wreck or gale.

I wish I was old Stormy's son,
I'd build me a ship of a thousand ton.

I'd fill her up with New England rum,
And all my shellbacks they would have some.

I'd sail this wide world 'round and 'round,
With plenty of money I would be found.

Old Stormy's dead and gone to rest,
*To my way hay, Stormalong, John!*
Of all the sailors he was the best,
*To my aye, aye, aye, aye, Mister Stormalong!*

# Shenandoah

THIS CAPSTAN chantey has, without question, the loveliest
melody of all sailor songs. It has, too, the greatest number of
variants, many of them muddled and most of them on the side of
gibberish. In some, Shenandoah is an Indian chief, a bright mulatto,
a savage maiden, and she has been mistaken for Sally Brown. In
Virginia, where there is a river by the name, Shenandoah means
"daughter of the stars," which gives a clue to the sailors' loving
the daughter: how the wide Missouri got in is a mystery.

The old sailors sang it "Shannadore" and "Mizzouray."

Oh, Shenandoah, I love your daughter,
*A-way, my rol-ling ri-ver!*
I'll take her 'cross yon rolling water.
*Ah, hah! We're bound away,*
*'Cross the wide Missouri!*

Oh, Shenandoah, I love your Nancy,
Oh, Shenandoah, she took my fancy.

Oh, Shenandoah, I long to hear you,
'Cross that wide and rol-ling riv-er.

Oh, Shenandoah, I'll ne'er forget you,
*Away, my rol-ling ri-ver!*
Till the day I die, I'll love you ever.
*Ah, hah! We're bound away,*
*'Cross the wide Missouri!*

# Paddy Get Back

A CAPSTAN chantey, called by Captain Bone, "The Liverpool
Song," that seems to be of a recent and questionable birth, possibly
one sired by sailors who went from sail to steam and back again
without heartbreak. The fact that the term chantey is used within
the song and firemen mentioned seems to warrant this conclusion.
It can be recalled that the Panama Canal was not opened to general
traffic until 1914 and up to that time even steamships had to double
Cape Horn to make the West Coast ports.

The air and words given here are from a recording in the
Archive of American Folksong in the Library of Congress.

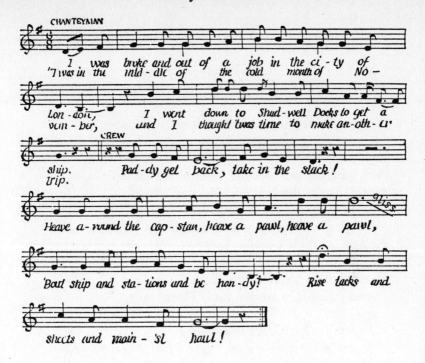

I was broke and out of a job in the city of London,
I went down to Shadwell Docks to get a ship.

*Paddy get back, take in the slack!*
*Heave away the capstan, heave a pawl! heave a pawl!*
*'Bout ship and stations and be handy,*
*Rise tacks and sheets and mains'l haul!*

There was a Yankee ship a-laying in the basin,
And they told me she was going to New York.

If I ever lay my hands on that shipping-master,
I'll murder him if it's the last thing that I do.

When the pilot left the ship 'way down the Channel,
Oh, the captain told us we were going around Cape Horn.

The mate and the second mate belonged in Boston,
And the captain hailed from Bangor down in Maine.

The three of them were rough-and-tumble fighters,
When not fighting amongst themselves they turned on us.

They called us out one night to reef the topsails,
Now belaying pins were flying around the deck.

And we came on deck and went to set the topsails,
Not a man in the bunch could sing a song.

We are tinkers, we are tailors, and the fireman also cooks,
And they couldn't sing a chantey unless they had the books.

Wasn't that a bunch of hoodlums,
For to take a ship around Cape Horn?

*Paddy get back, take in the slack!*
*Heave away the capstan, heave a pawl! heave a pawl!*
*'Bout ship and stations and be handy,*
*Rise tacks and sheets and mains'l haul!*

# Across the Western Ocean

THERE IS GOOD reason to believe that there was an earlier version of this westward bound capstan chantey. The Irish coming to America in droves left their impress on the songs, legends, and salty speech of the sailorman. The "Amelia" mentioned may have been the name of a vessel; there were two packets by that name but both were in the coastal service, there was a brig, *Amelia Strong,* and an English bark, *Amelia Packet.* It may have been a corruption of O'Malley or, quite likely, it was a girl by that name.

The Irish Army referred to in the second verse was probably the hordes leaving starving Ireland, though there was a sort of Irish-Army-in-Exile on the Continent (see "The Girl I Left behind Me"). Yet the term may have been ironic: sailors liked to refer to a large and unwieldy barge that had to be towed as an Irish man-of-war, and an Irish hurricane was rain and fog on a calm sea. An Irish pennant was any rope or sail that had broken loose and was blowing free in the wind.

On one of the packet ships, a storm came up and a devout Irishman assured the sailors that the waves were caused by the writhings of the snakes and serpents that St. Patrick had driven out of Ireland.

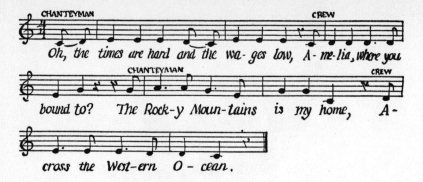

Oh, the times are hard and the wa-ges low, A-me-lia, where you bound to? The Rock-y Moun-tains is my home, A-cross the West-ern O-cean.

Oh, the times are hard and the wages low,
  *Amelia, where you bound to?*
The Rocky Mountains is my home,
  *Across the Western Ocean.*

The land of promise there you'll see,
  *Amelia, where you bound to?*
I'm bound across that Western sea,
  *To join the Irish army.*

To Liverpool I'll take my way,
  *Amelia, where you bound to?*
To Liverpool that Yankee school,
  *Across the Western Ocean.*

There's Liverpool Pat with his tarpaulin hat,
  *Amelia, where you bound to?*
And Yankee John, the packet rat.
  *Across the Western Ocean.*

Beware these packet ships, I say,
  *Amelia, where you bound to?*
They steal your stores and clothes away,
  *Across the Western Ocean.*

# We're All Bound to Go

THIS CAPSTAN chantey also dates from the great Irish emigration to America in the Forties and Fifties. Miss Joanna Colcord identifies William Tapscott as a Liverpool shipping agent. The *Henry Clay* was a famous packet, Ezra Nye, master, built in New York in 1845 for the Swallowtail Line to Liverpool. In 1846 she was wrecked on the New Jersey Monmouth coast with a loss of several lives but was brought off and within a few months put back on the old run. On September 5, 1849, she burned at her South Street pier. Her charred hulk was sold to the Collins Dramatic Line, which rebuilt and restored her to the Liverpool service. At the end of the Civil War she was operating as a freight packet.

Oh, as I walked down the Landing Stage,
All on a Summer's morn,
 *Heave away, my Johnny, heave away!*
It's there I spied an Irish girl
A-looking all forlorn.
 *And away, my Johnnie boys,*
 *We're all bound to go!*

"Oh, good morning, Mr. Tapscott,"
"Good morning, my girl," says he,
   *Heave away, my Johnny, heave away!*
"Have you got a packet ship
To carry me across the sea?"
   *And away, my Johnnie boys,*
   *We're all bound to go!*

"Oh, yes, I have a clipper ship,
She's called the *Henry Clay;*"
   *Heave away, my Johnny, heave away!*
"She sails today for Boston Bay,
She sails away at break of day."
   *And away, my Johnnie boys,*
   *We're all bound to go!*

"Oh, will you take me to Boston Bay,
When she sails away at break of day?"
   *Heave away, my Johnny, heave away!*
"I want to marry a Yankee boy,
And I'll cross the sea no more."
   *And away, my Johnnie boys,*
   *We're all bound to go!*

KEEP ON IT

# Paddy Works on the Railway

THIS CAPSTAN chantey shows that Jack could imitate the counting songs of the children. Many of the Irish emigrants went directly from the packets to the railway construction camps, and when Sailor Jack heard the wages Irish Paddy would get he followed along, at least for the cold, wintry months. Returning to the sea with the first breath of Spring, he brought the song back with him, half identifying himself with the Irish workers. The following version, placed in the Forties, is a fabrication made up of snatches in which the dates jump from the Forties to the Seventies and back again.

Oh, in eighteen hundred and forty-one,
My corduroy breeches I put on,
My time was nearly done.
> *To work upon the railway, the railway,*
> *I'm weary of the railway,*
> *Oh, poor Paddy works on the railway.*

Oh, in eighteen hundred and forty-two,
My corduroy breeches then were new,
I did not know what I should do.

Oh, in eighteen hundred and forty-three,
I sailed away across the sea,
I sailed away to Amerikee.

Oh, in eighteen hundred and forty-four,
I landed on the Columbia shore,
I had a pick-ax and nothing more.

Oh, in eighteen hundred and forty-five,
When Dan O'Connelly was still alive,
I worked in a railway hive.

Oh, in eighteen hundred and forty-six,
I found myself in a hell of a fix;
I changed my job to toting bricks.

Oh, in eighteen hundred and forty-seven,
When Dan O'Connelly went to heaven,
Little Paddy was going on eleven.

Oh, in eighteen hundred and forty-eight,
I found myself bound for the Golden Gate,
Gold was found in the western state.

Oh, in eighteen hundred and forty-nine,
I passed my time in the Black Ball Line.
And that's the end of my monkeyshine.
      *To work upon the railway, the railway,*
      *I'm weary of the railway,*
      *Oh, poor Paddy works on the railway.*

# Santa Anna
# or The Plains of Mexico

THIS IS a curious capstan chantey that must go unexplained. In some versions the roles of Santa Anna and General Taylor are reversed and it is the American who ran away. Jack, like a lot of other people, just didn't give a damn for historical fact. It is admitted that history is what happened and folklore is what the people think happened. This is folklore.

Oh, Santa Anna fought for fame,
*Hooray, Santa Anna!*
He fought for fame and gained his name,
*Along the plains of Mexico!*

General Taylor gained the day,
*Hooray, Santa Anna!*
And Santa Anna ran away,
*Along the plains of Mexico!*

# Maid of Amsterdam (A-Roving)

BACK IN 1608 Thomas Heywood, an English dramatist, wrote *The Rape of Lucrece* and in the production of the play this song was introduced. Heywood was something of a play-carpenter, he claimed to have written or "had a main finger in" no less than two hundred and twenty plays. No one can say whether Tom lifted the song from Jack or whether the reverse is true. What is known is that for over three hundred years the Maid has been a-roving and spreading ru-in across land and sea.

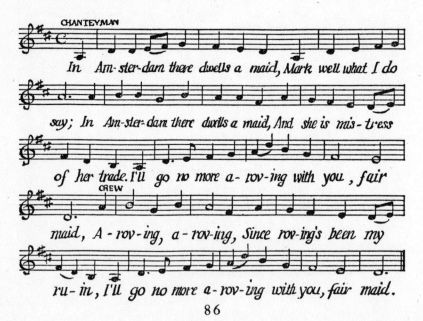

In Amsterdam there dwells a maid, Mark well what I do say; In Amsterdam there dwells a maid, And she is mis-tress of her trade. I'll go no more a-rov-ing with you, fair maid, A-rov-ing, a-rov-ing, Since rov-ing's been my ru-in, I'll go no more a-rov-ing with you, fair maid.

In Amsterdam there dwells a maid,
  Mark well what I do say;
In Amsterdam there dwells a maid,
  And she is mistress of her trade.

> *I'll go no more a-roving*
> *With you, fair maid,*
> *A-roving, a-roving,*
> *Since roving's been my ru-in,*
> *I'll go no more a-roving*
> *With you, fair maid!*

Her eyes are blue, her cheeks are red,
  Mark well what I do say;
Her eyes are blue, her cheeks are red,
  A wealth of hair is on her head.

I put my arm around her waist,
  Mark well what I do say;
I put my arm around her waist,
  Says she, "Young man, you're in some haste."

I took that girl upon my knee,
  Mark well what I do say,
I took that girl upon my knee,
  Says she, "Young man, you're rather free."

She swore that she'd be true to me,
  Mark well what I do say;
She swore that she'd be true to me,
  But spent my money both fast and free.

> *I'll go no more a-roving*
> *With you, fair maid,*
> *A-roving, a-roving,*
> *Since roving's been my ru-in,*
> *I'll go no more a-roving*
> *With you, fair maid!*

# The Banks of the Sacramento

*A Capstan chantey from the California clippers*

CHANTEYMAN — Sing and heave, and heave and sing, To me hoo-dah! To my hoo-dah

CHANTEYMAN — Heave and make the hand-spikes spring. To me hoo-dah, hoo-dah-

CREW — day! And it's blow, boys, blow, For Cal-i-for-ni-o. For there's

plen-ty of gold, So I've been told, On the banks of the Sa-cra-men-to.

Sing and heave, and heave and sing,
 *To me hoodah! To my hoodah!*
Heave and make the handspikes spring,
 *To me hoodah, hoodah, day!*

 *And it's blow, boys, blow,*
 *For Californi-o!*
 *For there's plenty of gold,*
 *So I've been told,*
  *On the banks of the Sacramento!*

From Limehouse Docks to Sydney Heads,
 *To me hoodah! To my hoodah!*
Was never more than seventy days.
 *To me hoodah, hoodah, day!*

We cracked it on, on a big skiute,
 *To me hoodah! To my hoodah!*
And the old man felt like a swell galoot.
 *To me hoodah, hoodah, day!*

 *And it's blow, boys, blow,*
 *For Californi-o!*
 *For there's plenty of gold,*
 *So I've been told,*
  *On the banks of the Sacramento!*

# Cape Cod Girls

THIS DITTY, sometimes bound for Australia, seems to be unknown to all active and retired mariners on Cape Cod. Yet every woman and child knows it and many have added verses of their own.

Cape Cod girls they have no combs,
*Heave away! Heave away!*
They comb their hair with codfish bones,
*We're bound for Californiay!*

Heave away, my bully, bully boys,
Heave away, and don't you make a noise.

Cape Cod boys they have no sleds,
They slide down dunes on codfish heads.

Cape Cod doctors they have no pills
They give their patients codfish gills.

Cape Cod cats they have no tails,
*Heave away! Heave away!*
They lost them all in sou'east gales.
*We're bound for Californiay!*

# Good-bye, Fare You Well

THIS AND the two following homeward bound chanteys were used at the capstan or windlass. All tell their own stories, all were sung with a spirit of exultation.

Oh, fare you well, I wish you well!
  *Good-bye, fare you well; good-bye, fare you well!*
Oh, fare you well, my bonny young lassies,
  *Hurrah, my boys, we're homeward bound!*

The billows roll, the breezes blow,
To us they're calling: sheet home and go!

We're homeward bound, and I hear the sound,
So heave on the caps'n and make it spin round.

Our anchor's aweigh and our sails they are set,
And the girls we are leaving we leave with regret.

She's a flash clipper packet and bound for to go,
  *Good-bye, fare you well; good-bye, fare you well!*
With the girls on her towrope she cannot say no.
  *Hurrah, my boys, we're homeward bound!*

91

# Time to Leave Her

Oh, the work was hard and the wages low, Leave her Johnny, leave her! We'll pack our bags and go below, It's time for us to leave her.

Oh, the work was hard and the wages low,
*Leave her, Johnny, leave her!*
We'll pack our bags and go below,
*It's time for us to leave her!*

The work was hard, the voyage was long,
The seas were high, the gales were strong.

The food was bad and the ship was slow,
But now ashore again we'll go.

92

It was growl you may but go you must,
It mattered not whether you're last or first.

I thought I heard the old man say,
"Just one more pull and then belay."

The sails are furled, our work is done,
  *Leave her, Johnny, leave her!*
And now on shore we'll have our fun.
  *It's time for us to leave her!*


Capstan chantey, often used, with a slight change of pace, as a pumping song.

# One Day More

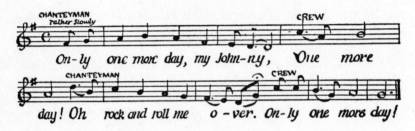

On-ly one more day, my John-ny, One more day! Oh rock and roll me o-ver. On-ly one more day!

Only one more day, my Johnny,
*One more day!*
Oh, rock and roll me over.
*Only one more day!*

Don't you hear the old man calling,
Can't you hear the pilot bawling.

Can't you hear those gals a-calling
Can't you hear the capstan pawling.

Put on your long-tailed blue, my Johnny,
For your pay is nearly due.

Only one more day, my Johnny,
*One more day!*
Oh, rock and roll me over.
*Only one more day!*

# Forecastle Songs

# The High Barbaree

CHARLES DIBDIN, a British editor and song writer, 1745–1814, is said to have written above twelve hundred songs, most of them for use by the Royal Navy. Among those that are still popular are "The High Barbaree," "Tom Bowline," and "Ben Backstay." Dibdin's great influence may be estimated from the fact that in 1803 the British government engaged him to write a series of songs designed "to keep alive the national feelings against the French."

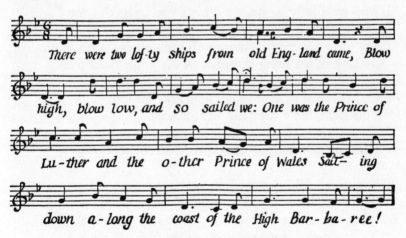

There were two lof-ty ships from old Eng-land came, Blow high, blow low, and so sailed we: One was the Prince of Lu-ther and the o-ther Prince of Wales Sail- ing down a-long the coast of the High Bar-ba-ree!

There were two lofty ships from old England came,
    *Blow high, blow low, and so sailed we:*
One was the *Prince of Luther* and the other *Prince of Wales,*
    **Sailing down along the coast of the High Barbaree!**

"Aloft there, aloft!" our jolly boatswain cries
  Blow high, blow low, and so sailed we:
"Look ahead, look astern, look aweather and alee,
    Look along down the coast of the High Barbaree!"

"There's nought upon our stern, there's nought upon our lee,"
  Blow high, blow low, and so sailed we:
"But there's a lofty ship to windward, she's sailing fast and free,
    Sailing down along the coast of the High Barbaree!"

"Oh, hail her, oh, hail her!" our gallant captain cried,
  Blow high, blow low, and so sailed we:
"Are you a man-of-war or a Yankee privateer?" asked he,
    "Cruising down along the coast of the High Barbaree!"

"Oh, I am not a man-of-war nor privateer," said she,
  Blow high, blow low, and so sailed we:
"But I am a deep-sea pirate, a-looking for my fee."
    Cruising down along the coast of the High Barbaree!

"If you are a jolly pirate, we'd have you come this way!"
  Blow high, blow low, and so sailed we:
"Bring out your quarter guns, we'll show these pirates play,"
    Cruising down along the coast of the High Barbaree!

'Twas broadside to broadside a long time we lay,
  Blow high, blow low, and so sailed we:
Until the *Prince of Luther* shot the pirate's masts away,
    Cruising down along the coast of the High Barbaree!

"Oh, quarter, Oh, quarter," those pirates then did cry,
  Blow high, blow low, and so sailed we:
But the quarter that we gave them—we sank them in the sea,
    Cruising down along the coast of the High Barbaree!

FLYING CLOUD

MAN OF WAR AND A CUTTER

# 'Way Down in Cuba

A WIDE SEARCH for this elusive Mississippi River song brought only the following:

> I've got a sister nine feet tall,
> > 'Way down in Cuba!
> Sleeps in the kitchen with her feet in the hall.
> > 'Way down in Cuba!
>
> I've got a girl friend, name is Jane,
> > 'Way down in Cuba!
> You can guess where she gives me a pain.
> > 'Way down in Cuba!

KEEP ON

# Tom Bowline

Here, a sheer hulk lies poor Tom Bow-line, The dar-ling of our crew; No more he'll hear the tem-pest howl-ing, For death has broach'd him to. His form was of the man-liest beau-ty, His heart was kind and soft; Faith-ful be-low, he did his du-ty, And now he's gone a-loft. And now he's gone a-loft.

Here, a sheer hulk, lies poor Tom Bowline,
   The darling of our crew;
No more he'll hear the tempest howling,
   For death has broach'd him to.
His form was of the manliest beauty,
   His heart was kind and soft;
Faithful below, he did his duty,
   And now he's gone aloft.

Tom never from his word departed,
   His virtues were so rare,
His friends were many, and true-hearted,
   His Poll was kind and fair:
And then he'd sing so blithe and jolly,
   Ah, many's the time and oft!
But mirth is turned to melancholy,
   For Tom is gone aloft.

Yet shall poor Tom find pleasant weather,
   When He, who all commands,
Shall give, to call life's crew together,
   The word to pipe all hands.
Thus Death, who kings and tars dispatches,
   In vain Tom's life has doff'd,
For, though his body's under hatches,
   His soul has gone aloft.

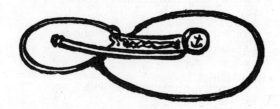

# Ben Backstay

Ben Backstay was our boatswain,
A very merry boy,
For no one half so merrily
Could pipe all hands ahoy,
And when unto his summons
We did not well attend,
No lad than he more merrily,
Could handle the rope's end.

  Singing chip chow, cherry chow,
  Fol de riddle ido.
  Singing chip chow, cherry chow,
  Fol de riddle ido.

While sailing once, our captain,
Who was a jolly dog,
Served out to all the company,
A double share of grog.

PRETTY POL

Ben Backstay he got tipsy,
All to his heart's content,
And he being half seas over,
Why overboard he went.

A shark was on the larboard bow,
Sharks don't on manners stand,
But grapple all they come near,
Just like your sharks on land.
We heaved Ben out some tackling
Of saving him some hope's,
But the shark had bit his head off,
So he couldn't see the ropes.

Without his head his ghost appeared
All on the briny lake;
He piped all hands ahoy and cried:
"Lads, warning by me take;
By drinking grog I lost my life,
So, lest my fate you meet,
Why, never mix your liquors, lads,
But always take them neat."

A HEART OF OAK

# The *Dreadnought*

THE *Dreadnought* was a clipper, 1413 tons, built in 1853 by New York owners at Newburyport, Massachusetts, for Captain Samuel Samuels, who superintended her construction. She made some remarkably fast passages between New York and Liverpool under the flag of the Red Cross Line. Captain Clark states that Captain Samuels believed in the use of an enterprising press agent, and as a result the *Dreadnought* became the best publicized of all the clippers. It is within reason to believe the publicist may have had a hand in the writing of the ballad. The ship went down while doubling Cape Horn in 1869.

I first heard the song during the years of the first World War, and the three who sang it ended each verse with the line, "She's

the Liverpool packet, Oh, Lord, let her go!" as a chorus which was
shouted rather than sung.

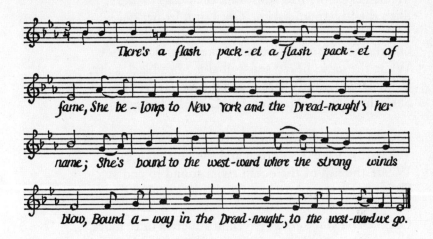

There's a flash packet, a flash packet of fame,
She belongs to New York and the *Dreadnought's* her name;
She's bound to the westward where the strong winds blow,
Bound away in the *Dreadnought*, to the westward we go.

The time for her sailing is now drawing nigh,
Farewell, pretty May, I must bid you good-bye,
Farewell to old England and all we hold dear,
Bound away in the *Dreadnought*, to the westward we'll steer.

Oh, the *Dreadnought* is pulling out of Waterloo Dock,
Where the boys and the girls to the pierheads do flock;
They will give us three cheers while their tears do flow,
Saying, "God bless the *Dreadnought*, where'er she may go!"

Oh, the *Dreadnought* is waiting in the Mersey so free,
Waiting for the *Independence* to tow her to sea;
For around that Rock Light where the Mersey does flow,
Bound away in the *Dreadnought*, to the westward we'll go.

Oh, the *Dreadnought's* a-bowlin' down the wild Irish Sea,
Where the passengers are merry, their hearts full of glee,
While her sailors like lions walk the decks to and fro,
She's the Liverpool packet, Oh, Lord, let her go!

Oh, the *Dreadnought's* a-sailin' the Atlantic so wide,
While the dark, heavy seas roll along her black sides,
With her sails neatly spread and the red cross to show,
She's the Liverpool packet, Oh, Lord, let her go!

Oh, the *Dreadnought's* becalmed on the banks of Newfoundland,
Where the water's so green and the bottom is sand;
Where the fish of the ocean swim round to and fro,
She's the Liverpool packet, Oh, Lord, let her go!

Oh, the *Dreadnought's* arrived in America once more,
Let's go ashore, shipmates, on the land we adore,
With wives and sweethearts so happy we'll be,
Drink a health to the *Dreadnought,* wherever she be.

Here's a health to the *Dreadnought,* to all her brave crew,
Here's a health to her captain, and her officers, too,
Talk about your flash packets, Swallowtail and Black Ball,
Then, here's to the *Dreadnought,* the packet to beat them all.

# The *Bigler*

THE GREAT LAKES sailors had adventures no less renowned than those of the salt-water men. Their voyages did not have the length of the clippers, but the storms on the lakes were of sufficient ferocity to wreck ships and drown sailors.

The following version is by Captain Asel Trueblood, of St. Ignace, Michigan, and is taken from a record in the Archive of American Folksong in the Library of Congress.

On the Sunday morning, just at the hour of ten,
When the tug *Mico Robert* towed the schooner *Bigler*, through
Lake Michigan.
Oh, there we made our canvas in the middle of the fleet,
And the wind hauled to the south'ard, boys, so we had to give her
sheet.

CHORUS:  Watch her, catch her, jump up in her ju-baju,
Give her sheet and let her go, the lads will pull her
through.

And don't you hear her howling when the wind was
   blowing free
On our down trip to Buffalo from Milwaukee.

The wind comes down from the south, southeast; it blows both
   stiff and strong,
You'd ought to've seen that little schooner *Bigler* as she pulled out
   Lake Michigan.
Oh, far beyond her foaming bows, the fiery lights aflame,
With every stitch of canvas and her course was wing and wing.

Passing by the Proctors the wind was blowing free,
Sailing by the Beavers with the Skillaglee on our lea;
Oh, we hauled her in full and bye as close as she would lie,
And we weathered Waugoshance to enter the Straits of Macki-
   naw.

At Huron we made Presque Isle Light and then we tore away,
The wind it being fair, for the Isle of Thunder Bay.
Then the wind it shifted and the night it came on dark,
The captain kept a sharp lookout for the light at Point aux Barques.

We passed the light and kept in sight of Michigan north shore,
A-boomin' for the river as we'd often done before.
When just abreast of Port Huron Light, both anchors we let go,
And the *Sweepstake* came 'longside and took the *Bigler* in tow.

She took the seven of us in tow, all of us fore and aft,
She towed us down to Lake St. Clare and stuck us on the flat.
Then eased the *Hunter's* tow line to give us all relief,
The *Bigler* fell astern and went into a boat called the *Maple Leaf.*

And then the *Sweepstake* towed us out beyond the river light,
Lake Erie for to roam and the blustering winds to fight.
The wind being from the south'ard, it blew a pretty gale,
And we took it as it came for we could not carry sail.

We made the Eau and passed Long Point, the wind now blowing
    free,
We bowled along the Canada shore, Port Colborne on our lee.
What is that that looms ahead? We knew as we drew near,
That blazing like a star, shone the light on Buffalo Pier.

And now we're safely moored in the Buffalo Creek at last,
And under Brigg's elevator the *Bigler* is made fast.
And in some lager beer saloon we'll let the bottle pass,
For we're all happy shipmates and we like a social glass.

~ SIGNALLING FOR A PILOT ~

CHINESE PIRATES

# Young Monroe at Gerry's Rock*

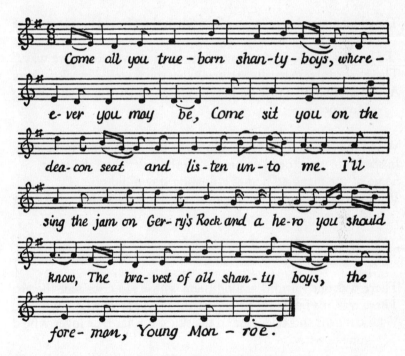

Come all you true-born shan-ty-boys, where-ever you may be, Come sit you on the dea-con seat and lis-ten un-to me. I'll sing the jam on Ger-ry's Rock and a he-ro you should know, The bra-vest of all shan-ty boys, the fore-man, Young Mon-roe.

Come all you true-born shanty-boys, wherever you may be,
Come sit you on the deacon seat and listen unto me.
I'll sing the jam on Gerry's Rock and a hero you should know,
The bravest of all shanty-boys, the foreman, Young Monroe.

*From *More Pious Friends and Drunken Companions.* Copyright, 1928, by Frank Shay.

It was on a Sunday morning, as you will quickly hear,
Our logs were piled mountain high, we could not keep them clear.
Our foreman said: "Come, cheer up, lads, with hearts relieved of
　　fear,
We'll break the jam on Gerry's Rock and for Saginaw we'll steer."

Now some of them were willing, while others they were not,
For to work on jams on Sunday they did not think we ought;
But six of our Canuck boys did volunteer to go
And break the jam on Gerry's Rock, with the foreman, Young
　　Monroe.

They had not rolled off many logs when they heard his clear voice
　　say:
"I'd have you lads on your guard, for the jam will soon give way."
These words were hardly spoken when the mass did break and go,
And it carried off those six brave lads, and their foreman, Young
　　Monroe.

When the rest of our shanty-boys, the sad news came to hear,
In search of their dead comrades, to the river they did steer.
Some of the mangled bodies a-floating down did go,
While crushed and bleeding near the bank was that of Young
　　Monroe.

They took him from his watery grave, smoothed back his raven
　　hair;
There was one fair girl among them whose sad cries rent the air;
There was one fair form among them, a maid from Saginaw town,
Whose moans and cries rose to the skies, for her true lover who'd
　　gone down.

For Clara was a nice young girl, the riverman's true friend;
She with her widowed mother dear, lived near the river's bend.
The wages of her own true love the boss to her did pay,
And the shanty-boys for her made up a generous purse next day.

They buried him with sorrow deep, 'twas on the first of May;
Come all you brave shanty-boys and for your comrade pray.
Engraved upon a hemlock tree that by the grave did grow,
Was the name and date of the sad fate of the foreman, Young
    Monroe.

Fair Clara did not long survive; her heart broke with her grief,
And scarcely two months later death came to her relief.
And when this time had passed away and she was called to go,
Her last request was granted, to rest beside Young Monroe.

Come all you brave shanty-boys: I would have you call and see
Those two green mounds by the riverside, where grows the hem-
    lock tree.
The shanty-boys cleared off the wood, by the lovers there laid
    low:
'Twas handsome Clara Vernon and our foreman, Young Monroe.

# I Come from Salem City

THIS IS THE argonauts' parody of Stephen Foster's "O, Susannah!" Unlike most parodies it has had a long and happy life. In hog-German it is quite amusing, beginning: Ich komm dem Salem City mit dem washbowl auf dem knee!

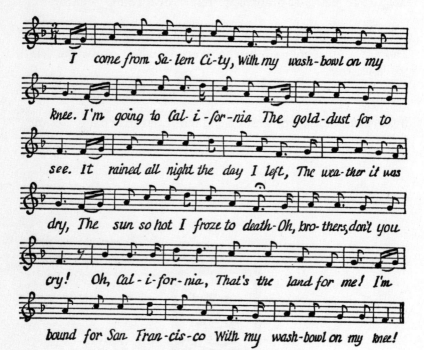

I come from Sa-lem Ci-ty, With my wash-bowl on my knee. I'm going to Cal-i-for-nia The gold-dust for to see. It rained all night the day I left, The wea-ther it was dry, The sun so hot I froze to death- Oh, bro-thers, don't you cry! Oh, Cal-i-for-nia, That's the land for me! I'm bound for San Fran-cis-co With my wash-bowl on my knee!

I came from Salem City,
    With my washbowl on my knee.
I'm going to California
    The gold dust for to see.
It rained all night the day I left,
    The weather it was dry,
The sun so hot I froze to death—
    Oh, brothers, don't you cry!

GOOD STUFF THIS!

Oh, California,
That's the land for me!
I'm bound for San Francisco
With my washbowl on my knee!

I jumped aboard the 'Liza ship
And traveled on the sea,
And every time I thought of home
I wished it wasn't me!
The vessel reared like any horse
That had of oats a wealth;
I found it wouldn't throw me, so
I thought I'd throw myself!

### Chorus

I thought of all the pleasant time
We've had together here,
I thought I ought to cry a bit,
But couldn't find a tear.
The pilot bread was in my mouth,
The gold dust in my eye,
And though I'm going far away,
Dear brothers, don't you cry!

### Chorus

I soon shall be in 'Frisco,
And there I shall look around,
And when I see the gold lumps there
I'll pick them off the ground.
I'll scrape the mountains clean, my boys,
I'll drain the rivers dry,
A pocketful of rocks bring home—
So, brothers, don't you cry!

# A-Cruising We Will Go

Behold upon the swelling seas
　　With streaming pennants gay,
Our gallant ship invites the waves,
　　While glory leads the way.

　　*And a-cruising we will go—oho, oho, oho!*
　　*And a-cruising we will go—oho, oho, oho!*
　　*And a-cruising we will go—o——oho,*
　　*And a-cruising we will go!*

You beauteous maids, your smiles bestow,
　　For if you prove unkind,
How can we hope to beat the foe?
　　We leave our hearts behind.

　　*When a-cruising we will go——*

See Hardy's flag once more display'd,
　　Upon the deck he stands;
Britannia's glory ne'er can fade,
　　Or tarnish in his hands.

　　***So a-cruising we will go——***

Britain to herself but true,
    To France defiance hurl'd:
Give peace, America, with you,
    And war with all the world.

*And a-cruising we will go—oho, oho, oho!*
*And a-cruising we will go—oho, oho, oho!*
*And a-cruising we will go—o——oho,*
*And a-cruising we will go!*

# We Be Three Poor Mariners

We be three poor mar-in-ers, New-ly come from the seas, We spend our lives in jeo-par-dy, while o-thers live at ease, Shall we go dance the Round, a-round, a-round? Shall we go dance the Round, a-round, a-round? And he that is a bul-ly boy, Come, pledge me on this ground, a-ground, a-ground!

We be three poor mariners, newly come from the seas,
We spend our lives in jeopardy, while others live at ease.
    Shall we go dance the Round, around, around?
    Shall we go dance the Round, around, around?
    And he that is a bully boy,
    Come, pledge me on this ground, aground, aground!

We care not for those martial men that do our states disdain;
But we care for those merchantmen that do our states maintain.
    Shall we dance this Round, around, around?
    Shall we dance this Round, around, around?
    And he that is a bully boy
    Come, pledge me on this ground, aground, aground!

The above song was first printed in 1609, and if the singer changes dance to drink he will have an excellent bar song.

SHE BLOWS!

# The Whale

It was in the year of for-ty-four, In
March the se-cond day, That our gal-lant ship her
an-chors weighed And for sea they bore a -
way Brave boys, And for sea they bore a - way.

It was in the year of forty-four,
In March the second day,
That our gallant ship her anchors weighed
And for sea they bore away,
Brave boys,
And for sea they bore away.

And when we came to far Greenland,
  And to Greenland cold we came,
Where there's frost and snow
  And the whalefishes blow,
    Brave boys,
  And the whalefishes blow.

Our bosun went to topmast high
  With his spyglass in his hand.
"A whale! There's a whalefish," he cried,
  "And she blows at every span,
    Brave boys,
  She blows at every span."

Our captain stood on the quarter-deck,
  And a brave little man was he.
"Overhaul, overhaul, on your davit tackles fall
  And launch your boats for sea,
    Brave boys,
  And launch your boats for sea."

We struck the whale, away he went,
  And he lashed out with his tail,
And we lost the boat and five good men,
  And we never got that whale,
    Brave boys,
  And we did not get that whale.

Oh, Greenland is an awful place,
  Where the daylight's seldom seen,
Where there's frost and snow,
  And the whalefishes blow,
    Brave boys,
  And the whalefishes blow.

It is usually conceded that "The Whale" originated with the English whalers and was to some extent taken over by the Americans. In the pure English versions there is a Captain Speedicut and many rambling and disconnected verses. In *Moby Dick* Herman Melville has a Nantucket sailor aboard the *Pequod* sing:

> "Our captain stood upon the deck,
>     A spy-glass in his hand,
> A-viewing of those gallant whales
>     That blew at every strand.
> Oh, your tubs in your boats, my boys,
>     And by your braces stand,
> And we'll have one of those fine whales,
>     Hand, boys, over hand!
>
> "So be cheery, my lads! may your hearts never fail!
> While the bold harpooner is striking the whale."

In the lore of the sea Americans were impatient with most European superstitions. They readily accepted the belief that beginning a voyage on Friday was tempting Fate: they rejected the idea of mermaids and that these ladies of the sea were omens of good luck. How two omens—one good, the other bad—got into the same verse passes understanding.

> On Friday morning we set sail,
> And our ship was not far from land,
> When there we saw a pretty maid,
> With a comb and glass in her hand,
>     Brave boys,
> With a comb and glass in her hand.

O, the captain went below,
For to light the cabin lamp;
   But he couldn't light the lamp
   Because the wick was too damn' damp.
Heave-ho, you sons of glory,
The Golden Gates are passed.

Let *go* the peak halyards,
Let *go* the peak halyards,
   My knuckles are caught in the falls.
   *Let go!* (shouted)

# Blow, Ye Winds

*Included through the courtesy of Miss Joanna C. Colcord.\**

'Tis advertised in Boston, New York and Buffalo,
Five hundred brave Americans, a-whaling for to go, singing,

CHORUS:  Blow, ye winds in the morning,
           And blow, ye winds, high-o!
           Clear away your running gear,
           And blow, ye winds, high-o!

\* From *Songs of American Sailormen*, by Joanna C. Colcord. Copyright, 1938, by W. W. Norton & Company, Inc.

They send you to New Bedford, that famous whaling port,
And give you to some land-sharks to board and fit you out.

They send you to a boarding-house, there for a time to dwell;
The thieves they there are thicker than the other side of hell!

They tell you of the clipper-ships a-going in and out,
And say you'll take five hundred sperm before you're six months
out.

It's now we're out to sea, my boys, the wind comes on to blow;
One half the watch is sick on deck, the other half below.

But as for the provisions, we don't get half enough;
A little piece of stinking beef and a blamed small bag of duff.

Now comes that damned old compass, it will grieve your heart
full sore.
For theirs is two-and-thirty points and we have forty-four.

Next comes the running rigging, which you're all supposed to
know;
'Tis "Lay aloft, you son-of-a-gun, or overboard you go!"

The cooper's at the vise-bench, a-making iron poles,
And the mate's upon the main hatch a-cursing all our souls.

The Skipper's on the quarter-deck a-squinting at the sails,
When up aloft the lookout sights a school of whales.

"Now clear away the boats, my boys, and after him we'll travel,
But if you get too near his fluke, he'll kick you to the devil!"

Now we have got him turned up, we tow him alongside;
We over with our blubber-hooks and rob him of his hide.

Now the boat-steerer overside the tackle overhauls,
The Skipper's in the main-chains, so loudly does he bawl!

Next comes the stowing down, my boys; 'twill take both night
    and day,
And you'll all have fifty cents apiece on the hundred and nine-
    tieth lay.

Now we are bound into Tonbas, that blasted whaling port,
And if you run away, my boys, you surely will get caught.

Now we are bound into Tuckoona, full more in their power,
Where the skippers can buy the Consul up for half a barrel of
    flour!

But now that our old ship is full and we don't give a damn,
We'll bend on all our stu'nsails and sail for Yankee land.

When we get home, our ship made fast, and we get through our
    sailing,
A winding glass around we'll pass and damn this blubber whaling!

# Song of the Fishes

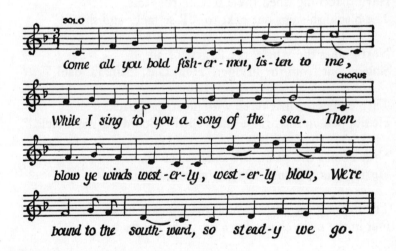

Come all you bold fisher-man, lis-ten to me,
While I sing to you a song of the sea. Then
blow ye winds west-er-ly, west-er-ly blow, We're
bound to the south-ward, so stead-y we go.

Come all you bold fishermen, listen to me,
While I sing to you a song of the sea.

CHORUS: Then blow ye winds westerly, westerly blow,
We're bound to the southward, so steady we go.

First comes the blue-fish a-wagging his tail,
He comes up on deck and yells: "All hands make sail!"

Next come the eels, with their nimble tails,
They jumped up aloft and loosed all the sails.

Next come the herrings, with their little tails,
They manned sheets and halliards and set all the sails.

Next comes the porpoise, with his short snout,
He jumps on the bridge and yells: "Ready, about!"

Next comes the swordfish, the scourge of the sea,
The order he gives is "Helm's a-lee!"

Then comes the turbot, as red as a beet,
He shouts from the bridge: "Stick out that foresheet!"

Having accomplished these wonderful feats,
The blackfish sings out next to: "Rise tacks and sheets!"

Next comes the whale, the largest of all,
Singing out from the bridge: "Haul taut, mainsail, haul!"

Then comes the mackerel, with his striped back,
He flopped on the bridge and yelled: "Board the main tack!"

Next comes the sprat, the smallest of all,
He sings out: "Haul well taut, let go and haul!"

Then comes the catfish, with his chuckle head,
Out in the main chains for a heave of the lead.

Next comes the flounder, quite fresh from the ground,
Crying: "Damn your eyes, chucklehead, mind where you sound!"

Along came the dolphin, flapping his tail,
He yelled to the boatswain to reef the foresail.

Along came the shark, with his three rows of teeth,
He flops on the foreyard and takes a snug reef.

Up jumps the fisherman, stalwart and grim,
And with his big net he scooped them all in.

CHORUS: Then blow ye winds westerly, westerly blow,
We're bound to the southward, so steady we go.

# Jack the Guinea Pig

When the anchor's weigh'd and the ship's unmoored,
And the landsmen lag behind, sir,
The sailor joyful skips aboard,
And, swearing, prays for a wind, sir!

*Towing here,*
*Yehoing there,*
*Steadily, readily,*
*Cheerily, merrily,*
*Still from care and thinking free,*
*Is a sailor's life at sea.*

When we sail with a fresh'ning breeze,
And the landsmen all grow sick, sir,
The sailor lolls, with his mind at ease,
And the song and the can go quick, sir!

*Laughing here,*
*Quaffing there,*
*Steadily, readily, etc.*

SWALLOWING THE ANCHOR

KEEP ON

When the wind at night whistles o'er the deep,
And sings to the landsmen dreary,
The sailor fearless goes to sleep,
Or takes his watch most cheery!

> *Boozing here,*
> *Snoozing there,*
> *Steadily, readily, etc.*

When the sky grows black and the wind blows hard,
And the landsmen skulk below, sir,
Jack mounts up to the top-sail yard,
And turns his quid as he goes, sir!

> *Hauling here,*
> *Bawling there,*
> *Steadily, readily, etc.*

When the foaming waves run mountains high,
And the landsmen cry, "All's gone, sir,"
The sailor hangs 'twixt sea and sky,
And he jokes with Davy Jones, sir!

> *Dashing here,*
> *Clashing there,*
> *Steadily, readily, etc.*

When the ship, d'ye see, becomes a wreck,
And the landsmen hoist the boat, sir,
The sailor scorns to quit the deck,
While a single plank's afloat, sir!

> *Swearing here,*
> *Tearing there,*
> *Steadily, readily,*
> *Cheerily, merrily,*
> *Still from care and thinking free,*
> *Is a sailor's life at sea.*

THE GIRL HE LEFT BEHIND

# Spanish Ladies

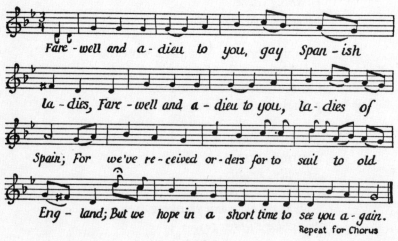

Fare-well and a-dieu to you, gay Span-ish la-dies, Fare-well and a-dieu to you, la-dies of Spain; For we've re-ceived or-ders for to sail to old Eng-land; But we hope in a short time to see you a-gain.

Repeat for Chorus

142

Farewell and adieu to you, gay Spanish ladies,
Farewell and adieu to you, ladies of Spain;
For we've received orders for to sail to old England;
But we hope in a short time to see you again.

*We'll rant and we'll roar like true British sailors,*
*We'll rant and we'll roar across the salt seas,*
*Until we strike soundings in the channel of old England,*
*From Ushant to Scilly is thirty-five leagues.*

Then we hove our ship to with the wind at sou'west, my boys,
We hove our ship to our soundings for to see;
So we rounded and sounded, and got forty-five fathoms,
We squared our mainyard, up channel steered we.

CHORUS

Now the first land we made it is called the Deadman,
Then, Ramshead off Plymouth, Start, Portland and Wight;
We passed by Beechy, by Fairleigh and Dungeness,
And hove our ship to, off South Foreland Light.

CHORUS

Then a signal was made for the grand fleet to anchor,
All in the Downs, that night for to meet;
Then stand by your stoppers, let go your shank-painters,
Haul all your clew garnets, stick out tacks and sheets.

CHORUS

So let every man toss off a full bumper,
Let every man toss off his full bowls;
We'll drink and be jolly and drown melancholy,
Singing, here's good health to all true-hearted souls.

# I Am a Brisk and Sprightly Lad

I am a brisk and sprightly lad,
But just come home from sea, sir.
  Of all the lives I ever led,
  A sailor's life for me, sir.

    *Yeo, yeo, yeo,*
    *Whilst the boatswain pipes all hands,*
    *With a yeo, yeo, yeo!*

What girl but loves the merry tar,
We o'er the ocean roam, sir.
In every clime we find a port,
In every port a home, sir.

But when our country's foes are nigh,
Each hastens to his guns, sir.
We make the boasting Frenchman fly,
And bang the haughty Dons, sir.

Our foes reduced, once more on shore,
And spend our cash with glee, sir.
And when all's gone we drown our care,
And out to sea again, sir.

    *Yeo, yeo, yeo,*
    *Whilst the boatswain pipes all hands,*
    *With a yeo, yeo, yeo!*

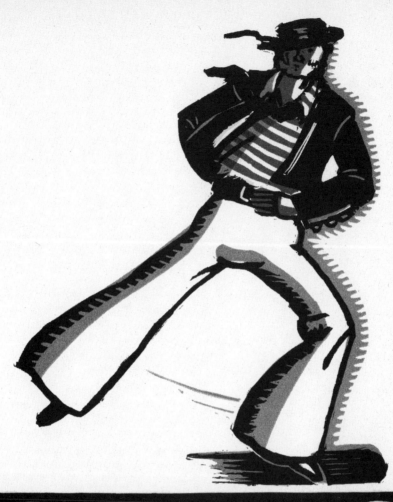

HE WAS A GAY
AND
SPRIGHTLY LAD

# Rolling Home

THIS BALLAD, so completely English, is a great favorite on the vessels of all nations. Several attempts have been made by eager patriots to give it a Yankee slant, such as "rolling home to dear old Boston" or to New York or some other two-syllable port but without any auricular success. Americans, letting go as the song deserves, still roll home to merry England.

up a-loft a-mid the rig-ging, Swift-ly

blows the fa-voring gale, Strong as spring-time in its

blos-som, Fill-ing out each bend-ing sail. And the

waves we leave be-hind us, Seem to mur-mur as they

rise, We have tar-ried here to bear you To the

CHORUS

land you dear-ly prize. Roll-ing home, roll-ing

home, roll-ing home a-cross the sea; Roll-ing

home to dear old Eng-land, Roll-ing

home, dear land, to thee!

Up aloft amid the rigging,
Swiftly blows the favoring gale,
Strong as springtime in its blossom,
Filling out each bending sail.
And the waves we leave behind us,
Seem to murmur as they rise,
We have tarried here to bear you,
To the land you dearly prize.

*Rolling home, rolling home,*
*Rolling home across the sea;*
*Rolling home to dear old England,*
*Rolling home, dear land, to thee!*

Full ten thousand miles behind us,
And a thousand miles before,
Ancient ocean waves to waft us
To the well-remembered shore.
Newborn breezes swell to send us
To our childhood's welcome skies,
To the glow of friendly faces
And the glance of loving eyes.

*Rolling home, rolling home,*
*Rolling home across the sea;*
*Rolling home to dear old England,*
*Rolling home, dear land, to thee!*

# Home, Dearie, Home

*Included through the courtesy of Miss Joanna C. Colcord.\**

Oh, Bos-ton's a fine town with ships in the bay, and

I wish in my heart it was there I was to-day, I

wish in my heart I was far a-way from here,

CHORUS

Sit-ting in my par-lor and talk-ing to my dear. Then it's

home, dear-ie, home, it's home I want to be and it's

home, dear-ie home, a-cross the rol-ling sea. Oh, the

oak and the ash and the bon-ny elm tree,

They're all a-grow-in' green in my own coun-try.

\* From *Songs of American Sailormen*, by Joanna C. Colcord. Copyright, 1938, by W. W. Norton & Company, Inc.

150

Oh, Boston's a fine town, with ships in the bay,
And I wish in my heart it was there I was today,
I wish in my heart I was far away from here,
A-sitting in my parlor and talking to my dear.

> Then it's home, dearie, home, it's home I want to be,
> And it's home, dearie, home, across the rolling sea,
> Oh, the oak and the ash and the bonny ellum tree,
> They're all a-growin' green in my own countree.

In Baltimore a-walking a lady I did meet,
With her baby on her arm as she walked down the street,
And I thought how I sailed, and the cradle standing ready,
And the pretty little babe that has never seen its daddy.

CHORUS

> And if it's a girl, oh, she shall live with me,
> And if it's a boy, he shall sail the rolling sea;
> With his tarpaulin hat and his little jacket blue,
> He shall walk the quarter-deck as his daddy used to do.

W. E. Henley, the English poet, liked the song so well that he
changed it to read Falmouth instead of Boston and the bonny elm
tree became the birken tree. In the third verse he tosses the as yet
unborn child right onto the deck of the Royal Navy:

O, if it be a lass, she shall wear a golden ring;
And if it be a lad, he shall fight for his king:
With his dirk and his hat and his little jacket blue,
He shall walk the quarter-deck as his daddy used to do.

The American Navy has a roistering version of the chorus:

Home, boys, home, it's home we ought to be!
  Home, boys, home, in God's countree!
The apple and the oak and the weeping willow tree,
  Green grows the grass in North Amerikee!

And lastly it became the many-versioned "Bell-Bottom Trousers" of the clubhouses and bull sessions.

# Bell-Bottom Trousers

When I was a serving maid, down in Drury Lane,
My master was so kind to me, my mistress was the same.
Then came a sailor, home from the sea,
And he was the cause of all my misery.

*Singing* *

Bell-bottom trousers, coat of navy blue,
He can climb the rigging as his daddy used to do.

He asked for a candle to light him up to bed,
He asked for a pillow to place beneath his head;
And I, like a silly girl, thinking it no harm,
Jumped into the sailor's bed to keep the sailor warm.

*Singing*

Bell-bottom trousers, coat of navy blue,
He can climb the rigging as his daddy used to do.

Early in the morning, before the break of day,
He handed me a five-pound note and this to me did say:
"Maybe you'll have a daughter, maybe you'll have a son,
Take this, my darling, for the damage I have done."

*Singing*

Bell-bottom trousers, coat of navy blue,
He can climb the rigging as his daddy used to do.

"If you have a daughter, bounce her on your knee,
But if you have a son send the rascal out to sea.
Singing bell-bottom trousers, coat of navy blue,
He'll climb the rigging as his daddy used to do."

* Spoken flatly.

PAINTING THE LILY

# Homeward Bound

To Pen-sa-co-la town we'll bid a-dieu, To love-ly Kate and
pret-ty Sue, Our an-chor's weighed and our sails un-furled, We're
bound for to plough this wa-tery world. You know we're out-ward.
bound, Hur-rah, we're out-ward bound.

To Pensacola town we'll bid adieu,
To lovely Kate and pretty Sue.
Our anchor's weighed and our sails unfurled,
We're bound for to plough this watery world.

*You know we're outward bound,*
*Hurrah, we're outward bound!*

153

The wind blows hard from the east-nor'east,
Our ship sails ten knots at least,
The skipper will our wants supply,
And while we've grog we'll ne'er say die.

And should we touch at Malabar,
Or any other port so far,
Our skipper will tip the chink,
And just like fishes we will drink.

And now our three years it is out,
It's very near time we back'd about;
And when we're home, and do get free,
Oh, won't we have a jolly spree.

*You know we're homeward bound,*
*Hurrah, we're homeward bound!*

And now we'll haul into the docks,
Where all the pretty girls come in flocks,
And one to the other they will say,
"Here comes Jack with his three years' pay!"

And now we'll haul to the "Dog and Bell,"
Where there's good liquor for to sell,
In comes old Archer with a smile,
Saying, "Drink, my lads, it's worth your while."

But when our money's all gone and spent,
And none to be borrowed nor none to be lent,
In comes old Archer with a frown,
Saying, "Get up, Jack, let John sit down.

*I know you're outward bound."*
*Hurrah, we're outward bound!*

CROSSING THE LINE

HOME FOR CHRISTMAS

# Wardroom Ballads

TAKING A PRIZE

# The Yankee Man-of-War

Sometimes *The Stately Southerner*

AMERICAN SAILORMEN have taken over many songs that
were written for the patriotic uses of the British. There is one
American song that survives principally because of its popularity
among the English, who seem to prefer the title "The Stately
Southerner."

Cruising in the *Ranger*, eighteen guns, Captain John Paul Jones,
in 1778, conducted a series of punishing raids on the English
coast, capturing merchantmen, burning the shipping at White-
haven and other points, and finally taking captive the British
twenty-gun *Drake* that had been sent out to stop him. The British
sent more and bigger ships, and the song celebrates the *Ranger's*
escape.

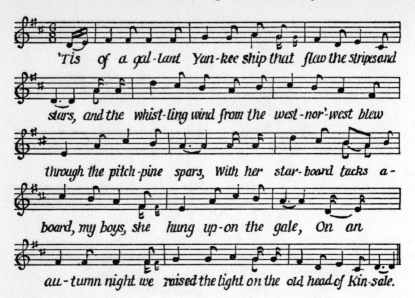

'Tis of a gallant Yankee ship that flew the stripes and stars,
And the whistling wind from the west-nor'west blew through the
　　pitch-pine spars,
With her starboard tacks aboard, my boys, she hung upon the gale,
On an autumn night we raised the light on the old head of Kinsale.

It was a clear and cloudless night, and the wind blew steady and
　　strong,
As gayly over the sparkling deep our good ship bowled along;
With the foaming seas beneath her bow the fiery waves she spread,
And bending low her bosom of snow, she buried her lee cat-head.

There was no talk of short'ning sail by him who walked the poop,
And under the press of her pond'ring jib, the boom bent like a
　　hoop!
And the groaning waterways told the strain that held her stout
　　main-tack,
But he only laughed as he glanced abaft at a white and silv'ry track.

A DAY AT THE SEA SHORE

The mid-tide meets in the channel waves that flow from shore to
shore,
And the mist hung heavy upon the land from Featherstone to Dun-
more,
And that sterling light in Tusker Rock where the old bell tolls
each hour,
And the beacon light that shone so bright was quench'd on Waterford Tower.

The nightly robes our good ship wore were her own topsails
three,
Her spanker and her standing jib—the courses being free;
"Now, lay aloft! my heroes bold, let not a moment pass!"
And royals and topgallant sails were quickly on each mast.

What looms upon our starboard bow? What hangs upon the
breeze?
'Tis time our good ship hauled her wind abreast the old Saltee's.
For by her ponderous press of sail and by her consorts four
We saw our morning visitor was a British man-of-war.

Up spoke our noble Captain then, as a shot ahead of us past—
"Haul snug your flowing courses! lay your topsail to the mast!"
Those Englishmen gave three loud hurrahs from the deck of their
covered ark,
And we answered back by a solid broadside from the decks of our
patriot bark.

"Out booms! out booms!" our skipper cried, "out booms and give
her sheet,"
And the swiftest keel that was ever launched shot ahead of the
British fleet,
And amidst a thundering shower of shot with stun'sails hoisting
away,
Down the North Channel Paul Jones did steer just at the break of
day.

# Ye Parliament of England

## *War of 1812*

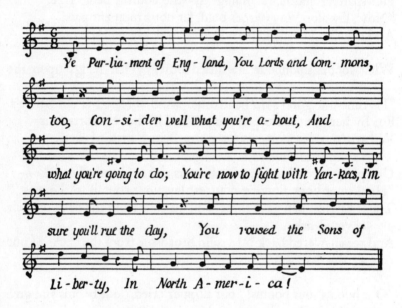

Ye Par-lia-ment of Eng-land, You Lords and Com-mons, too, Con-si-der well what you're a-bout, And what you're going to do; You're now to fight with Yan-kees, I'm sure you'll rue the day, You roused the Sons of Li-ber-ty, In North A-mer-i-ca!

Ye Parliament of England,
  You Lords and Commons, too,
Consider well what you're about,
  And what you're going to do;
You're now to fight with Yankees,
  I'm sure you'll rue the day,
You roused the Sons of Liberty,
  **In North America!**

You first confined our commerce,
    And said our ships shan't trade,
You next impressed our seamen,
    And used them as your slaves;
You then insulted Rodgers,
    While ploughing o'er the main,
And had we not declared war,
    You'd have done it o'er again!


You thought our frigates were but few
    And Yankees could not fight,
Until brave Hull your *Guerrière* took
    And banished her from your sight.
The *Wasp* then took your *Frolic*,
    We'll nothing say to that,
The *Poictiers* being of the line,
    Of course she took her back.


The next, your *Macedonian*,
    No finer ship could swim,
Decatur took her gilt-work off,
    And then he sent her in.
The *Java*, by a Yankee ship
    Was sunk, you all must know;
The *Peacock* fine, in all her plume,
    By Lawrence down did go.


Then next you sent your *Boxer*,
    To box us all about,
But we had an *Enterprising* brig
    That beat your *Boxer* out;
We boxed her up to Portland,
    And moored her off the town,
To show the Sons of Liberty
    The *Boxer* of renown.

The next upon Lake Erie,
  Where Perry had some fun,
You own he beat your naval force,
  And caused them for to run;
This was to you a sore defeat,
  The like ne'er known before—
Your British squadron beat complete—
  Some took, some run ashore.

There's Rodgers, in the *President*,
  Will burn, sink, and destroy;
The *Congress*, on the Brazil coast,
  Your commerce will annoy;
The *Essex*, in the South Seas,
  Will put out all your lights,
The flag she waves at her mast-head—
  "Free Trade and Sailors' Rights."

Lament, ye Sons of Britain,
  For distant is the day,
When you'll regain by British force,
  What you've lost in America;
Go tell your king and parliament,
  By all the world 'tis known,
That British force, by sea and land,
  By Yankees is o'erthrown!

Use every endeavor,
  And strive to make a peace,
For Yankee ships are building fast,
  Their navy to increase;
They will enforce their commerce;
  The laws by heaven are made,
That Yankee ships in time of peace
  To any port may trade.

# The *Constitution* and the *Guerrière*

OF ALL OUR wars, that of 1812 was the most productive of songs: the naval songsters are full of them, and even at this late date many are still in favor in the wardrooms of the Navy. The old charge so often leveled against Americans that they are over-boastful has much in it save when uttered by the British. There were two great engagements in that war, the first won by the Americans, the second by the British, and the reader can decide which service crowed the loudest. Both songs were written to the music of "A Drop of Brandy, O!"

The fight between the *Constitution* and the *Guerrière* took place off the New England coast, August 19, 1812. In less than half an hour the *Guerrière*, fifty guns, commanded by Captain Dacres, was a wreck not worth towing to port and was blown up. The *Constitution*, forty-four guns, was commanded by Captain Isaac Hull. It was in this battle that the American sailors, seeing the solid British shot bouncing off the live oak sides of their vessel, named her "Old Ironsides."

It ofttimes has been told,
That the British seaman bold
Could flog the tars of France so neat and handy, oh!
But they never found their match,
Till the Yankees did them catch,
Oh, the Yankee boys for fighting are the dandy, oh!

The *Guerrière*, a frigate bold,
On the foaming ocean rolled,
Commanded by proud Dacres the grandee, oh!
With as choice an English crew,
As a rammer ever drew,
Could flog the Frenchmen two to one so handy, oh!

When this frigate hove in view,
Says proud Dacres to his crew,
"Come, clear ship for action and be handy, oh!
To the weather gage, boys, get her,"
And to make his men fight better,
Gave them to drink, gunpowder mixed with brandy, oh!

Then Dacres loudly cries,
"Make this Yankee ship your prize,
You can in thirty minutes, neat and handy, oh!
Twenty-five's enough I'm sure,
And if you'll do it in a score,
I'll treat you to a double share of brandy, oh!"


The British shot flew hot,
Which the Yankee answered not,
Till they got within the distance they called handy, oh!
"Now," says Hull unto his crew,
"Boys, let's see what we can do,
If we take this boasting Briton we're the dandy, oh!"


The first broadside we poured
Carried her mainmast by the board,
Which made this lofty frigate look abandoned, oh!
Then Dacres shook his head,
And to his officers said,
"Lord! I didn't think those Yankees were so handy, oh!"


Our second told so well,
That their fore and mizzen fell,
Which dous'd the royal ensign neat and handy, oh!
"By George," says he, "we're done,"
And they fired a lee gun,
While the Yankees struck up Yankee Doodle Dandy, oh!


Then Dacres came on board,
To deliver up his sword,
Tho' loath he was to part with it, it was so handy, oh!
"Oh, keep your sword," says Hull,
"For it only makes you dull,
Cheer up and let us have a little brandy, oh!"

Now fill your glasses full,
And we'll drink to Captain Hull,
And so merrily we'll push about the brandy, oh!
John Bull may toast his fill,
But let the world say what they will,
The Yankee boys for fighting are the dandy, oh!


The following year, on June first, while the *Chesapeake*, Captain James Lawrence, was lying in Boston Harbor, the *Shannon*, Captain P. V. Broke, came up with the express design of fighting the American. Captain Lawrence accepted the challenge and sailed out to meet the enemy. He and his chief officers were mortally wounded, and it was at this moment that Lawrence uttered his immortal words, "Don't give up the ship!" Carried to his cabin, he said: "Go on deck and order them to fire faster and fight the ship till she sinks. Never strike. Let the colors wave while I live." But the *Chesapeake* was taken by assault and Lawrence carried a prisoner to Halifax, where he died.

# The *Shannon* and the *Chesapeake*

*Included through the courtesy of Arch H. Ferguson.\**

Now the *Chesapeake* so bold
Sailed from Boston we've been told,
For to take the British frigate neat and handy, O!
   The people in the port
   All came out to see the sport
And the bands were playing "Yankee Doodle Dandy, O!"

The British frigate's name,
Which for the purpose came
To cool the Yankee courage neat and handy-o,
   Was the *Shannon*—Captain Broke,
   All her men were hearts of oak.
And at fighting were allowed to be the dandy-o.

\* From *Sea Songs and Shanties*, collected by W. B. Whall. Fourth Edition.
Published by Brown, Son & Ferguson, Ltd., Glasgow.

The fight had scarce begun
Ere they flinch-ed from their guns,
Which at first they started working neat and handy-o.
Then brave Broke he waved his sword,
Crying, "Now, my lads, aboard,
And we'll stop their playing 'Yankee Doodle Dandy-o.'"

They no sooner heard the word,
Than they quickly jumped aboard,
And hauled down the Yankee colours neat and handy-o;
Notwithstanding all their brag,
Now the glorious British flag
At the Yankee mizzen peak was quite the dandy-o.

Here's a health, brave Broke, to you,
To your officers and crew,
Who aboard the *Shannon* frigate fought so handy-o;
And may it always prove,
That in fighting and in love,
The British tar forever is the dandy-o.

# Charge the Can Cheerily

*Copied from the original in the Public Library of the City of Boston*

Now coil up your nonsense 'bout England's great Navy,
   And take in your slack about oak-hearted Tars;
For frigates as stout, and as gallant crews have we,
   Or how came her *Macedon* deck'd with our stars?
Yes—how came her *Guerrière*, her *Peacock*, and *Java*,
   All sent broken ribb'd to Old Davy of late?
How came it? why, split me! than Britons we're braver,
   And that shall they feel it whenever we meet.


CHORUS:    *Then charge the can cheerily;*
            *Send it round merrily;*
   *Here's to our country and captains commanding;*
           *To all who inherit*
            *Of Lawrence the spirit,*
  *"Disdaining to strike while a stick is left standing."*

Now coil up your non-sense 'bout Eng-land's great Na-vy, And take in your slack a-bout oak-heart-ed Tars; For fri-gates as stout, and as gal-lant crews have we, Or how came her Ma-ce-don deck'd with our stars? Yes,- how came her Guer-riere, her Pea-cock, and Ja-va, All sent bro-ken ribb'd to Old Da-vy of late? How came it? Why, split me! than Bri-tons we're bra-ver, And that shall they feel it wher-ev-er we meet. Then charge the can

CHORUS

cheer-i-ly; Send it round mer-ri-ly: Here's to our coun-try and cap-tains com-mand-ing; To all who in-her-it of Law-rence the spir-it, "Dis-dain-ing to strike while a stick is left stand-ing."

Now, if unawares, we should run (a fresh gale in)
   Close in with a squadron, we'd laugh at 'em all;
We'd tip master Bull such a sample of sailing,
   As should cause him to fret like a pig in a squall;
We'd show the vain boaster of numbers superior,
   Though he and his slaves at the notion may sneer,
In skill, as in courage, to us they're inferior;
   For the longer they chase us the less we've to fear.

CHORUS

But should a Razee be espied ahead nearly;
   To fetch her we'd crowd ev'ry stitch we could make;
Down chests and up hammocks would heave away cheerily,
   And ready for action would be in a shake;
For her swaggering cut, though, and metal not caring,
   Till up with her close should our fire be withheld;
Then pour'd in so hot that her mangled crew, fearing
   A trip to the bottom, should speedily yield.

CHORUS

Britannia, although she beleaguers our coast now,
   The dread of our wives and our sweethearts as well,
Of ruling the waves has less reason to boast now,
   As Dacres, and Carden, and Whinyates can tell:
Enroll'd in our annals live Hull and Decatur,
   Jones, Lawrence, and Bainbridge, Columbia's pride;
The pride of our Navy, which sooner or later,
   Shall on the wide ocean triumphantly ride.

    *Then charge the can cheerily;*
    *Send it round merrily;*
  *Here's to our country and captains commanding;*
    *To all who inherit*
    *Of Lawrence the spirit,*
  *"Disdaining to strike while a stick is left standing."*

# Nancy Lee

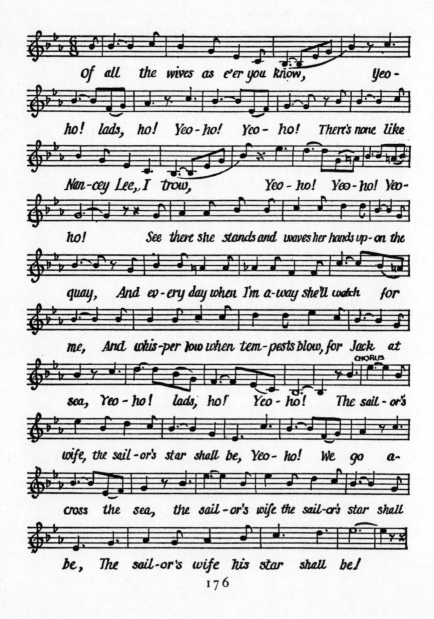

Of all the wives as e'er you know, Yeo-

ho! lads, ho! Yeo-ho! Yeo-ho! There's none like

Nan-cey Lee, I trow, Yeo-ho! Yeo-ho! Yeo-

ho! See there she stands and waves her hands up-on the

quay, And ev-ery day when I'm a-way she'll watch for

me, And whis-per low when tem-pests blow, for Jack at

sea, Yeo-ho! lads, ho! Yeo-ho! The sail-or's

wife, the sail-or's star shall be, Yeo-ho! We go a-

cross the sea, the sail-or's wife the sail-or's star shall

be, The sail-or's wife his star shall be!

Of all the wives as e'er you know,
 Yeo-ho! lads, ho! Yeo-ho! Yeo-ho!
There's none like Nancy Lee, I trow,
 Yeo-ho! Yeo-ho! Yeo-ho!
See there she stands and waves her hands upon the quay,
And every day when I'm away she'll watch for me,
And whisper low when tempests blow, for Jack at sea,
 Yeo-ho! lads, ho! Yeo-ho!

CHORUS

 The sailor's wife the sailor's star shall be,
  Yeo-ho! We go across the sea;
 The sailor's wife the sailor's star shall be,
  The sailor's wife his star shall be!

The harbor's past, the breezes blow,
 Yeo-ho! lads, ho! Yeo-ho! Yeo-ho!
'Tis long ere we come back, I know.
 Yeo-ho! Yeo-ho! Yeo-ho!
But true and bright from morn till night my home will be,
And all so neat, and snug and sweet, for Jack at sea,
And Nancy's face to bless the place, and welcome me.
 Yeo-ho! lads, ho! Yeo-ho!

CHORUS

The bosun pipes the watch below,
 Yeo-ho! lads, ho! Yeo-ho! Yeo-ho!
Then here's a health afore we go,
 Yeo-ho! Yeo-ho! Yeo-ho!
A long, long life to my sweet wife, and mates at sea,
And keep our bones from Davy Jones, where-e'er we be,
And may you meet a mate as sweet as Nancy Lee.
 Yeo-ho! lads, ho! Yeo-ho!

# The Norfolk Girls

Our top-sails reef'd and filled a-way, All snug a-loft we know, De- spite the storm we'll still be gay, A- mong our friends be- low. Come ga- ther round and lis- ten, then, with spi - rits warm and true; Here's a health to all the Nor- folk girls, And Ports- mouth maid- ens, too.

**CHORUS**

Here's a health to all the Nor- folk girls, And Ports-mouth maid- ens, too, There's a health to all the Nor - folk girls, And Ports-mouth maid- ens, too.

Sir Henry Morgan

NEXT IS SIR HENRY ~

Our topsails reef'd and filled away,
All snug aloft we know,
Despite the storms we'll still be gay,
Among our friends below.
Come gather round and listen, then,
With spirits warm and true;
Here's a health to all the Norfolk girls,
And Portsmouth maidens, too.

Here's a health to all the Norfolk girls,
  And Portsmouth maidens, too,
Here's a health to all the Norfolk girls,
  And Portsmouth maidens, too.

May the darksome eye of loveliness,
And that of ocean's ray,
Shed only tears of happiness
Forever and for aye.
Fill up, tho' far away from home,
And foreign scenes we view,
We cherish still the Norfolk girls,
And the Portsmouth maidens, too.

Chorus

May the cheek whereon reposes
Emotion young and dear,
Still wear the hue of roses
Thro' each succeeding year.
We'll drink to by-past scenes, and hope
Some day again to view,
The lovely girls of Norfolk, and
The Portsmouth maidens, too.

Chorus

And if we never backward go,
Borne home on ocean's breast,

But find among the caves below
A sailor's place of rest;
Still ere we close our eyes and pass
Beneath the depths of blue,
We'll think of all the Norfolk girls,
And Portsmouth maidens, too.

CHORUS

Should the foe appear before us,
To our guns we'll fondly cling,
While our stars are gleaming o'er us,
Shall their notes of freedom ring.
While life's warm stream is flowing,
 Our eager pulses through,
We'll fight for home, the Norfolk girls,
And Portsmouth maidens, too.

CHORUS

Fill up, fill up, yet once again,
Before we say good night,
From every glass its sweetness drain,
To friendship's steady light.
May peace around our kindred dwell,
All beings loved and true,
The lovely girls of Norfolk,
And the Portsmouth maidens, too.

CHORUS

Good night, good night, our pillows now
With pleasant thoughts we'll press,
And dream some hand rests on our brow,
Its slumbering to bless.
Amid delightful reveries
That fancy brings to view,

Perhaps we'll meet the Norfolk girls,
And Portsmouth maidens, too.

Here's a health to all the Norfolk girls,
And Portsmouth maidens, too,
Here's a health to all the Norfolk girls,
And Portsmouth maidens, too.

# The Flash Frigate

I sing of a fri-gate, a fri-gate of fame, And
in the West In-dies she bore a great name, For
cru-el, hard treat-ment of ev-ery de-gree, Like
slaves in the gal-leys we ploughed the salt sea.

I sing of a frigate, a frigate of fame,
And in the West Indies she bore a great name,
For cruel, hard treatment of every degree,
Like slaves in the galleys we ploughed the salt sea.

At four in the morning our day's work begun;
"Come, lash up your hammocks, boys, every one."
Seven turns with the lashing so neatly must show,
And all of one size through a hoop they must go.

The next thing we do is to holystone the decks,
Mizzen-topmen from the forehatch their buckets must fetch,
And its fore and main topmen so loudly they bawl,
Come, fetch up your holystones, squilgees and all.

The decks being scrubbed and the rigging coiled down,
It's clean up your bright work which is found all around,
Your gun-caps and aprons so neatly must shine,
And in white frocks and trousers you must all toe the line.

The next thing we hear is "All hands to make sail!"
"Way aloft!" and "Lay out!" and "Let fall!" is the hail,
Oh, your royals and your skysails and moonsails so high,
At the sound of the call your skyscrapers must fly.

But now, my brave boys, comes the best of the fun:
"All hands about ship and reef topsails," in one.
Oh, it's "lay aloft, topmen," as the helm goes down,
And it's "clew down your topsails," as the mainyard swings round.

"Trice up, and lay out, and take two snug reefs in one,"
And all in one moment this work must be done.
Then man your head braces, topsail-halliards and all,
And hoist away topsails as you let go and haul.

Our second lieutenant, you all know him well,
He comes up on deck and cuts a great swell.
Oh, it's "bear a hand here," and "bear a hand there."
And at the lee gangway he serves out our share.*

Now, all you bold seamen who plough the salt sea,
Beware this frigate wherever she be,
For they'll beat you and bang you till you ain't worth a damn,
And send you an invalid to your own native land.

H.M.S. *Pique*, frigate, was assigned for many years to the West
Indies station. She had the name of a "blood ship," and her vices
were celebrated chiefly by the American Navy.

* of the rope's end.

# Miscellaneous Songs
## and Ballads

# The *Flying Cloud*

THIS BALLAD achieved a certain degree of popularity in the shore dives and music halls patronized by sailormen that it never deserved. The *Flying Cloud*, without doubt the greatest of the clippers, was never in the slave trade nor given to piratical practices: her life is an open book and an inspiring one to all Americans. No captain named Moore ever commanded her, and there are no records of another ship with the same name. The song's closing lines are reminiscent of "The Ballad of Captain Kidd," which follows it.

My name is Edward Hallahan and you must understand,
I came from County Waterford and Ireland's happy land.
When I was young and in my prime, fair fortune on me smiled,
My parents reared me tenderly, I was their only child.

My name is Ed-ward Hall-a-han and you must un-der-
stand, I came from Coun-ty Wa-ter-ford and
Ire-land's hap-py land. When I was young and
in my prime, fair for-tune on me smiled, My
pa-rents reared me ten-der-ly, I was their on-ly child.

My father bound me to a trade in Waterford's fair town,
He bound me to a cooper there, by name of William Brown,
I served my master faithfully for eighteen months or more,
Then I shipped on board the *Ocean Queen*, belonging to Tramore.

When we came unto Bermuda's isle, there I met with Captain
  Moore,
The commander of The *Flying Cloud*, hailing from Baltimore.
He asked me if I'd ship with him, on a slaving voyage to go,
To the burning shores of Africa, where the sugar cane does grow.

It was after some weeks' sailing we arrived on Africa's shore,
Five hundred of those poor slaves, from their native land we tore,
We made them walk in on a plank, and we stowed them down
  below
Scarce eighteen inches to a man was all they had to go.

The plague and fever came on board, swept half of them away;
We dragged the bodies up on deck and hove them in the sea.
It was better for the rest of them that they had died before,
Than to work under brutes of planters in Cuba forevermore.

It was after stormy weather we arrived off Cuba's shore,
And we sold them to the planters there to be slaves forevermore.
For the rice and the coffee seed to sow beneath the broiling sun,
There to lead a wretched lonely life till their career was run.

It's now our money is all spent, we must go to sea again,
When Captain Moore he came on deck and said unto us men:
"There is gold and silver to be had if with me you'll remain,
And we'll hoist the pirate flag aloft and scour the Spanish Main."

We all agreed but three young men who told us them to land,
And two of them were Boston boys, the other from Newfound-
    land.
I wish to God I'd joined those men and went with them on shore,
Than to lead a wild and reckless life, serving under Captain Moore.

The *Flying Cloud* was a Yankee ship of five hundred tons or more,
She could outsail any clipper ship hailing out of Baltimore.
With her canvas white as driven snow, and on it there's no specks,
And forty men and fourteen guns she carried on her decks.

It's oft I've seen that gallant ship with the wind abaft her beam,
With her royals and her stunsails set, a sight for to be seen;
With the curling waves at her clipper bow, a sailor's joy to feel,
And the canvas taut in the whistling breeze, logging fourteen off
    the reel.

We sank and plundered many a ship down on the Spanish Main,
Caused many a wife and orphan in sorrow to remain;
To them we gave no quarter, but gave them watery graves
For the saying of our captain was, that dead men tell no tales.

Pursued we were by many a ship, by frigates and liners, too,
Till at last a British man-of-war, the *Dungeness*, hove in view;
She fired a shot across our bow, as we sailed before the wind,
Then a chain shot cut our mainmast down and we fell far behind.

Our crew they beat to quarters as she ranged up alongside,
And soon across our quarter-deck there ran a crimson tide.
We fought till Captain Moore was killed and twenty of our men,
Till a bombshell set our ship on fire; we had to surrender then.

It's next to Newgate we were brought, bound down in iron chains,
For the sinking and the plundering of ships on the Spanish Main.
The judge he found us guilty, we were condemned to die;
Young men, a warning take by me, and shun all piracy.

Then fare you well, old Waterford, and the girl that I adore,
I'll never kiss your cheek again, or squeeze your hand no more.
For whiskey and bad company first made a wretch of me;
Young men, a warning by me take, and shun all piracy.

# The Ballad of Captain Kidd

My name was William Kidd, when I sailed, when I sailed,
  My name was William Kidd, when I sailed,
My name was William Kidd; God's laws I did forbid,
  And so wickedly I did, when I sailed.

My parents taught me well, when I sailed, when I sailed,
  My parents taught me well, when I sailed,
My parents taught me well, to shun the gates of hell,
  But against them I rebelled, when I sailed.

I'd a Bible in my hand, when I sailed, when I sailed,
  I'd a Bible in my hand, when I sailed,
I'd a Bible in my hand, by my father's great command,
  And I sunk it in the sand, when I sailed.

I murdered William Moore, as I sailed, as I sailed,
  I murdered William Moore, as I sailed,
I murdered William Moore, and laid him in his gore,
  Not many leagues from shore, as I sailed.

I was sick and nigh to death, as I sailed, as I sailed,
  I was sick and nigh to death, as I sailed,
I was sick and nigh to death and I vowed with every breath,
  To walk in wisdom's ways, when I sailed.

I thought I was undone, as I sailed, as I sailed,
  I thought I was undone, as I sailed,
I thought I was undone, and my wicked glass had run,
  But health did soon return, as I sailed.

My repentance lasted not, as I sailed, as I sailed,
  My repentance lasted not, as I sailed,
My repentance lasted not, my vows I soon forgot,
  Damnation was my lot, as I sailed.

I spied three ships from France, as I sailed, as I sailed,
  I spied three ships of France, as I sailed,
I spied the ships of France, to them I did advance,
  And took them all by chance, as I sailed.

I spied three ships from Spain, as I sailed, as I sailed,
  I spied three ships from Spain, as I sailed,
I spied the ships of Spain, I looted them for gain,
  Till most of them were slain, as I sailed.

I'd ninety bars of gold, as I sailed, as I sailed,
  I'd ninety bars of gold, as I sailed,
I'd ninety bars of gold and dollars manifold,
  With riches uncontrolled, as I sailed.

Thus being o'ertaken at last, as I sailed, as I sailed,
  Thus being o'ertaken at last, as I sailed,
Thus being o'ertaken at last, and into prison cast,
  And sentence being passed, I must die.

Farewell, the raging main, I must die, I must die,
  Farewell, the raging main, I must die,
Farewell, the raging main, to Turkey, France and Spain,
  I shall never see you again, for I must die.

To the Execution Dock, I must go, I must go,
  To the Execution Dock, I must go,
To the Execution Dock, while many thousands flock,
  But I must bear the shock, and must die.

Come all ye young and old and see me die, see me die,
  Come all ye young and old and see me die,
Come all ye young and old, you're welcome to my gold,
  For by it I've lost my soul, and must die.

Take a warning now by me, for I must die, I must die,
  Take a warning now by me, for I must die,
Take a warning now by me and shun bad company,
  Lest you come to hell with me, for I must die.

# The Female Smuggler

*Included through the courtesy of Arch H. Ferguson.* *

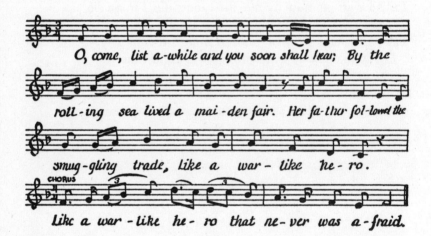

O, come, list a-while and you soon shall hear; By the
roll-ing sea lived a mai-den fair. Her fa-ther fol-lowed the
smug-gling trade, like a war-like he-ro.

CHORUS
Like a war-like he-ro that ne-ver was a-fraid.

O, come, list awhile, and you soon shall hear,
By the rolling sea lived a maiden fair.
Her father followed the smuggling trade,
Like a war-like hero.

Chorus: Like a war-like hero that never was afraid.

* From *Sea Songs and Shanties*, collected by W. B. Whall. Fourth Edition.
Published by Brown, Son & Ferguson, Ltd., Glasgow.

BLACKBEARD!

Now, in sailor's clothing young Jane did go,
Dressed like a sailor from top to toe;
Her aged father was the only care
Of this female smuggler,

       Of this female smuggler who never did despair.

With her pistols loaded she went aboard.
And by her side hung a glittering sword,
In her belt two daggers; well armed for war
Was this female smuggler,

       Was this female smuggler, who never feared a scar.

Now they had not sail-ed far from the land,
When a strange sail brought them to a stand.
"These are sea robbers," this maid did cry,
"But the female smuggler,

       But the female smuggler will conquer or will die."

Alongside, then, this strange vessel came.
"Cheer up," cried Jane, "we will board the same;
We'll run all chances to rise or fall,"
Cried this female smuggler,

       Cried this female smuggler who never feared a ball.

Now they killed these pirates and took their store,
And soon returned to old Eng-a-land's shore.
With a keg of brandy she walked along,
Did this female smuggler,

       Did this female smuggler, and sweetly sang a song.

Now they were followed by the blockade,
Who in irons strong did put this fair maid.

But when they brought her for to be ter-ried,
This young female smuggler,

   This young female smuggler stood dress-ed like a bride.

Their commodore against her appeared,
And for her life she did greatly fear.
When he did find to his great surprise
'Twas a female smuggler,

   'Twas a female smuggler had fought him in disguise.

He to the judge and the jury said,
"I cannot prosecute this maid,
Pardon for her on my knees I crave,
For this female smuggler,

   For this female smuggler so valiant and so brave."

Then this commodore to her father went,
To gain her hand he asked his consent.
His consent he gained, so the commodore
And the female smuggler,

   And the female smuggler are one for evermore.

# Little Mohee

IT WOULD BE nothing short of criminal negligence to leave this ballad out of a book of sailors' songs, even if it could be proved that no deep-water sailor ever sang the song. So much for the sailors' loss: it is a great folksong and is sung in the Kentucky mountains, the Texas plains, and all along the Shining Mountains. It is also a great favorite among the sailors on the Great Lakes.

The words and music were taken from a recording in the Archive of American Folksong of the Library of Congress.

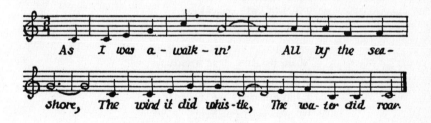

As I was a-walkin'
All by the seashore,
The wind it did whistle,
The water did roar.

As I sat a-musing
Myself on the grass,
Who should come by me
But a young Indian lass.

She came and sat by me,
Took hold of my hand,
And said, "You're a stranger
And in a strange land.

But if you will follow,
You're welcome to come
And dwell in the cottage
That I call my home."

The sun was past sinking
Far over the sea,
As I wandered along with
My little Mohee.

She asked me to marry
And offered her hand
Saying, "Father's the chieftain
All over this land.

My father's the chieftain
And ruler can be,
I'm his only daughter,
My name is Mohee."

"Oh, no, my dear maiden,
That never can be,
I have a dear sweetheart
In my own country.

I will not forsake her,
I know she loves me;
Her heart is as true
As any Mohee."

The last time I saw her
She knelt on the sand;
Just as my boat passed her
She waved me her hand.

Saying, "When you get over
With the girl that you love,
Remember the Mohee
In the mountains above."

And when I have landed
With the girl that I love,
Both friends and relations
Gathered 'round me once more.

I gazed all about me,
Not one did I see,
That did really compare
With my little Mohee.

The girl I had trusted
Proved untrue to me,
So I'll turn my courses
Back over the sea.

I'll turn my high courses,
Backwards I'll flee,
I'll go spend my days with
My little Mohee.

# The Nantucket Skipper

NEW ENGLAND'S coast long had a fleet of packets, sloops, and schooners that operated between Boston and their home ports, carrying passengers, freight, and the mail. There are many stories of those rugged little vessels, but one, that of a Nantucket skipper, who day or night could remain in his bunk and give his position, is worth retelling. James T. Fields, a distinguished writer and editor, put it into verse.

Many a long, long year ago,
Nantucket skippers had a plan
Of finding out, though 'lying low,'
How near New York their schooners ran.

They greased the lead before it fell,
And then, by sounding through the night,
Knowing the soil that stuck, so well,
They always guessed their reckoning right.

A skipper gray, whose eyes were dim,
Could tell by *tasting*, just the spot;
And so below he'd dowse the glim,—
After, of course, his 'something hot.'

Snug in his berth, at eight o'clock,
This ancient skipper might be found.
No matter how his craft would rock,
He slept; for skippers' naps are sound.

The watch on deck would now and then
Run down and wake him, with the lead;
He'd up and taste, and tell the men
How many miles they went ahead.

One night 'twas Jotham Marden's watch,
A curious wag,—the pedler's son;
And so he mused (the wanton wretch):
"Tonight I'll have a grain of fun!

We're all a set of stupid fools
To think the skipper knows by *tasting*
What ground he's on,—Nantucket schools
Don't teach such stuff, with all their basting!"

And so he took the well-greased lead
And rubbed it o'er a box of earth
That stood on deck,—a parsnip bed;
And then he sought the skipper's berth.

"Where are we now, sir? Please to taste."
The skipper yawned, put out his tongue;
Then oped his eyes in wondrous haste,
And then upon the floor he sprung!

The skipper stormed and tore his hair,
Thrust on his boots, and roared to Marden:
"Nantucket's sunk, and here we are
Right over old Marm Hackett's garden."

# Brother Noah

Brother Noah, Brother Noah,
May I come into the Ark of the Lord
For it's growing very dark and it's raining very hard?
    Halleloo, halleloo, halleloo, hallelujah!

No, you can't sir, no, you can't, sir,
You can't come into the Ark of the Lord,
Though it's growing very dark and it's raining very hard.
    Halleloo, halleloo, halleloo, hallelujah!

Very well, sir, very well, sir,
You can go to the dickens with your darned old scow,
'Cause it ain't goin' to rain very hard anyhow.
   Halleloo, halleloo, halleloo, hallelujah!

That's a lie, sir, that's a lie, sir,
You can darn soon tell that it ain't no sell,
'Cause it's sprinklin' now and it's goin' to rain like hell.
   Halleloo, halleloo, halleloo, hallelujah!

# The Girl I Left Behind Me

The dames of France are fond and free, And Flem-ish lips are will-ing; And soft the maids of I-ta-ly, And Span-ish eyes are thrill-ing; Still, though I bask be-neath their smile, Their charms fail to bind me, And my heart goes back to E-rins Isle, To the girl I left be-hind me.

The dames of France are fond and free,
  And Flemish lips are willing;
And soft the maids of Italy,
  And Spanish eyes are thrilling;
Still, though I bask beneath their smile,
  Their charms fail to bind me.
And my heart goes back to Erin's Isle,
  To the girl I left behind me.

For she's as fair as Shannon's side,
  And purer than its water,
But she refused to be my bride
  Though many years I sought her.
Yet, since to France I sailed away,
  Her letters oft remind me,
That I promised never to gainsay
  The girl I left behind me.

She says: "My own dear love come home,
  My friends are rich and many;
Or else, abroad with you I'll roam,
  A soldier stout as any;
If you'll not come, nor let me go,
  I'll think you have resigned me."
My heart nigh broke when I answered "No,"
  To the girl I left behind me.

For never shall my true love brave
  A life of war and toiling,
And never as a skulking slave
  I'll tread my native soil on.
But were it free or to be freed,
  The battle's close would find me
To Ireland bound, nor message need
  From the girl I left behind me.

# Rollicking Bill the Sailor

Who's that a-knocking at my door?
  Cried the fair young maiden.
Who's that a-knocking at my door?
  Cried the fair young maiden.

It's me, myself, and nobody else!
  Cried Rollicking Bill the Sailor.
It's me, myself, and nobody else!
  Cried Rollicking Bill the Sailor.

I'll come down and let you in,
  Cried the fair young maiden.
I'll come down and let you in,
  Cried the fair young maiden.

I need a place for me to sleep,
  Cried Rollicking Bill the Sailor.
I need a place for me to sleep,
  Cried Rollicking Bill the Sailor.

But we have only one bed!
  Cried the fair young maiden.
But we have only one bed!
  Cried the fair young maiden.

# The Fire Ship*

As I strolled out one eve-ning, out for a night's ca-reer, I
spied a lof-ty fire-ship and af-ter her did steer. I
hoist-ed her my sig-a-nals which she ve-ry quick-ly knew; And
when she seed my bunt-ing fly she im-med-iate-ly hove
to-o-o. She's a dark and a rol-ling eye, And her
hair hung down in ring-a-lets. She was a nice girl, a
de-cent girl, But one of the ra-kish kind.

CHORUS

* From *Drawn from the Wood*. Copyright, 1929, by Frank Shay.

211

As I strolled out one evening, out for a night's career,
I spied a lofty fire ship and after her did steer.
I hoisted her my siganals which she very quickly knew;
And when she seed my bunting fly she immediately hove to.

CHORUS:     She's a dark and rolling eye,
            And her hair hung down in ringalets.
            She was a nice girl, a decent girl,
            But one of the rakish kind.

"Oh, sir, you must excuse me for being out so late,
For if my parents knew of it, sad would be my fate.
My father he's a minister, a good and honest man,
My mother she's a Methodist, and I do the best I can."

CHORUS

I took her to a tavern and I treated her to wine,
Little did I think she belonged to the rakish kind.
I handled her, I dandled her, and found to my surprise,
She was nothing but a fire ship, rigged up in a disguise.

CHORUS

# Christofo Columbo *

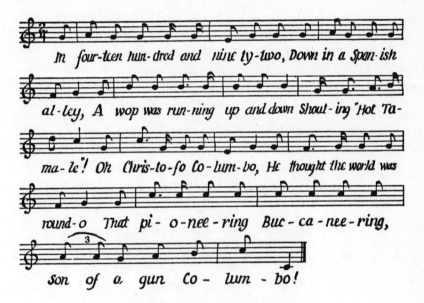

In fourteen hundred and ninety-two, Down in a Spanish alley, A wop was running up and down Shouting "Hot Tamale"! Oh Christofo Columbo, He thought the world was round-o That pioneering Buccaneering, Son of a gun Columbo!

In fourteen hundred and ninety-two,
   Down in a Spanish alley,
A wop was running up and down
   Shouting, "hot tamale!"

Oh, Christofo Columbo,
   He thought the world was round-o;
That pioneering, buccaneering,
   Son-of-a-gun, Columbo!

* From *My Pious Friends and Drunken Companions*. Copyright, 1927, by Frank Shay.

Columbus came from Italee,
   He was full of pink confetti;
He showed the Queen of Spain
   How to manage her spaghetti.

     Oh, Christofo Columbo,
     Knew that land could be found-o;
     That heathen-hating, navigating,
     Son-of-a-gun, Columbo!

He rushed up to the Queen one day,
   Said: "Give me ships and cargo,
I'll be a sea-going son-of-a-gun
   If I don't bring back Chicago!"

     Oh, Christofo Columbo,
     He thought the world was round-o;
     That encroaching, queen-approaching,
     Son-of-a-gun, Columbo!

The Queen she said to Ferdinand,
   "His scheme sounds like a daisy."
"To hell with him," said Ferdinand,
   "I think the wop is crazy!"

     Oh, Christofo Columbo,
     He thought the world was round-o;
     That pioneering, buccaneering,
     Son-of-a-gun, Columbo!

"It isn't ships or men he wants,
   For something else he's shootin',
And if he hangs around you much
   He'll lose his head right tootin'."

Oh, Christofo Columbo,
Knew the gold could be found-o;
That brave sea-faring, never-caring,
Son-of-a-gun, Columbo!

Said Columbo: "Now, Isabelle,
Don't act so gosh-darned funny;
I need the ships and men
So pony up the money!"

Oh, Christofo Columbo,
He knew ships could be found-o;
That always-busted, never trusted,
Son-of-a-gun, Columbo!

Said Isabelle: "Now wait awhile,
And cut out this flam-flimmin';
You've only asked for ships and men
But how about some wimmin?"

Oh, Christofo Columbo,
He knew the world was round-o;
This goll-durning, woman-spurning,
Son-of-a-gun, Columbo!

On the day they sailed away,
The people thought them crazy.
Columbus said: "No janes on board,
The sailors won't get lazy."

Oh, Christofo Columbo,
He never could be bound-o;
That woman-hating, captivating,
Son-of-a-gun, Columbo!

In fourteen hundred and ninety-two,
    Across the broad Atlantic;
The sailors all were filled with grief,
    Their wives were nearly frantic.

    Oh, Christofo Columbo,
    He knew the world was round-o;
    That family-breaking, history-making,
    Son-of-a-gun, Columbo!

In fourteen hundred and ninety-two,
    The doctors were not many;
The only one they had on board
    Was a gosh-darned quack named Benny.

    Oh, Christofo Columbo,
    He knew the world was round-o;
    That philosophic, philanthropic,
    Son-of-a-gun, Columbo!

Columbo's ears ached him one day,
    But Benny was quite placid.
He filled up both Columbo's ears
    With hot mercuric acid.

    Oh, Christofo Columbo,
    Knew doctors could be drowned-o;
    That democratic and autocratic,
    Son-of-a-gun, Columbo!

They anchored near San Salvydor,
    In search of women and booty;
A pretty girl stood on the shore,
    Columbo said: "Do your duty!"

Oh, Christofo Columbo,
Found here was solid ground-o;
That stop-your-shoving, woman-loving,
Son-of-a-gun, Columbo!

The sailors jumped into the surf,
　And shed their shirts and collars;
Columbo said: "The first one there
　Will get a hundred dollars."

Oh, Christofo Columbo,
Knew where he was bound-o;
That woman-baiting, captivating,
Son-of-a-gun, Columbo!

He settled down to stay awhile,
　But things were not so pretty;
The sailors started getting drunk
　Which really was a pity.

Oh, Christofo Columbo,
Got to where he was bound-o;
That heavy-headed, ever-dreaded,
Son-of-a-gun, Columbo!

One day they loaded him in chain,
　And shipped him back to Spain.
Columbo said: "I'm done for good,
　These doings give me a pain."

Oh, Christofo Columbo,
Proved the world was round-o;
That pioneering, persevering,
Son-of-a-gun, Columbo!

When Columbo got back to Sunny Spain,
 He told them of bonanzas.
They answered him: "We notice, Wop,
 You ain't got no bananas!"

Oh, Christofo Columbo,
 He showed the world was round-o;
That poorly-treated, badly cheated,
Son-of-a-gun, Columbo!

THE END

ON LEAVE

# A
# Sailor's Treasury

*Being the Myths and Superstitions, Lore,
Legends and Yarns, the Cries, Epithets,
and Salty Speech of the American Sailorman
in the Days of Oak and Canvas*

## By FRANK SHAY

*Decorations by EDWARD A. WILSON*

"He had but little learning except what he had
picked up from the sun and the sea."—*Moby Dick*

# Foreword

"Literacy has helped seamanship very little indeed."

*Samuel Eliot Morison*

SUPERSTITIONS anywhere can be considered man's first grop-
ing attempt to make sense of his observations and experiences. The
sea, the great mystery of creation, produced phenomena that de-
fied any but mystical answers. Ignorance and fear, man's imagination and his tendency to exaggerate his experiences, form the great
body of maritime folklore. Science has the correct answer; superstition is the popular answer.

In the making of a superstition there are definite elements. These
are, in the order of their importance, optical illusions, hallucina-
tions, mistaken imagination, and the reverie or plain daydream.
Deliberate deception is easily detected. Modern man, looking unexpectedly and for the first time at a waterspout, or seeing St.
Elmo's lights, might easily be inclined to attribute either to the
supernatural.

It would be an easy matter to prove that most of these superstitions and legends are basically foreign, to trace them back to the
Greeks, the Egyptians, or the natives of the Pacific Islands. All of
us are of foreign stock, and the great majority of men serving before the mast in American ships were of foreign birth. The effort
here has been to bring together the folklore, regardless of origin,
that was part of the culture of the native American sailorman in
the days of oak and canvas.

# I

# Seeing Things at Sea

## *Myths, Superstitions, Omens, and Weather Lore*

"There is a majesty in the might of the great deep, that
has a tendency to keep open the avenues of that dependent credulity which more or less besets the mind
of every man. The confusion between things which are
explicable and the things which are not, gradually brings
the mind of the mariner to a state in which any exciting
and unnatural sentiment is welcome."

*James Fenimore Cooper*

# The Phantom Islands of the Atlantic

UNTIL 1873 the entirely imaginary Island of Brazil, lying off the coast of Ireland and in the steamer's track from New York to London, was noted on the charts of the British Admiralty.* As late as 1609, two years after the founding of Jamestown, Virginia, the Bermudas were believed to be entirely populated by demons and were known as the Isles of the Devils. In *Life*, December 6, 1948, Dod Osborne, captain of the *Girl Pat*, told of the reappearing islands off the coast of Africa that he had come across in 1936.

The belief in phantom and floating islands dates from the earliest times. They were not only floating but also unattainable islands. The early mariner knew only what he could see with his naked eye; beyond all horizons lurked strange lands, mystery, and danger. Beyond his sight were the Sea of Solitude, the Sea of Darkness or Gloom (*mare tenebrosum*)—even the Devil's Sea.

Not until the early fifteenth century, when expeditions were sent out by Prince Henry of Portugal, was the myth disproved that any mariners bold enough to pass Cape Bojador on the coast of Africa, a little south of the Canaries, would turn black as Moors, a little farther they would be burned to a crisp, and beyond that the sun came down in liquid fire.

* E. E. Hale, American Antiquarian Society Proceedings, Oct. 1873.

> Whoe'er would pass the Cape of Nun,
> Shall turn again or else be gone.

Cape Bojador was eventually passed in 1434 by Gil Eames, who returned unbrowned to tell of the adventure.

Prince Henry, called "the Navigator," opened the way for Columbus and the other great discoverers: he was the means of destroying many myths, but by no means all of them. Quite a few persist to this day.


## The Enchanted Islands

> "There life is easiest unto man; no snows nor
> wintry storms, or rain at any time."
>
> *Proclus*

The sailor's belief in islands that mysteriously appeared and disappeared is an ancient one. In the beginning these were supposed to be earthly paradises, but in time they took on more mundane and even malevolent characteristics.

"The green isles of the ocean, however, were supposed to be the abode of the souls of virtuous Druids, who could not enter the Christian heaven, but were permitted to enjoy this paradise of their own. Gaffran, a distinguished British chieftain of the fifth century, went on a voyage with his family to discover these islands, but he never returned." *

A sixth-century Irish monk also went in search of the islands.

"But a more widespread tradition was the voyage of St. Brandon, an early saint. He sailed, with twelve fellow-monks, in search of the Isles of the Blessed. He was fabled to have found the holy island, inhabited by twenty-four monks. Besides he found an island of birds (fallen angels), an island of sheep, an island of fiends, who attacked him. This is like the Island of Birds and Island of Sheep, in the Arabian Nights. One version of this story calls the islands *Hy-Breasil*." †

The legend of St. Brandon's Island is one of the most singular and

---

* Jones, *Credulities, Past and Present.*
† Michel, *Voyage Merveilleux de St. Brandan.* Quoted from Bassett, *Sea Phantoms.*

persistent illusions on record. Even today men standing on the coast of Ireland see the great island at dawn or sunset; and the inhabitants of the Canaries, at the same moments, see what they believe is the same island. They see a mountainous island about ninety leagues in length, lying far to the westward. It is to be seen only at intervals, and only in clear weather. To some it appears to be a hundred leagues away, to others less than half that distance.

So many eyewitnesses of credibility have testified to having seen it, and the testimony of the inhabitants of different islands agreed so well, that for long its existence was generally believed, and geographers inserted it in their maps. On one early map it appears no less than three times in as many different positions. As the Isle of Dragons it was supposed to be on the coast of Africa. On the map of Pizigani, it is called Hy-Brazil and lies west of northern France; it is accompanied by a cut of two ships and a dragon eating a man, with a legend stating that one cannot sail further on account of monsters.*

It is laid down on the globe of Martin Behaim, projected in 1492, and it will be found in most of the maps of the time of Columbus, placed about two hundred leagues west of the Canaries. During the time Columbus was making his representations to the court of Portugal, an inhabitant of the Canaries applied to Joao II for a vessel to go in search of this island. In the archives of the Torre de Tombo also, there is a record of a contract made by the crown of Portugal with Fernando de Ulmo, cavalier of the royal household, and captain of the island of Tercera, wherein he undertook to go at his own expense in quest of an island or islands, or Terra Firma, supposed to be the island of the Seven Cities, on condition of having jurisdiction over the same for himself and his heirs, allowing one-tenth of the revenues to the king. This Ulmo, finding the expedition beyond his capacity, associated with one Juan Alfonso del Estreito in the enterprise. They were bound to be ready to sail with two caravels in the month of March, 1487. The fate of their enterprise is unknown.†

The belief in this island continued long after the time of Columbus. It was repeatedly seen, and by various persons at a time, always

* Winsor, *Narrative and Critical History of America.*
† Irving, *The Life and Voyages of Christopher Columbus.*

in the same place and of the same form. In 1526 an expedition set off for the Canaries in search of it, commanded by Fernando de Troya and Fernando Alvarez. They cruised in the correct direction but in vain, and their failure ought to have undeceived the public.

"The phantasm of the island, however," says Vieira, "had such a secret enchantment for all who beheld it, that the public preferred doubting the good conduct of the explorers, than their own senses." *

In 1570 the appearances were so repeated and clear, that again a universal fever of curiosity was awakened among the people of the Canaries, and it was determined to send forth another expedition. That they might not appear to act upon light grounds, an exact investigation was first made of all the persons of talent and credibility who had seen these apparitions of land, or who had other proofs of its existence.

Alonzo de Espinosa, governor of the island of Ferro, accordingly made a report in which more than one hundred witnesses, several of them persons of the highest respectability, deposed that they had beheld the unknown island about forty leagues to the northwest of Ferro, that they had contemplated it with calmness and certainty and had seen the sun set behind one of its points.

Testimonials of still greater force came from the islands of Palma and Teneriffe. There were certain Portuguese who affirmed that, being driven about by a tempest, they had come upon the island of St. Brandon. Pedro Villa, who was the pilot of the vessel, affirmed that having anchored in a bay, he landed with several of his crew. They drank fresh water in a brook, and beheld in the sand the print of footsteps, double the size of those of ordinary men, and the distance between them was in proportion.†

They found a cross nailed to a neighboring tree, near to which were three stones placed in the form of a triangle, with signs of a fire having been made between them, probably to cook food. Having seen many cattle and sheep grazing in the neighborhood, two of their party armed with lances went into the woods in pursuit of them. Night was approaching, the heavens began to darken, and a heavy wind arose. The men aboard the ship cried out that she was

* Irving, *The Life and Voyages of Christopher Columbus.*
† *Ibid.*

dragging her anchor, whereupon Villa entered the boat and hurried on board. In an instant they lost sight of the land, as though it had been swept away in the hurricane. When the storm had passed away and the sea and sky were again serene, they searched in vain for the island. Not a trace of it was to be seen and they had to go on with their voyage, lamenting the loss of their two companions who had been abandoned in the woods.

Another mariner, Marcos Verde, had a similar experience many years later. His men had anchored in what they thought the harbor of the island of St. Brandon, only to be overtaken by a severe storm and driven out to sea and forever out of sight of the beautiful and hidden island.

Testimony collected again in 1570 seemed so satisfactory that another expedition, commanded by Fernando de Villalobos, regidor of the island, was fitted out at the island of Palma. However, it proved equally fruitless. Thirty-five years later, in 1605, they sent another vessel on the quest, this one commanded by Gaspar Perez de Acosta, an accomplished pilot, accompanied by the padre Lorenzo Pinedo, a holy Franciscan friar, skilled in natural science. St. Brandon refused to reveal his island to either monk or mariner. After cruising about in every direction, sounding, observing the skies, the clouds, the winds, everything that could furnish proof, they returned without having seen anything to authorize a hope.

Over a century elapsed without any new attempt to seek the elusive island. Every now and then the public mind had been agitated by fresh reports of its having been seen. Lemons and other fruits and the green branches of trees which floated to the shores of the Canaries were pronounced to be from the enchanted groves of St. Brandon. At length, in 1721, public infatuation again rose to such a height that a fourth expedition was sent, commanded by Don Gaspar Dominguez, a man of probity and talent. As this expedition was one of solemn and mysterious import, two holy friars were sent along as apostolic chaplains. They made sail from the island of Teneriffe toward the end of October, leaving the populace in an indescribable state of anxiety. The ship, however, returned from the cruise as unsuccessful as all its predecessors.

In a letter written from the island of Gomera, in 1759, by a Franciscan monk, the writer tells of having seen it from the village of

Alaxero at six in the morning of the third of May. It appeared to consist of two lofty mountains, with a deep valley between; and on contemplating it with a telescope, the valley or ravine appeared filled with trees. He summoned the curate Antonio Joseph Manrique, and upward of forty other persons, all of whom saw it plainly.

Such are the principal facts existing relative to the island of St. Brandon. Its reality was for a long time a matter of firm belief. Repeated voyages and investigations failed to prove its nonexistence; the people took refuge in the supernatural. They maintained that the island was rendered inaccessible to mortals by Divine Providence or by diabolical magic. Most of them inclined to the former. All kinds of extravagant fancies were indulged in concerning it, some even confounding it with the fabled Island of the Seven Cities. Some of the Portuguese imagined it to be the abode of their lost king Sebastian. The Spaniards believed that Roderick, the last of their Gothic kings, had fled thither from the Moors after the disastrous battle of the Guadalete. Others suggested it might be the seat of the terrestrial paradise, the place where Enoch and Elijah remained in a state of blessedness until the final day, and that it was made at times apparent to the eyes but unattainable to the feet of mortals.

A learned priest, known only as Feyjoo, has given a philosophical solution to this problem. He attributes all these appearances, which have been so numerous and well authenticated as to admit of no doubt, to certain atmospherical deceptions, like that of the fata morgana, seen at times in the Straits of Messina, where the city of Reggio and its surrounding country are reflected in the air above the neighboring sea, a phenomenon which likewise has been witnessed in front of the city of Marseilles. As to the tales of mariners who had landed on these forbidden shores, and been hurried away in whirlwinds and tempests, the good father puts them down as sheer fabrications.*

## Hy-Brasil

Early geographers often confused this island with that of St. Brandon. Certain trees floating on the shores of Europe were prized

* Irving, *The Life and Voyages of Christopher Columbus.*

because they were of Brazil-wood, and were believed to have come from it, the wood being well known long before the South American Brazil was discovered.

While it is known that these pre-fifteenth-century islands were geographical fancies, it was easy and only natural to transfer their names to the real discoveries.

## Antillia, the Island of the Seven Cities

"One of the popular traditions concerning the ocean, which were current during the time of Columbus, was that of the Island of the Seven Cities. It was recorded in an ancient legend, that at the time of the conquest of Spain by the Moors, when the inhabitants fled in every direction to escape from slavery, seven bishops, followed by a great number of their people, took shipping and abandoned themselves to their fate on the high seas. After tossing about for some time, they landed upon an unknown island in the midst of the ocean. Here the Bishops burnt the ships, to prevent desertion by their followers, and founded seven cities. Various pilots of Portugal, it was said, had reached that island at different times, but had never returned to give any information concerning it, having been detained according to subsequent accounts, by the successors of the bishops to prevent pursuit. At length, according to common report, at the time Prince Henry of Portugal was prosecuting his discoveries, several sea-faring men presented themselves one day before him, and stated they had just returned from a voyage, in the course of which they had landed upon this island. The inhabitants, they said, spoke their language and carried them immediately to church, to ascertain whether were Catholics, and were rejoiced at finding them of the true faith. They then made earnest inquiries, to know whether the Moors still retained possession of Spain and Portugal. While part of the crew were at church, the rest gathered sand on the shore for the use of the kitchen, and found to their surprise that one third of it was gold. The islanders were anxious that the crew should remain with them a few days, until the return of their governor who was absent; but the mariners, afraid of being detained, embarked and made sail. Such was the story they told to Prince Henry, hoping to receive reward for their intelligence. The Prince, it is said, expressed displeasure * at their hasty departure from the island, and ordered them to return and procure further information; but the men, apprehensive, no doubt, of having the falsehood of their tale discovered, made their escape, and nothing more was heard of them.

"This story had much currency. The Island of the Seven Cities was identified with the island mentioned by Aristotle as having been discovered by the Carthaginians, and was put down in the early maps about the time of Columbus, under the name of Antillia.†

"At the time of the discovery of New Spain, extravagant reports were brought to Hispaniola of the civilization of the country; that the people wore clothing; that their houses and temples were solid, spacious, and often magnificent; and that crosses were occasionally found among them. Juan de Grijalva, being dispatched to explore the coast of Yucatan, reported that in sailing along it, he beheld with great wonder, stately and beautiful edifices of lime and stone, and many high towers that shone at a distance. For a time the old tradition of the Seven Cities was revived." ‡

The geographer Toscanelli, in his letter to Columbus, suggested Antillia as a port of call likely to prove useful on the way to India. When Columbus reached Hispaniola he believed he had discovered the famous island, whence the name of Antilles was given to the group.

## The Island of Satan's Hand

The most malevolent of the phantom islands in the Sea of Darkness took the shape of a human hand greatly enlarged. This strange island never showed itself in fair weather, making its appearances only in fogs and dirty weather, or at night. No man ever sought this island. It was supposed to be located near Antillia, but unlike other islands in the group, it was always surrounded by chilly mists and cold weather. It was generally believed that this island constantly changed its location and that it was really the hand of some monstrous demon of the deep, reaching up and plucking men and even whole boats. The victims, once grasped, were never seen again.

* See Sanceau, *Henry the Navigator.*
† It is on Martin Behaim's globe of 1492.
‡Irving, *The Life and Voyages of Christopher Columbus.*

The island was on the map of Bianco, projected in 1436, as Yd. laman Satanaxio, the Island of the Hand of Satan.

## The Bermudas

"For the Islands of the Bermudas, otherwise called the Isles of the Devils, every man knoweth that hath heard or read of them, they were never inhabited by any Christians, but were esteemed and reputed a most prodigious and inchanted place, affording nothing but gusts, storms and foul weather; which made every mariner and navigator to avoid them as Scylla and Charybdis, or as they would shun the devil himself. . . . Sir George Somers espied the land, which they judged it should be the dreadful coast of the Bermudas, which island men of all nations said and supposed to be enchanted and inhabited with witches and devils, which grew by reason of accustomed monstrous thunder-storms and tempests near to these islands. . . . Marryat says there was a sailor tradition that the crust of these islands was so thin, that there was constant danger of breaking through. . . . The Colony of Virginia supplemented this account thus: 'These islands of the Bermudas have long been accounted an inchanted place, and *a desert inhabitation for devils;* but all the fairies of the rock were but a flock of birds, and all the devils that haunted the woods were but herds of swine.' " *

Coryatt, in his *Crudities* (1611) reports

> Of the Bermudas, the example such,
> Where not a ship until this time darst touch,
> Kept, as suppos'd by hell's infernal dogs;
> Our fleet found there most honest courteous hogs.

## The Isle of the Amazons

Originally there were two of these islands: one, Feminea, inhabited solely by women; the other, Masculea, by men alone. The legend was probably started by Marco Polo, but the latter island held no interest for sailors, and they ignored and forgot it.

The legend of the Isle of Women was enlarged upon and amplified in many ways. All the inhabitants were young, tall, beauti-

* Quoted from Bassett, *Sea Phantoms.*

ful, and very passionate, and for three months each year they welcomed the intimate companionship of all males, especially sailors. There was no toil required of the visitors, the island dripped with fruit and honey, and the entire time was to be spent in amorous dalliance. At the end of three months the visitors would be asked to leave, and to take with them all male children that had reached adolescence.

Columbus believed in the existence of this legendary island. On his homeward passage in 1493, he determined to visit it and bring five or six of the women to his sovereigns. He had placed it as the island now known as Martinique, and he set his course for it. However, the condition of the *Nina* and *Pinta* was such—both were making water—that on second thought he considered the women they might collect not to be worth the dangerous delay.

## The Isle of Demons

This island is shown on many ancient maps; on that of Sebastian Cabot, laid out in 1544, it appears as the *Isla de demonios*. The island was believed to have been located in the Gulf of St. Lawrence and to have been discovered by Sieur Jean Roberval, the wealthy French explorer.

Roberval led a large expedition to found a colony in Canada: in his company was a niece of his and her old nurse. In the course of the voyage the commander learned that his relative had been seduced by a young man of the company, and as punishment he ordered that the niece, her nurse, and her lover be placed ashore on the Island of Demons. The young woman's two companions soon died, and after more than two years she was rescued by a fishing vessel and taken back to France.

One account of her adventures is illustrated with a picture of a young woman shooting wild beasts. Her story is told by Margaret of Navarre, in the Heptameron, Novel LXVII.*

## The Lost City of New England

Though not one of the enchanted islands, Norumbega belongs among them. David Ingram, a sailor with Sir John Hawkins, was set

* Winsor, *Narrative and Critical History of America*, Vol. 4, 1884.

ashore in the Gulf of Mexico, probably for lying. He claimed that with two Indian companions, he made his way far to the northward, where he came upon Norumbega, a city built entirely of silver and crystal. He was found by Champlain and returned to his home, where he related, very convincingly, the yarn of his travels and the great prize he had found.

Sir Walter Raleigh, Sir Humphrey Gilbert, and other explorers and geographers believed his story, and many expeditions were fitted out to bring the great treasure to Britain. The most careful search failed to find the wonder city, and it early became known as "the lost city of New England."

## Against the Wind: The Ghostly Fleet

### The Flying Dutchman

THOSE who have seen or heard of the vessel known as *The Flying Dutchman* are of several minds as to the curse under which she sails: they agree only on her principal cruising ground. The American sailor was content with the simple legend of the Dutch captain who, homeward bound, met with long-continued head winds at the Cape of Good Hope. He swore that he would not put back but would strive till the day of doom, if necessary, to double the Cape. He was taken at his word, and there he still beats but never succeeds in rounding Table Bay.

To English mariners the cause of her wandering is a retributive curse. She was a treasure ship, bound homeward from the East Indies, and in a fit of rage, because of his inability to take the vessel around the point, the captain murdered the pilot. In retribution a plague broke out and the crew sailed the ship in vain from port to port, offering as the price of shelter the whole of the ship's wealth. Excluded from every harbor for fear of contagion, the ship was doomed to sail the open seas forever. It is an omen of ill luck to see her.

The French add a supernatural note to the legend.

"There was formerly a ship's captain who believed neither in saints, nor God, nor anything else. 'Twas a Dutchman, I know not from what city. He sailed one day to go south. All went well as far as the latitude of the Cape of Good Hope, but there he got a hard blow. The ship was in great danger. Every one said to the captain, 'Captain, put in shore, or we are all lost.' The captain laughed at the fears of his crew and his passengers; he sang, songs horrible enough to call down a hundred times the thunderbolts on his masts. Then as the captain scoffed at the tempest, a cloud opened and a huge figure descended upon the poop. 'Twas the Everlasting Father. Every one was afraid; the captain continued to smoke his pipe; he did not even raise his cap when the figure addressed him. 'Captain,' it said, 'You are out of your head.' 'And you are a very uncivil fellow,' said the captain, 'I don't ask anything of you; get out or I'll blow your brains out.' The venerable person replied nothing, but shrugged his shoulders. Then the captain seized one of his pistols, cocked it, and aimed it at the cloud-figure. The shot, instead of wounding the white-bearded form, pierced the captain's hand; that worried him a little, you may believe. He jumped up to hit the old man a blow in the face with his fist, but his arm dropped paralyzed with palsy. The tall figure then said: 'You are accursed, Heaven sentences you to sail forever, without being able to put into port or harbor. You shall have neither beer nor tobacco, you shall drink gall at all times, you shall chew red-hot iron for your quid, your boy shall have a horned forehead, a tiger's jaw, and a skin rougher than a sea-dog's. You shall eternally watch, and shall not sleep when sleepy, because when you close your eyes a long sword shall pierce your body. And since you love to torment sailors, you shall persecute them, for you shall be the evil one of the sea; you shall wander ceaselessly throughout all latitudes; you shall have neither rest nor fine weather; you shall have the tempest for a breeze; the sight of your ship which shall hover about to the end of time, will bring misfortune to those who see it.' 'I defy you!' was the sole reply of the captain. The Holy Father disappeared, and the captain found himself alone on the deck, with the ship's boy disfigured as predicted. The crew had disappeared with the figure in the cloud.

"Since then the Voltigeur sails about in heavy weather, and his whole pleasure is in doing ill to poor sailors. 'Tis he who sends them white squalls, who wrecks ships or leads them on false courses. There are those who say that *The Flying Dutchman* often has the audacity to visit passing ships; then there is war in the caboose, wine sours, and all food becomes beans. Often he sends letters on board ships he meets, and if the captain reads them, he is lost; he becomes a madman and his ship dances in the air, and finishes by turning over while pitching violently. The Voltigeur paints himself at will, and changes six times a day, so as not to be recognized. He has sometimes the appearance of a heavy Dutch camel, who can hardly bluff his heavy quarters into the wind. At others, he becomes a corvette, and scours the seas as a light corsair." *

Almost abruptly the French legend makes the cursed vessel a punishment ship.

"His crew are accursed as well as he, for 'tis a gang of hardened sinners. All sailor shirkers, rogues dying under the cat, and cowards, are on board his ship. Look out for squalls, my lads, and if you don't do your duty, you will find yourselves on board the Dutchman, and there is work, believe me. It is always 'tack ship' because it is necessary to be everywhere at the same time. No pastime there, but hunger, thirst and fatigue, everyone trembling, indeed, for if one should complain, there are officers who have whips ending in lashes as sharp as a razor . . . and this lash will last through all eternity." †

"She was painted yellow, of yellow were the dim churchyard lines that I marked her hull was coated with. She was low in the bows with a great spring aft, crowned by a kind of double poop, one above another, and what I could see of the stern was almost pear-shape, supposing the fruit inverted with the stalk sliced off. She had three masts each with a large protected circular top, resembling turrets, sails of the texture of cobwebs hung from her square-yards." ‡

"But Heaven help the ship near which the demon sailor steers!
The doom of those is sealed, to whom the Phantom Ship appears,
They'll never reach their destin't port, they'll never see their homes
    no more,
They who see the Flying Dutchman never, *never* reach the
    shore." §

* Jal, *Scènes de la vie maritime*. Quoted in Bassett, *Wander-Ships*.
† *Ibid.*
‡ Russell, *A Voyage to the Cape*.
§ O'Reilly, *Songs from the Southern Seas*.

From an English log of 1835: "We had been in dirty weather as the sailors say, for several days, and to beguile the afternoon, I commenced after-dinner narratives to the French officers and passengers (who were strangers to the eastern seas) current about the Flying Dutchman. The wind which had been freshening now blew a stiff gale, and we proceeded on deck to see the crew make our bark all snug for the night. The clouds, dark and heavy, coursed with rapidity across the bright moon, whose lustre is so peculiar in the southern hemisphere, and we could see a distance of from eight to ten miles on the horizon. Suddenly the second officer, a fine Marseilles sailor, who had been among the foremost in the cabin in laughing at and ridiculing the story of the Flying Dutchman ascended the weather rigging, exclaiming, '*Voila le volant Hollandais!*' The captain sent for his night glass and soon observed, 'It is very strange, but there is a ship bearing down on us with *all sail* set, while we dare scarcely show a pocket-handkerchief to the breeze.' In a few minutes the stranger was visible to all on deck, her rig plainly discernible, and people on her poop; she seemed to near us with the rapidity of lightning, and apparently wished to pass under our quarter for the purpose of speaking. The captain, a resolute Bordeaux mariner, said it was quite incomprehensible and sent for the trumpet to hail an answer, when in an instant, and while we were all on the *qui vive*, the stranger totally disappeared, and was seen no more."

During the years 1879–1882 the two sons of Edward, Prince of Wales, one of them later George V, were on a cruise in H.M.S. *Bacchante*, and they kept a diary rather than a log. An entry during 1881 related:

"At 4 A.M. the Flying Dutchman crossed our bows. A strange, red light, as of a phantom ship all aglow, in the midst of which light the masts, spars and sails of a brig two hundred yards distant stood out in strong relief as she came up. The look-out man on the forecastle reported her as close on the port bow, where also the officer of the watch from the bridge clearly saw her, as did also the quarter-deck midshipman, who was sent forward at once to the forecastle; but on arriving there no vestige of any sign whatever of any material ship was to be seen either near or right away to the horizon, the night being clear and the sea calm. Thirteen persons altogether saw her, but whether it was Van Diemen or the Flying Dutchman, or who, she must remain unknown, The *Tourmaline* and *Cleopatra*, who were sailing on our starboard bow, flashed to ask whether we had seen the strange red light." *

> "Repelled from port to port, they sue in vain
> And track with slow, unsteady sail the main,
> Where ne'er the bright and buoyant wave is seen
> To streak with wandering foam the sea-weeds green.
>
> .    .    .    .    .    .    .    .
>
> The Spectre-Ship, in livid glimpsing light,
> Glares baleful on the shuddering watch at night,
> Unblest of God and man!"

John Leyden

## The Carmilhan

Only Longfellow and Brewer have recorded the legend of the *Carmilhan*, and the latter confuses it with the Dutchman, placing the vessel off the Cape of Good Hope. The New England poet combines three myths in his poem: the phantom ship, the imaginary islands known as the Three Chimneys, and, finally, the kobold, one named Klaboterman.

> "There is a Spectre Ship," quoth he,
> "A ship of the Dead that sails the sea,
>     And is called the *Carmilhan*.
> A ghostly ship, with a ghostly crew,
>     In tempests she appears;
> And before the gale, or against the gale,
> She sails without a rag of sail,
>     Without a helmsman steers.
> She haunts the Atlantic north and south,
>     But mostly the mid-sea. . . ."

The captain of the *Valdemar*, who listens to the legend, declares he would like nothing better than to meet this evil ship, and he later does, making an effort to run it down with his own vessel. His ship passes right through the phantom, but the *Valdemar* is wrecked.

> "The storm and night were passed, the light
>     To streak the east began;

* *The Cruise of the Bacchante, 1879–82.*

The cabin-boy, picked up at sea,
Survived the wreck, and only he,
To tell of the *Carmilhan*." *

## *The Dead Ship of Harpswell*

One living legend exists in many versions. Though she sails no more, there are those, even today, who claim to have seen the Dead Ship, seen through her sails as though they were cobwebs, through the green oak sheathing of her hull they saw her stout frames: no crew was on her deck, no master on the quarterdeck, and no helmsman at her wheel. She came in with the wind, and, without tack of sail, or turn of helm or tide, she sailed stern fore toward the sea again. Her coming foretold death, and in the dead ship's wake the burial boat followed shortly.

The dead ship is known to be the *Dash*, one of the most successful privateers of the Maine coast. "Her speed is legendary. Rigged at first as a topsail schooner, it was later discovered that she could carry a greater spread of canvas and her rig was changed to an hermaphrodite brig—that is, square-rigged forward and schooner-rigged aft. With this she carried a ringtail, a light sail bent on a long sliding spar which was fitted to her main boom. This, when hoisted to the gaff as needed, increased the size of her mainsail by one-third. It has been said of her that 'She never suffered defeat, never attacked an enemies' ship in vain, was never injured by a hostile shot and knew no equal in speed.'

"On her last cruise tragedy struck. Having taken leave of his bride of a few months, Captain Porter, aged twenty-four, sailed from Portland in company with the *Champlain*, a new privateer, for a trial of speed. At the end of the first day the *Dash* had her all but hull down. Night came on, and with it a squall. The light of the *Dash* disappeared in the scud. Finding the water shoaling, the *Champlain* altered her course. The *Dash* was never again seen. She is believed to have foundered on George's Bank. With her were lost the Captain, his two brothers, and a crew of sixty able men." †

Unlike the Palatine, the *Dash* returned, not on each anniversary

* H. W. Longfellow, *Tales of a Wayside Inn*.
† W. H. Rowe, *The Maritime History of Maine*.

of her destruction, but when "any of those who loved the lads" were about to die. The legend was put into verses by one Kenlin Lufkin and was found in the *Lewiston Journal*, January 28, 1905, where it was noted "as in an old newspaper." *

> You have heard of the ship that sails the bay,
>   With night for helmsman and death in tow,
> And that glides to sea as he comes ashore
>   And speeds on his errand of woe.
>
> It was in the year of Eighteen Twelve
>   They launched the *Dash* from a Freeport yard,
> She sails the bay as the 'Dead Ship' now,
>   You have heard her doom from the Quaker bard.
>
> She was manned by a crew of gallant lads
>   As ever a vessel's deck had trod,
> A score and a hundred of them all—
>   And their fate is known to none but God.
>
> They all belonged to the towns around,
>   They were brothers and cousins and comrades, too,
> Full armed and equipped they put to sea,
>   And the skies were never a softer blue.
>
> But weeks and months and years sped on,
>   And hearts grew hopeless and cheeks grew pale,
> And eyes are dim that have watched so long
>   To catch a glimpse of her home bound sail.
>
> But when any of those who loved the lads
>   Are ready to slip their moorings here,
> And sail away to the unknown port
>   You will see the Dead Ship gliding near.

* From a letter of Mr. William Hutchinson Rowe. The verses are quoted in Mr. Rowe's *Shipbuilding Days in Casco Bay, 1727–1890* and are used here with Mr. Rowe's permission. See also "The Sources of Whittier's 'The Dead Ship of Harpswell,'" by Kenneth Scott, *The American Neptune*, July, 1946.

And the ship and the life go out with the tide.
And the captain paused for a while, then said
"They are most all gone and the Dead Ship soon
Will come no more for the souls of the dead."

## The Burning Palatine

"Some time during the last century—even the year is uncertain—an emigrant ship bound for Philadelphia came upon the American coast, only to be driven off to sea again by stress of weather. The emigrants were substantial and thrifty Dutch people of the better class, who had brought all their property along with them to their new home, whither many of their countrymen had preceded them. Some of them are even alleged to have been wealthy. It was in the dark and dreary season of midwinter, when the voyage, already long, was thus disastrously lengthened. With the coast in sight, but unable to gain her port, the ship, buffeting the frozen seas, was driven northward far out of her course; while scenes were being enacted on board, the bare thought of which makes the blood run cold. The captain had died, or had been murdered, at sea, before the vessel came in sight of the land. All discipline was at an end; and the ship's crew then began a system of cold-blooded robbery, to which the act of boldly hoisting the black flag and of cutting the throats of their miserable victims would have been mercy indeed. The wretches armed themselves; and having taken possession of the water and provisions, with a refined cruelty demanded from the famishing emigrants twenty guilders for a cup of water, and fifty rix-dollars for a biscuit. To save their lives the poor passengers were obliged to beggar themselves. Those who could not or would not comply with the atrocious demand were allowed to starve, and their emaciated bodies were coolly thrown into the sea. The ship soon became a floating hell. Having plundered their victims of everything that they possessed of value, the inhuman crew finally took to the boats; and deserting the stricken ship, they left her to the mercy of the winds and waves. With no one left on board to navigate her, the doomed ship drifted on. Days of despair were succeeded by nights of terror. She was now a madhouse, tenanted only by maniacs or the unburied corpses of those who had died from famine or disease.

"One calm Sunday morning the *Palatine* struck on the northern-most reef of Block Island. But her voyage was not to end here. The wreckers manned their boats and humanely rescued all those who had survived starvation, except one woman, who had gone stark mad, and who now refused to leave the wreck.

"The ship, having only touched on the reef, floated off again with the rising tide; and the wreckers, who surrounded the grimy hulk like vultures the carcass of a noble stag, now making their boats fast to it, towed her to a neighboring cove, in order that they might dismantle her at their leisure. But before this could be done a gale sprang up; when the wreckers, seeing that the ship, in spite of their efforts, would be blown off to sea, set her on fire; and she was soon in flames.

"Enveloped in fire from truck to deck, the *Palatine* drove out into the thickening darkness of a stormy sea,—an object of dread even to those who had so recklessly applied the torch. But this feeling was turned into deeper horror when the frenzied shrieks borne to their ears from the burning ship told the lookers-on that a human being was perishing miserably in the flames before their eyes.

"These appalling sounds were supposed to proceed from the maniac woman, who had been forgotten in the excitement of the moment. The *Palatine* drifted away, and burned to the water's edge. And so ends the dismal tale of the actual ship.

"But it is now averred that on very night twelvemonth, the anniversary of the same storm, the islanders were affrighted by the startling and sublime spectacle of a ship on fire in the offing, which, as the gale rose, drifted before it, and gradually faded from their sight, exactly as the ill-fated *Palatine* had done. Year after year the same strange sight continued to keep the fate of the *Palatine* fresh in the memory of every man, woman, and child upon the island." *

J. G. Whittier's poem "The *Palatine*" was written in 1867 and two years after publication he received a letter from Benjamin Corydon, of Napoli, N.Y., then in his ninety-second year, in which he wrote in part:

"She was seen once a year on the same night of the year on which the murders occurred, as long as any of the wreckers were living; but never after all were dead. I must have seen her eight or ten times

* Drake, *New England Legends and Folklore.*

—perhaps more—in my early days. It is seventy years or more since she was last seen. My father lived right opposite Block Island, on the mainland, so we had a fair view of her as she passed down by the island, then she would disappear. She resembled a full-rigged ship, with her sails all set and all ablaze. It was the grandest sight I ever saw in all my life."

Across the strait, on Long Island, the same ship appears in legend:

" 'Tis the Phantom Ship, that, in darkness and wrath,
  Ploughs evermore the waste ocean path,
  And the heart of the mariner trembles in dread,
  When it crosses his vision like a ghost of the dead." *

## The New Haven Ghost Ship

The name of this vessel is unknown. When she was launched in January, 1647, with a Captain Lamberton in command, the harbor was choked with ice. A channel five miles long had to be cut to open water and the vessel was towed stern first, a humiliating procedure, out to sail off as best she might in a heavy fog, the last ever seen of her.

The legend has the *imprimatur* of Cotton Mather,† one of the noisier Bible-thumpers of our early days, who had it from the Rev. James Pierpont, minister of New Haven. In June of the same year about an hour before sunset, a ship sailed into the harbor against the wind. The people gathered on the shore and cheered the return of the missing ship. Captain Lamberton stood on her poop pointing seaward with his sword.

On she came, with a cloud of canvas
  Right against the wind that blew,
Until the eye could distinguish
  The faces of the crew.

Then fell her straining topmasts,
  Hanging tangled in the shrouds,

* Ayres, *Legends of Montauk.*
† *Magnalia Christi Americana.*

And her sails were loosened and lifted,
And blown away like clouds.

And the masts, with all their rigging,
Fell slowly, one by one,
And the hulk dilated and vanished,
As a seamist in the sun!

And the people who saw this marvel
Each said unto his friend,
That this was the mould of their vessel,
And thus her tragic end.*

## Salem's Specter Ships

Old Salem had many legends of phantom ships, most of them transient and now, save in the works of the New England poets, generally forgotten. Salem ships went everywhere, and it is quite reasonable to assume that many of the legends came in unlisted in the manifest.

"The spectre ship of Salem, with the dead men in her shrouds,
Sailing sheer above the water, in the loom of morning clouds." †

In one there are lovers, a strange man and a girl of great beauty, who were passengers on a vessel bound for England. So strange was their conduct that they were supposed to be witches and the other passengers feared to sail in the vessel. The ship sailed on a Friday and never reached her destination. Months later, after a storm of three days, the vessel reappeared with only the lovers on her deck. It took a fervent prayer from a minister to make her disappear.

Another legend, almost a phantom itself, tells of the ghost ship that brings the souls of proper Salem people who have died elsewhere back to their home port.

*The Salem Ghost Ship* ‡    We were all Salem men aboard the brig *Neptune*, and we were ending a sixteen months' voyage on the short-

* H. W. Longfellow, "The Ship of the Dead."
† J. G. Whittier, "The Garrison of Cape Ann."
‡ From *Woman's Day*, copyright, 1948, by Frank Shay.

est day of the year, well in time for Christmas. Only a sailorman knows that great joy and only a Salem man can fully savor the cup. Salem's a town that holds its people wherever they roam, and though many of us travel far and long we remain Salem men until death. An old legend has it that no matter where his body dies, the spirit of a true Salem man always returns.

Captain Abner Low had taken two of us boys with him on the voyage that was to last eight to nine months, and Jack Somers was in the captain's watch, the starboard, and I was in the second, or larboard, under the mate. The Old Man, who had sailed with Captain Bowditch, was known as a maker of sailors, and at fourteen we were taking a year out from school to see what we were made of.

*Neptune's* was the usual Salem run, to Madeira for wine, trading along Africa's west coast, round the cape to Madagascar and on to the Arabian ports for coffees, the Indian ports, to China for teas, silks and nankeens, Sumatra for pepper and, finally, Manila for cigars. Then we beat across the Pacific to Juan Fernandez for water and fresh provisions, and doubling Cape Stiff crossed the Atlantic to Antwerp.

The afterguard did not share its secrets with us boys, but we sensed from the high good humor of the Old Man and the supercargo that the owners would find our adventure a profitable one. We had started out with the usual Yankee cargo of rum, Lowell cottons, codfish, cheese, clocks, furniture and shoes, and we were returning with a rich haul of plunder from Europe, Africa and Asia.

There I was, not yet fifteen, returning from a voyage that had doubled both capes; I was familiar with strange ports, I who had yet to see Boston, which was but sixteen miles from old Salem. Not only that, but I had some eighty silver dollars due me, and few were the shoremen who could show that wealth after sixteen months' work. None of it had to go for presents, for I had in my bag, silk for a dress for my mother, a carved meerschaum pipe for my father, a Chinese doll for my sister and genuine Calcutta bandannas for all my relatives.

In the carpenter's cuddy there was a Javanese parrot, and for myself I had several pieces of scrimshaw which I had traded for tobacco with a passing whaler. Best of all, I could inform my parents that, with their permission, I was not returning to school; Captain

Low had asked Jack Somers and me to sign on as able seamen for his next voyage.

Each Tuesday and Friday night, the captain had us boys to the cabin, where he instructed us in arithmetic and the simpler problems of navigation. That was book learning; our more practical education was in the hands of the sailmaker, an elderly sailorman known to us only as "Sails." It was from this character we learned to knot, reeve and splice, to hand, reef and steer and not to run when an officer gave an order but to jump. From Old Sails we learned the lore of the sea, the legends and superstitions and the salty speech. His favorite topic was the ghost ships. He had, he insisted, seen them all, the *Flying Dutchman*, the *Carmilhan* of the Baltic, the Dead Ship, of Orr's Island, up Maine way, the *Palatine*, of Block Island, and both the schooners, *Breeze* and *Jessie*.

We thought at the time he was pulling our legs. But long before we'd put the first patches on our sea breeches we were scanning the horizon for a glimpse of a phantom ship. Many were the watches below we spent on the cold wintry deck while doubling the Cape of Good Hope looking for the *Dutchman*. Old Sails had primed us how to handle him should her captain hail us.

"Do not speak to him," he said. "If he asks your position shrug your shoulders; if he asks have you letters for him shake your heads; if he asks for water point to the sea and if for food throw him an iron belaying pin. His last appeal will be for you to take letters for his dearly beloved wife. Beware, do not take them, for neither you nor your ship will ever reach a port to deliver them. Best of all is to make believe you do not see or hear him."

Now returning to Salem, about to put our feet on the first rung of the ladder that leads to the quarterdeck, to the command of our own ships, we had but one regret, we had seen no ghostly ships, which to any boy's way of thinking was a serious matter.

The Old Man always boasted of his ship. *Neptune*, he claimed, could tack in a sixteen-quart pail of water, so responsive that she could be brought into port by a couple of knowledgeable boys; and now she was doing just that: I was at the helm and Jack Somers was on lookout. We were entering Salem Harbor under reefed topsails, riding a following easterly of moderate gale strength. It was the first dog of the watch and darkness had already fallen. The pilot, Mr.

Cates, was beside me and the captain had retired to his cabin. The mate, a young chap whose wife had birthed a child while we were at sea, was everywhere, singing his song:

> O, Salem is a fine town with ships in the bay,
> And it's there in my heart I wish I were today;
> And I thought as I sailed of the cradle standing ready
> For the pretty little baby that has never seen its daddy.

Old Sails, a privileged character, was standing near the wheel, and the crew, bags packed and ready to go ashore, lined the rails looking for the first lights of home. We would make a running moor, take in our canvas, and warp into our berth. The men were laughing and telling each other what they'd be having for supper.

We had passed Peach's Point and were inside Kettle Bottom; and the pilot was giving his orders in his quiet voice, with me repeating them loud and strong with the added "sir." In a few moments the bell would be struck and Jack would sound off briskly. Both of us knew the Old Man would be expecting the pilot's compliment on the smart handling of his vessel.

"Ease her a bit to port, lad," said Mr. Cates.

"To port, sir!" I snapped, and then two bells were struck and I listened for Jack Somer's cry. It came promptly out of the darkness.

"Two bells, sir, and all lights are burning brightly!" Then he screamed: "Astern! Look astern! Ship ho!"

Thoughtlessly I turned and looked aft. A great ship, under full sail, four times the size of *Neptune*, was bearing down upon us. For a moment I wondered what maniac was her master and then I threw the helm over hard to port, believing I could throw the brig over enough to ease a dead-on crash. The wheel was roughly taken from my hands and I was crowded off the grating.

The wheel spun back to its old position, and a calm voice was saying, "Steady, lad, steady!"

I must have been cringing, waiting for the crash that could not be avoided. She'd strike us on our starboard quarter and we'd find ourselves swimming for the Triangles, our ship at the bottom.

The crash did not come. Lifting my head I saw the giant vessel tack slightly and come along our starboard counter, crowding us, but with no splintering of wood against wood, no rush of water—and she was making fifteen knots to our eight—no creaking and straining of ropes and canvas, only a grim and glowing silence. Every sail was set, every rope taut or coiled and flemished on her deck; her anchor was stowed as for a long voyage, all Bristol fashion yet with not a sailor in sight.

I thought I could see her masts through her sails, as though they were cobwebs; then I looked at her hull and I could see her stout frames through the sheathing of green oak; she carried no cargo, there were no men in her fo'c'sle; and then I saw there was no one at her helm.

The strange ship seemed to fade away, rather than to sail out of our ken, as though she had entered a dense fog bank. There was a funny sensation in the pit of my stomach and then my attention was distracted by a sound, as though a heavy sea boot was being drawn out of soft mud, and I looked about. In the faint gleam cast by the binnacle light I could see it came from Old Sails, who was sucking his breath, his eyes bugging out of his gaunt features, his knees shaking in terror.

Mr. Cates was pressing a silver pocket flask on the old man and saying, in his quiet voice:

"It's the Ghost Ship. A proper Salem man has died somewhere and the ship is bringing his spirit home to Salem, home for Christmas."

## The Ghost of the Great Eastern

During the building of this monster steamship (London, 1854–57), it was whispered about the shipyard that, unfortunately, one of the riveters had been sealed up in one of the compartments of her double hull. No one knew just which compartment, and equally no one expected the builders to take the big ship apart just to release a workman presumed already dead.

Later, sailors on watch in the quiet nights, especially during the churchyard trick, insisted they could hear the luckless riveter still working at his trade, hammering away with might and main. Only they claimed that he was demanding a much belated release. On one occasion, in 1862, when the vessel was entering the port of New

York, she scraped her hull on an uncharted submerged rock. Although a large hole was torn in the outer skin, the vessel was able to dock. A diver sent down to appraise the damage returned to the surface shivering with fright, saying that he had heard the riveter hammering away. A spiritualist was engaged to investigate, and he confirmed the presence of the riveter "in body and in spirit."

The *Great Eastern* was a hard luck ship; she never paid her way, and eventually she became a coal hulk at Gibraltar. In 1887 she was broken up, and legend has it, the knackers found the riveter's skeleton.

## The Ghosts of the Georges Banks

In a terrific gale on the Georges Banks, the *Haskell*, a fisherman out of Gloucester, broke loose from her moorings and crashed into the *Andrew Johnson*, of the same port, sinking her and drowning all hands aboard her. For years after, whenever the *Haskell* returned to the Georges, the drowned men of the *Andrew Johnson* would come aboard at midnight and go through the dumb show of fishing over her side. At last the *Haskell* had to be retired because no crew could be recruited in Gloucester to sail her.*

## Navy Ghosts

It was a belief in the old Navy that when a man was hanged at the yardarm, at midnight of the same day the ghost of the executed man would return the hail from the yardarm at which he had been hanged.

## Luck of Ships

There is a story of an unnamed grain ship, a Great Lakes three-master, that lost her luck on a run to Buffalo. A man, named Bill, had fallen to his death from the masthead, and on the following day another had lost his life. On arriving at Buffalo the men went ashore as soon as they were paid off. They were not returning because,

* W. H. Bishop, "Fish and Men in the Maine Islands," *Harper's Magazine*, September, 1880.

they said, the ship had lost her luck. While the vessel was discharging her cargo at an elevator the story got around and the grain-trimmers refused to work her.

When the ship was unloaded she was ordered to Cleveland to take on coal but could not sign a crew. The captain managed to get a new crew by going to a crimp, who ran them in from salt water. They came aboard two-thirds drunk and the mate was steering them to the forecastle, when one of them stopped and, pointing aloft, said:

"What have you got a figurehead on the masthead for?"

The mate looked aloft and then turned white.

"It's Bill," he cried, and with that the whole lot did a pierhead jump, even the mate.

The captain managed to sign on another crew and sailed for Cleveland, but he never got there: his vessel was sunk by a steamer off Dunkirk.

## Gloucester's Alice Marr

Captain John Ackman named his vessel for his promised bride and sailed for the Banks, as have so many other fishermen, never to return. Fair Alice and others haunted the shore for a sight of the vessel they all believed would return.

> "Ever as rolls the year around,
> Bringing again her sailing day,
> Rises her hull from the depths profound,
> And slowly cruises the outer bay.
>
> Not a word of her master's fate,
> Only a glimmer of sail and spar;
> Not a word of her crew or mate—
> This is the ghost of the 'Alice Marr.' " *

## The Storm Ship of the Hudson †

The news from the fort, therefore, brought all the populace down to the battery, to behold the wished-for sight. It was not ex-

---

* E. Norman Gunnison, "The Phantom Boat."
† Irving, "The Storm Ship," in *Bracebridge Hall.*

actly the time when she had been expected to arrive, and the circumstance was a matter of some speculation. . . .

In the meantime, the ship became more distinct to the naked eye: she was a stout, round Dutch-built vessel, with high bow and poop, and bearing Dutch colors. The evening sun gilded her bellying canvas, as she came riding over the long waving billows. The sentinel who had given notice of her approach, declared, that he got first sight of her when she was in the centre of the bay; and that she broke suddenly on his sight, just as if she had come out of the bosom of the black thunder-cloud. The bystanders looked at Hans Van Pelt, to see what he would say to this report: Hans Van Pelt screwed his mouth closer together, and said nothing; upon which some shook their heads, and others shrugged their shoulders.

The ship was now repeatedly hailed, but made no reply, and, passing by the fort, stood on up the Hudson. A gun was brought to bear on her, and, with some difficulty, loaded and fired by Hans Van Pelt, the garrison not being expert in artillery. The shot seemed absolutely to pass through the ship, and to skip along the water on the opposite side, but no notice was taken of it! What was strange, she had all her sails set, and sailed right against the wind and tide, which were both down the river. Upon this Hans Van Pelt, who was likewise harbor-master, ordered his boat and set off to board her; but after rowing two or three hours, he returned without success. Sometimes he would get within one or two hundred yards of her, and then, in a twinkling, she would be half a mile off. Some said it was because his oarsmen, who were rather pursy and short-winded, stopped every now and then to take breath, and spit on their hands; but this, it is probable, was a mere scandal. He got near enough, however, to see the crew; who were all dressed in Dutch style, the officers in doublets and high hats and feathers: not a word was spoken by any one on board: they stood as motionless as so many statues, and the ship seemed as if left to her own government. Thus she kept on, away up the river, lessening and lessening in the evening sunshine, until she faded from sight, like a little white cloud melting away in the summer sky.

.     .     .     .     .     .     .     .     .     .

Messengers were despatched to different places on the river; but they returned without any tidings—the ship had made no port. Day after day, and week after week, elapsed, but she never returned down the Hudson. As, however, the council seemed solicitous for intelligence, they had it in abundance. The captains of the sloops seldom arrived without bringing some report of having seen the strange ship at different parts of the river; sometimes near the Palisadoes; sometimes off Croton Point, and sometimes in the highlands; but she never was reported as having been seen above the highlands. The crews of the sloops, it is true, generally differed among themselves in their accounts of these apparitions; but they may have arisen from the uncertain situations in which they saw her. Sometimes it was by the flashes of the thunder storm lighting up a pitchy night, and giving glimpses of her careering across Tappaan Zee, or the wide waste of Haverstraw Bay. At one moment she would appear close upon them, as if likely to run them down, and would throw them into great bustle and alarm; but the next flash would show her far off, always sailing against the wind. Sometimes on quiet moonlight nights, she would be seen under some high bluff of the highlands, all in deep shadow, excepting her top-sails glittering in the moonbeams; by the time, however, that the voyagers would reach the place, there would be no ship to be seen; and when they had passed on for some distance, and looked back, behold! there she was again with her top-sails in the moonshine! Her appearance was always just after, or just before, or just in the midst of unruly weather; and she was known by all the skippers and voyagers of the Hudson, by the name of "the storm ship."

.    .    .    .    .    .    .    .    .    .    .    .

. . . Old Hans Van Pelt, who had been more than once to the Dutch colony at the Cape of Good Hope, insisted that this must be the Flying Dutchman which had so long haunted Table Bay, but, being unable to make port, had now sought another harbor. Others suggested, that, if it really was a supernatural apparition, as there was every natural reason to believe, it might be Hendrick Hudson, and his crew of the *Half-Moon*. . . .

## A Great Lakes Ghost

Great Lakes sailors, in the dead of wild, stormy nights, sight a one-stacker sailing easily through the storm. They know her as the

*Bannockburn*, a freighter, lost on Lake Superior with twenty-two men aboard. She had sailed from Duluth on a winter morning and was sighted by a passing ship the following evening. That was the last seen of her until she reappeared as a phantom, a vessel destined to sail on but never to reach port.*

## Hudson River Phantoms

"The ancient traditionists of the neighborhood, however, religiously ascribed these sounds to a judgment upon one Rumbout Van Dam, of Spiting Devil, who had danced and drank late one Saturday night, at a Dutch quilting frolic, at Kakiat, and set off alone for home in his boat, on the verge of Sunday morning; swearing he would not land until he reached Spiting Devil, if it took him a month of Sundays. He was never seen afterward, but is often heard plying his oars across the Tappan Sea, a Flying Dutchman on a small scale, suited to the size of his cruising-ground; being doomed to ply between Kakiat and Spiting Devil till the day of judgment, but never to reach the land." †

\* D. T. Bowen, *Lore of the Lakes.*
† Irving, *Chronicles of Wolfert's Roost.*

## Sea Creatures

### Mermaids and Mermen

THE belief in these imaginary marine beings was never strongly held by American seamen. They were, quite naturally, attracted to the female of the species, but mermen and marmachler, or merchildren, were out of the picture. They did sing:

> On Friday morning we set sail,
> And our ship was not far from land,
> When there we saw a pretty maid,
> With a comb and glass in her hand,
>     Brave boys,
> With a comb and glass in her hand.

They did not know of the Nereids, the fifty daughters of Nereus, the prophetic old sea god of great kindliness. His daughters were of great beauty and lived in the depths of the sea in a coral grotto richly furnished and decorated in gold and silver. Born seers, they were friendly to mariners and often acted as pilots through dangerous straits; they showed a great partiality to the human race. When the treacherous pilot had run Vasco da Gama's ship aground, three of the Nereids, Nerine, Doto, and Nyse, lifted up the vessel and turned it round.

At times they appeared clothed and at others nude. They disported themselves on the waves, along with sea monsters, and were seen riding on the backs of dolphins or seated in chariots drawn by Tritons, the trumpeters of the sea. The most distinguished of the sisters were Amphitrite, Thetis, and Galatea.

From the Greek fables these legendary ladies spread throughout the world; they were known to the Hindus, the Mongolians, the Vikings, and even the Indians of North, Central, and South America. In the passing of time they were given the form of a woman from the waist up, with the lower half the tail of a fish. Many claimed to have seen one or more and were promptly put down as liars.

"The *fifteenth* [June 15, 1608], all day and night cleere sunshine; the wind at east; the latitude at noone 75 degrees, 7 minutes. We held westward by our account 13 leagues. In the afternoon the sea was asswaged; and the wind being at east we set sayle, and stood south and by east, and south south-east as we could. This morning, one of our companie looking over boord saw a mermaid, and calling up some of the companie to see her, one more came up, and by that time shee was come close to the ship's side, looking earnestly on the men: a little after, a sea came and overturned her: from the navill upward, her backe and breasts were like a woman's, as they say that saw her; her body as big as one of us; her skin very white; and long haire hanging downe behinde, of colour black: in her going down they saw her tayle, which was like the tayle of a porposse, and speckled like a macrell. Their names that saw her, were Thomas Hilles and Robert Rayner." *

The redoubtable Captain John Smith saw a mermaid, or thought he saw one, in 1614 in the West Indies. What he could see of her from the deck he examined critically: she was swimming about with extraordinary grace. Her eyes, he thought, were too round, her

* From "A Second Voyage or Employment of Master Henry Hudson," in *Henry Hudson, the Navigator*, London, Hakluyt Society, 1860.

finely shaped nose too short and her well-formed ears too long, but, all in all, a very attractive woman. Just as Captain John was about to lose his heart the lady turned over, revealing below the waist the tail of a fish.

In 1881 a dispatch from New Orleans announced the capture of a mermaid in Aspinwall Bay and the bringing of her to New Orleans:

"This wonder of the deep is in a fine state of preservation. The head and body of a woman are very plainly and distinctly marked. The features of the face, eyes, nose, mouth, teeth, arms, breasts and hair are those of a human being. The hair on its head is of a pale, silky blonde, several inches in length. The arms terminate in claws closely resembling an eagle's talons, instead of fingers with nails. From the waist up, the resemblance to a woman is perfect, and from the waist down, the body is exactly the same as the ordinary mullet of our waters, with its scales, fins and tail perfect. Many old fishermen and amateur anglers who have seen it pronounce it unlike any fish they have ever seen. Scientists and savants alike are 'all at sea' respecting it, and say that if the mermaid be indeed a fabulous creature, they cannot class this strange comer from the blue waters."

The real answer seems to be that in 1881 P. T. Barnum was still alive and active.

## Kobolds

The belief in these invisible little evildoers never interested American seamen, but several instances of them and their peculiar powers have been recorded. During World War II there was much talk by aviators of gremlins, little men who interfered with the smooth performance of planes and even committed, at times, acts that resulted in serious accidents. Kobolds and gremlins are members of the large family of familiars, each with characteristics of their own, and known as elves, gnomes, nereids, nymphs, trolls, brownies, pixies, goblins, djinns, and many other names.

To sailors and miners they are known as kobolds, and, in the case of the miners, they are believed to take over the mines as soon as the humans leave. While they are in possession of the mine they change the course of seams and the locations of galleries, and hide tools and other things. The lumberjacks of the northern woods have a similar character whom they call Sock Saunders, a chap who dulls freshly sharpened axes and tries to make life more complicated for the loggers.

The sailor's kobold was called Klaboterman, and his roving area was the Baltic, where he was sometimes heard but rarely seen. Those who have seen him say he sits on the bowsprit of a phantom ship named the *Carmilhan*, dressed in yellow, wearing a nightcap and smoking a cutty pipe.*

> And one was spinning a sailor's yarn
>   About Klaboterman,
> The Kobold of the sea; a sprite
> Invisible to mortal sight,
>   Who o'er the rigging ran.
>
> Sometimes he hammered in the hold,
>   Sometimes upon the mast,
> Sometimes abeam, sometimes abaft,
> Or at the bows he sang and laughed,
>   And made all tight and fast.
>
> He helped the sailors at their work,
>   And toiled with jovial din;
> He helped them hoist and reef the sails,
> He helped them stow the casks and bales,
>   And heave the anchor in.
>
> But woe unto the lazy louts,
>   The idlers of the crew;
> Them to torment was his delight,
> And worry them by day and night,
>   And pinch them black and blue.
>
> And woe to him whose mortal eyes
>   Klaboterman behold.
> It is a certain sign of death!—
> The cabin-boy here held his breath,
>   And felt his blood run cold.†

* Brewer, *The Reader's Handbook*.
† H. W. Longfellow, "The Ballad of the *Carmilhan*," from *Tales of a Wayside Inn*.

"The captains of the river craft talk of a little bulbous-bottomed Dutch goblin, in trunk hose and sugar-loaf hat, with a speaking trumpet in his hand, which they say keeps about the Dunderberg. They declare they have heard him, in stormy weather, in the midst of the turmoil, giving orders in Low Dutch for the piping up a fresh gust of wind, or the rattling off of another thunder-clap. That sometimes he has been seen surrounded by a crew of little imps in broad breeches and short doublets; tumbling head-over-heels in the rack and mist, and playing a thousand gambols in the air; or buzzing like a swarm of flies about Anthony's Nose, and that, at such times, the hurry-scurry of the storm was always greatest. One time, a sloop, in passing by the Dunderberg, was overtaken by a thunder-gust, that came scouring around the mountain, and seemed to burst just over the vessel. Though tight and well ballasted, yet she labored dreadfully, until the water came over the gunwale. All the crew were amazed, when it was discovered that there was a little white sugar-loaf hat on the mast-head, which was known at once to be that of the Heer of the Dunderberg. Nobody, however, dared climb to the mast-head, and get rid of this terrible hat. The sloop continued laboring and rocking, as if she would have rolled her mast overboard. She seemed in continual danger either of upsetting or of running ashore. In this way she drove quite through the highlands, until she had passed Pollopol's Island, where, it is said, the jurisdiction of the Dunderberg potentate ceases. No sooner had she passed this bourne, than the little hat, all at once, spun up into the air like a top, whirled up all the clouds into a vortex, and hurried them back to the summit of the Dunderberg, while the sloop righted herself, and sailed on as quietly as if in a mill-pond. Nothing saved her from utter wreck, but the fortunate circumstance of having a horse-shoe nailed against the mast, a wise precaution against evil spirits, which has since been adopted by all the Dutch captains that navigate this haunted river." *

"There is another story told of this foul-weather urchin, by Skipper Daniel Ouslesticker, of Fish-Kill, who was never known to tell a lie. He declared, that in a severe squall, he saw him seated astride his bowsprit, riding the sloop ashore, full butt against Anthony's Nose; and that he was exorcised by Dominie Van Gieson, of Esopus, who happened to be on board, and who sung the hymn of St. Nich-

* Irving, "The Storm Ship," in *Bracebridge Hall*.

olas; whereupon the goblin threw himself up in the air like a ball, and went off in a whirlwind, carrying away with him the nightcap of the Dominie's wife; which was discovered next Sunday morning hanging on the weathercock of Esopus church steeple, at least forty miles off! After several events of this kind had taken place, the regular skippers of the river, for a long time, did not venture to pass the Dunderberg, without lowering their peaks, out of homage to the Heer of the mountain; and it was observed that all as paid this tribute of respect were suffered to pass unmolested." *

## Sea Serpents

Many of the known sea serpents have been reported by shore birds, and one of the truly honest of this breed observed that he had "never been that drunk." But all seamen know of these maiden-devouring, man-swallowing monsters of the deep, and they fear them and their powers. For almost a century and a half scientists have been trying to disprove the existence of the serpent, but they have been working against great odds, against the sworn and witnessed words of honorable mariners, men whose words have seldom been questioned. Scientists in many instances do not credit their own eyes, and should they come upon a sea serpent unexpectedly would probably charge it to something they had eaten, an illusion, or a hallucination. In the face of hard evidence they call it a myth, a superstition.

* *Ibid.*

"In that day the Lord with his sore and great and strong sword shall punish Leviathan the piercing serpent, even Leviathan that crooked serpent, and he shall slay the dragon that is in the sea" (Isaiah 27:1).

St. Brandon, on his famous voyage, "told of the grete fiss, he named Jasconye, which laboureth nyght and daye to put his tayle in his mouth, but for greetness he may not."

And in Scandinavian mythology the great Midgaard serpent, Jormundgandr, sits at the bottom of the sea, forever trying to bite his own tail, and is said to be so large that he can encircle the world. The Hindus tell of Odonto-tyrannus, the serpent of the Ganges, who swallowed elephants without chewing them.

"All seamen say that there is a sea serpent two hundred feet long, and twenty feet thick, who comes out at night to devour cattle. It has long black hair hanging down from its head, and flaming eyes, with sharp scales on its body." *

Let us get down to the days of iron men and wooden ships:

From a statement made by a Kennebec shipmaster in 1818, and sworn to before a justice of the peace in Kennebec county, Maine, it would seem that the notable sea serpent and the whale are sometimes found in conflict. At six o'clock in the afternoon of June 21, the packet *Delia*, was plying between Boston and Hallowell; when Cape Ann bore west southwest about two miles, steering north-northeast, Captain Shubael West, and fifteen others on board with him, saw an object directly ahead which he had no doubt was the sea serpent, or the creature so often described under that name, engaged in a fight with a large humpback whale that was endeavoring to elude the attack.

The serpent threw up its tail perpendicularly from twenty-five to thirty feet, striking the whale with tremendous blows rapidly repeated, which were distinctly heard and very loud for two or three minutes. They then both disappeared, moving in a west-southwest direction, but after a few minutes reappeared inshore of the packet, and about under the sun, the reflection of which was so strong as to prevent their seeing so distinctly as at first, when the serpent's fearful blows with his tail were repeated and clearly heard as before.

They again went down for a short time, and then came up to the

* Olaus Magnus, *History of the Goths.*

surface under the packet's larboard quarter, the whale appearing first and the serpent in pursuit, which was again seen to shoot up its tail as before, which it held out of water some time, waving it in the air before striking, and at the same time, while its tail remained in this position, it raised its head fifteen or twenty feet, as if taking a view of the surface of the sea. After being seen in this position a few minutes, the serpent and the whale again sank and disappeared, and neither was seen again by any on board. It was Captain West's opinion that the whale was trying to escape, as it spouted but once at a time on coming to the surface, and the last time it appeared it went down before the serpent came up.*

"The captain, officers and crew of the bark *Pauline*, of London, also made deposition before a magistrate in 1875, that they saw, in July, an immense serpent twined about a large sperm whale, that whirled the latter over as if it had been a toy, and finally carried it down to the sea-depths. Again, later, by a few days, they saw a similar monster, skimming along the sea, head and neck out of the water several feet." †

The years 1817 to 1819 were marked by a great rash of sea serpents, all reported from Massachusetts Bay, from Cape Ann to Plymouth. Save for the already quoted affidavit of the master of the packet *Delia*, all the reports were made by landsmen. Despite the fact that the ineffable Captain Marryat, in writing of a monster, makes one of his characters say: "Nor has the animal been seen before or since, except by Americans, who have much better eyes than the people of Europe boast of," most of the credible accounts are from British sources. Captain M'Quhae's report is a classic.

"Her Majesty's Ship *Daedalus*, Hamoaze, Oct. 11 [1848]
"Sir,— In reply to your letter of this day's date, requiring information as to the truth of a statement published in *The Times* newspaper, of a sea-serpent of extraordinary dimensions having been seen from Her Majesty's ship *Daedalus*, under my command, on her passage from the East Indies, I have the honour to acquaint you, for the information of my Lords Commissioners of the Admiralty, that at 5 o'clock P.M. on the 6th of August last, in latitude 24' 44' S., and

* Cheever, *The Whale and His Captors.*
† Bassett, *Sea Phantoms.*

longitude 9' 22' E., the weather dark and cloudy, wind fresh from the N.W., with a long ocean swell from the S.W., the ship on the port tack heading N.E. by N., something very unusual was seen by Mr. Sartoris, midshipman, rapidly approaching the ship from before the beam. The circumstance was immediately reported by him to the officer of the watch, Lieut. Edgar Drummond, with whom and Mr. William Barrett, the Master, I was at the time walking the quarter-deck. The ship's company were at supper.

"On our attention being called to the object it was discovered to be an enormous serpent, with head and shoulders kept about four feet constantly above the surface of the sea, and as nearly as we could approximate by comparing it with the length of what our main-topsail yard would show in the water, there was at the very least 60 feet of the animal à fleur d'eau, no portion of which, to our perception, used in propelling it through the water, either by vertical or horizontal undulation. It passed rapidly, but so close under our lee quarter, that had it been a man of my acquaintance I should have easily recognised his features with the naked eye; and it did not, either in approaching the ship or after it had passed our wake, deviate in the slightest degree from its course to the S.W., which it held on at the pace of from 12 to 15 miles per hour, apparently on some determined purpose.

"The diameter of the serpent was about 15 or 16 inches behind the head, which was, without any doubt, that of a snake, and it was never, during the 20 minutes that it continued in sight of our glasses, once below the surface of the water; its colour a dark brown, with yellowish white about the throat. It had no fins, but something like the mane of a horse, or rather a bunch of seaweed, washed about its back. It was seen by the quartermaster, the boatswain's mate, and the man at the wheel, in addition to myself and the officers above mentioned.

"I am having a drawing of the serpent made from a sketch taken immediately after it was seen, which I hope to have ready for transmission to my Lords Commissioners of the Admiralty by to-morrow's post.

"I have, &c

"Peter M'Quhae, Captain.

"To Admiral Sir W. H. Gage, G. C. H. Devonport."

The captain and officers of the ship *Castilian* saw a serpent near St. Helena, in the evening of December 12, 1857. Their affidavit affirms:

"At 6.30 P.M., strong breezes and cloudy, ship sailing about 12 miles per hour. While myself and officers were standing on the lee side of the poop, looking towards the island, we were startled by the sight of a huge marine animal which reared its head out of the water within 20 yards of the ship, when it suddenly disappeared for about half a minute, and then made its appearance in the same manner again, showing us distinctly its neck and head about 10 or 12 feet out of the water.

"Its head was shaped like a long nun buoy, and I suppose the diameter to have been seven or eight feet in the largest part, with a kind of scroll, or tuft of loose skin, encircling it about two feet from the top; the water was discoloured for several hundred feet from its head, so much so that on its first appearance, my impression was that the ship was in broken water, produced, as I supposed, by some volcanic agency since the last time I passed the island, but the second appearance completely dispelled those fears, and assured us that it was a monster of extraordinary length, which appeared to be moving slowly towards the land.

"The ship was going too fast to enable us to reach the mast-head in time to form a correct estimate of its extreme length, but from what we saw from the deck we conclude it must have been over 200 feet long. The boatswain and several of the crew who observed it from the topgallant forecastle state that it was more than double the length of the ship, in which case it must have been 500 feet; be that as it may, I am convinced it belonged to the serpent tribe; it was of dark colour about the head, and was covered with several white spots. Having a press of canvas on the ship at the time, I was unable to round to without risk, and therefore was precluded from getting another sight of this leviathan of the deep.

"George Hanry Harrington, Commander
"William Davies, Chief Officer
"Edward Wheeler, Second Officer."

These honorable seamen, reporting only what they had seen with their own eyes, and supported by credible witnesses, were shortly answered by an equally honorable mariner. In *The Times* of February 12, 1858, there was published a letter from a merchant captain, Frederic Smith, of the ship *Pekin*. Wrote Captain Smith:

"In your paper of the 5th inst. is a letter from Captain Harrington, of the ship *Castilian*, stating his belief that he had seen the great sea serpent near St. Helena. His confidence is strengthened from the fact of something similar having been seen by Her Majesty's ship *Daedalus* near the same position. The following circumstance, which occurred on board the ship *Pekin*, then belonging to Messrs. T. & W. Smith, on her passage from Moulmein, may be of some service respecting this 'queer fish.'

"On December the 28th, 1848, being then in lat. 26 S., long. 6 E., nearly calm, ship having only steerage way, saw about half-a-mile on port beam a very extraordinary-looking thing in the water of considerable length. With the telescope we could plainly discern a huge head and neck, covered with a long shaggy-looking kind of mane, which it kept lifting at intervals out of the water. This was seen by all hands and declared to be the great sea-serpent.

"I determined on knowing something about it, and accordingly lowered a boat, in which my chief officer and four men went, taking with them a long small line in case it should be required. I watched them very anxiously, and the monster seemed not to regard their approach. At length they got close to the head. They seemed to hesitate, and then busy themselves with the line, the monster all the time ducking its head, and showing its great length. Presently the boat began pulling towards the ship, the monster following slowly.

"In about half-an-hour they got alongside; a tackle was got on the mainyard, and it was hoisted on board. It appeared somewhat supple when hanging, but so completely covered with snaky-looking barnacles about eighteen inches long, that we had it some time on board before it was discovered to be a piece of gigantic seaweed, 20 feet long, and 4 inches diameter; the root end of which appeared when in the water like the head of the animal, and the motion given by the sea caused it to seem alive. In a few days it dried up to a hollow tube, and as it had a rather offensive smell was thrown overboard.

"I had only been a short time in England when the *Daedalus* arrived and reported having seen the great sea-serpent—to the best of my recollection near the same locality, and which I have no doubt was a piece of the same weed. So like a huge living monster did this appear, that had circumstances prevented my sending a boat to it I should certainly have believed I had seen the great sea snake."

The reader will have to take his own position, with the shipmasters who saw the sea serpent, with him who saw only an attenuated weed, or with the zoologists who insist to this day that it is only a myth.

# Fire and Water

## Corposant, Ampizant, or St. Elmo's Fire

FREQUENTLY a luminous ball appears on the ends of yardarms or mastheads, due to the air being surcharged with electricity. Science has not yet dispelled the sailors' belief in the supernatural character of these lights. Ancient seamen feared them, but later sailors, especially those of the Roman Catholic faith, regarded them as the Holy Ghost, *corpus sancti*. On different occasions the crews of Columbus and Magellan observed the phenomenon and rejoiced, convinced that St. Elmo, their patron saint, was near at hand.

The general belief among the old sailing-ship men was that it was a good omen if the corposant was seen to rise, and the opposite if it descended to a lower position. It meant personal ill luck if the light shone directly into a sailor's face. To some the appearance of a single corposant was a signal of bad luck, and two or more at the same time were of good omen. Others believed they preceded or followed rain, and Dana, in *Two Years before the Mast*, records that the one he saw was followed by rain. Melville, in *Moby Dick*, says that all the men avoided oaths while they were burning. And Davis, in *The American Nimrod*, writes that whalers called the light Ampizant, and had a superstition that it was the spirit of some sailor who had died on board the vessel on which it appeared.

## Phosphorescence

Foreign sailors had many explanations for this; one was that they were the reflections of the flames of hell and marked its temporary location. American sailors referred to it as witches' oil and let it go at that.

## Waterspouts

This phenomenon of the sea, a column of whirling spray and moisture reaching from the sea to the clouds, still strikes terror into the hearts of lubbers. In the imaginations of early seamen it was the work of a dragon, or of the devil; later sailors said it was God replenishing the clouds. Until very recently it was thought a waterspout could be destroyed by artillery fire. Mediterranean sailors believe that a gesture with a knife, a black-handled knife, will destroy them.

"During the voyages of Columbus, the mariners were terrified at the waterspouts; and despairing of all human means to avert them, repeated passages from St. John the Evangelist, and when the spouts passed close to the ships without injuring them, the trembling crew attributed their escape to the miraculous efficacy of their quotations from the scripture." *

* Jones, *Credulities, Past and Present.*

## Witches and Wizards

"IN that Ilonde is sortilege and witchcraft, for women there sell the shipmen wynde, as it were closed under thre knotes of threde, so that the more wynde he would have, the more knotes, he must undo." *

An enduring belief in the power of certain persons to raise winds and storms has existed from the earliest times and is far from being extinct even today. European folklore is shot with legends of women, who on land sold fair or foul weather to mariners, and of men, usually a member of the ship's company, who held equally malevolent powers and made grim use of them.

### Witches

European witches were strictly commercial, offering for cash in hand a variety of winds and weather, and the means of purveying these were usually strings or cords with knots. The purchaser, once at sea and becalmed, opened the first knot for a light breeze, the second for a moderate, and the last for a strong breeze. In addition to the knotted strings they also sold charms and amulets and, sometimes, cauls. American witches were purely malevolent and were

* Polychronicon (1387).

held responsible for many losses at sea. Only one, Moll Pitcher, put her alleged power on a commercial basis.

In Liverpool there was an old Negro woman, by the name of de Squak, whose house was much frequented by American sailors. She had two black cats with green eyes and nightcaps on their heads, and she would feel the sailor's pulse before telling him what was going to befall him.*

Polly Twichell, of Casco Bay, was, in the seventeenth century, charged with raising storms and wrecking ships at sea, and a ship going from London to Virginia in 1674 was said to have encountered storms and other disasters from the machinations of the weird sisterhood. During the same century Margaret Jones, of Charlestown, was executed for witchcraft, and shortly thereafter the ship in which her husband was seeking refuge in the Barbados commenced to roll violently while at anchor in smooth water, continuing for twelve hours. Finally the husband of the executed witch was threatened with arrest if he did not stop the ship's rolling, and did so upon being shown the sheriff's warrant.†

Mrs. Eunice Cole, of Hampton, in New Hampshire, was charged with being a witch as early as 1656 but was not imprisoned until twenty-four years later. Known as Goody Cole, she was, for that quarter of a century, the terror of the people of the town, who believed she had sold herself body and soul to the devil.‡

Goody Cole was believed responsible for one of the great sea tragedies of her time. A large party of the townspeople sailed out of the river for a day's pleasure of fishing at sea. As they sailed past the mouth of the river they could see the witch, seated in front of her hut, at her spinning wheel.

> "She's cursed," said the skipper; "speak her fair:
> I'm scary always to see her shake
> Her wicked head, with its wild gray hair,
> And nose like a hawk, and eyes like a snake."

The skipper had answered a merry girl who cried "Fie on the witch!" But Goody Cole answered:

* Melville, *Redburn* (1849).
† Massachusetts Historical Collections.
‡ Drake, *New England Legends and Folklore*.

"Oho!" she muttered, "ye're brave today!
But I hear the little waves laugh and say.
'The broth will be cold that waits at home,
For it's one to go, but another to come!' "

They dropped their lines in the lazy tide,
Drawing up haddock and mottled cod;
They saw not the Shadow that walked beside,
They heard not the feet with silence shod.
But thicker and thicker a hot mist grew,
Shot by lightnings through and through;
And muffled growls, like the growl of a beast,
Ran along the sky from west to east.

.    .    .    .    .    .

The skipper hauled at the heavy sail:
  "God be our help!" he only cried,
As the roaring gale, like the stroke of a flail,
  Smote the boat on its starboard side.

.    .    .    .    .    .

Suddenly seaward swept the squall;

.    .    .    .    .    .

But far and wide as eye could reach,
No life was seen upon wave or beach;
The boat that went out at morning never
Sailed back again into Hampton River.*

Moll Pitcher was a witch by birth. The daughter of John Dimond, of Marblehead, she was married to Robert Pitcher, a shoemaker, and went to live with him in Lynn. "During the fifty years
that Moll pursued her trade . . . her most valued clients came from
the opulent seaports that are within sight of High Rock. The common sailor and the master, the cabin-boy and the owner, equally
resorted to her humble abode to know the luck of a voyage. It is
asserted that many a vessel has been deserted when on the eve of
sailing, in consequence of Moll's unlucky vaticination. She was also
much besought by treasure-seekers—a rather numerous class in her

* Whittier, "The Wreck at Rivermouth."

day, whose united digging along the coast of New England would, if usefully directed, have reclaimed for cultivation no inconsiderable area of virgin soil. For such applicants the witch had a short and sharp reply. 'Fools!' she would say; 'if I knew where money was buried, do you think I would part with the secret?' " *

John Dimond, Moll's father, was a wizard in Marblehead. "In proof of this it is said that he was in the habit of going to the old burying-ground on the hill whenever a violent gale at sea arose, and in that lonely place, in the midst of the darkness and the storm, to astound and terrify the simple fisherfolk in the following manner. He would direct vessels then at sea how to weather the roughest gale,—pacing up and down among the gravestones, and ever and anon, in a voice distinctly heard above the howling of the tempest, shouting out his orders to the helmsman or the crew, as if he were actually on the quarter-deck, and the scene all before him. Very few doubted his ability to bring a vessel safely into port." †

## Wizards

Wizards and sorcerers resembled witches in that they claimed control over wind and weather. Some of these were landsmen dispensing good and bad weather for a price or as a gift. Aeolus, who lived on a floating island, gave Ulysses upon his departure a fair wind and all the other winds in a leathern bag. There is a similar Great Lakes legend of an Indian wizard who kept winds in bags, and another from farther north of a Cree medicine man who sold winds, three kinds, all for a pound of tobacco.

In 1711 Sir Hovenden Walker led an expedition against the French at Quebec that ended in a series of disasters, all credited to Jean Lavallée, a wizard living on the Isle of Orleans in the St. Lawrence. Walker's fleet was met by a storm of Lavallée's making and the ships dispersed and sailed back across the Atlantic, pursued by fogs and more storms. The flagship, *Edgar*, blew up as it reached Spithead, and nearly the entire crew perished.

"The Great Wiggins Storm," an event prophesied by a Canadian weather wizard in 1882, failed to materialize, but it succeeded in

* Drake, *New England Legends and Folklore.*
† *Ibid.*

keeping many Atlantic ships at their wharves in New York and Boston because they were unable to ship crews until the period of Wiggins' predicted storm had passed. And Gloucester fishermen incurred losses of many thousands of dollars because they superstitiously accepted the Canadian's prophecy.*

The wizards who operated at sea were, for the greater part, Finns and Laplanders. The earliest charge against them that has come to light was made by Olaus Magnus, in his *History of the Goths* (1658), in which he alludes to their trade in winds; and Cotton Mather, in *Magnalia Christi Americana* (1702) writes of "a Laplander . . . who can with looks and words or works, bewitch other people, or sell wind to mariners." Edward B. Tylor, in *Primitive Culture* (1871), speaks of "the sorcerers' art, practiced especially by Finn wizards, of whose uncanny power over the weather our sailors have not to this day forgotten their old terror."

In 1857 a sailor was tried in England for the killing of a mulatto at sea on the *Ruby Castle*. His defense was that he thought the man a Finn and so put him out of the way of doing harm.†

⚓

"The night after this event, when I went to the galley to get a light, I found the cook inclined to be talkative, so I sat down on the spars, and gave him opportunity to hold a yarn. I was the more inclined to do so, as I found he was full of the superstitions once more common among seamen, and which the recent death had waked up in his mind. He talked about George's having spoken of his friends, and he said he believed few men died without having a warning of it, which he supported by a great many stories of dreams, and of unusual behaviour of men before death. From this he went on to other superstitions, the *Flying Dutchman*, etc., and talked rather mysteriously, having something evidently on his mind. At last he put his head out of the galley and looked carefully about to see if anyone was within hearing, and, being satisfied on that point, asked me in a low tone,—

" 'I say! you know what countryman 'e carpenter be?'

* Drake, *New England Legends and Folklore.*
† Jones, *Credulities, Past and Present.*

" 'Yes,' said I, 'he's a German.'

" 'What kind of a German?' said the cook.

" 'He belongs to Bremen,' said I.

" 'Are you sure o' dat?' said he.

"I satisfied him on that point by saying he could speak no language but the German and English.

" 'I'm plaguey glad o' that,' said the cook. 'I was mighty 'fraid he was a Fin. I tell you what, I been plaguey civil to dat man all the voyage.'

"I asked him the reason for this, and found that he was fully possessed with the notion that Fins are wizards, and especially have power over winds and storms. I tried to reason with him about it; but he had the best of all arguments, that from experience, at hand, and was not to be moved. He had been to the Sandwich Islands in a vessel in which the sail-maker was a Fin, and could do anything he was of a mind to. This sail-maker kept a junk bottle in his berth, which was always just half-full of rum, though he got drunk upon it nearly every day. He had seen him sit for hours together, talking to this bottle, which he stood up before him on the table. The same man cut his throat in his berth, and everybody said he was possessed.

"He had heard of ships, too, beating up the Gulf of Finland against a head wind, and having a ship heave in sight astern, overhaul, and pass them, with as fair a wind as could blow, and all studding-sails out, and find she was from Finland.

" 'Oh, oh!' said he; 'I've seen too much o' dem to want to see 'm 'board a ship. If they can't have der own way, dey'll play the d—l wid you.'

"As I still doubted, he said he would leave it to John, who was the oldest seaman aboard, and would know, if anybody did. John, to be sure, was the oldest, and at the same time the most ignorant, man in the ship; but I consented to have him called. The cook stated the matter to him, and John, as I anticipated, sided with the cook, and said that he himself had been in a ship where they had a head wind for a fortnight, and the captain found out at last that one of the men, with whom he had had some hard words a short time before, was a Fin, and immediately told him if he didn't stop the head wind he would shut him down in the fore-peak. The Fin would not give in, and the captain shut him down in the fore-peak, and would not give him anything to eat. The Fin held out for a day and a half, when he could not stand it any longer, and did something or other which brought the wind round again, and they let him up.

" 'Dar,' said the cook, 'what you tink o' dat?'

"I told him I had no doubt it was true, and that it would have been odd if the wind had not changed in fifteen days, Fin or no Fin." *

* Dana, *Two Years before the Mast.*

# Jonahs and Kittle Cargoes

## Jonahs

"SO they took up Jonah, and cast him forth into the sea: and the sea ceased from her raging." And there begins and ends the historical record of a human being having been jettisoned because his presence was considered dangerous to the ship. Many men have been suspected and threatened, but only one other, and he by his own act, went for this reason to Davy Jones's locker.

The belief in Jonahs, sometimes Jonas, was tightly held: if all went well on a voyage the forecastle heard only yarns and ballads. When there was a series of misadventures or misfortunes due to wind and weather, or especially for some unexplained reason, a Jonah was suspected and a search started.

The ship *President*, one of the original Charleston coastal packets, bound for New York, ran into severe weather off Hatteras. One of the crew, believing himself a Jonah, declared the storm had been brought on by his wickedness and jumped overboard from the rigging. The storm subsided for a while but revived with renewed fury. The crew, accepting their mate's estimate of himself, decided his chest must follow him. After that there was another lull and still another return of the gale. The crew was convinced that some of the dead man's effects still remained aboard, and his shoes were found under his bunk. After they were thrown overboard the storm finally ended.*

Within their own ranks the crew believed that Finns and cross-eyed men (swivel-eyed, to them) had the makings of Jonahs. All Finns were wizards, which are quite as bad as Jonahs, and a cross-eyed man at the wheel was nothing short of tempting fate. Passengers carrying umbrellas or little black bags or wearing unusual garb were suspect. More specifically, men and women of the cloth were feared because of their black habits and their office of consoling the dying and burying the dead. A deeper grievance against the clerics was that the devil, the maker of storms, was their sworn enemy and sent tempests to destroy them.

Heretics, too, were feared. Captain John Smith records that he was deemed a Jonah while on a voyage to Rome: "They would never have fair weather while I, a heretic, was on board." And John Lloyd Stephens, the American archeologist, wrote that his vessel was becalmed and that the crew charged it was due to his being a heretic.

The actor, Holcroft, tells that the sailors thought him a Jonah because he was an actor. In the next sentence he probably reveals the situation. On Easter Sunday, while walking the quarter-deck, reading a play aloud (or was he rehearsing?), several of the crew approached and one asked him what he was reading.

"By the holy father, I know you are a Jonas, and the ship will never see land till you are tossed overboard, you and your plays."

*Bibles as Jonahs*   This is one of the unexplained mysteries of the sea. Sailors, as a rule, did not carry a Bible with their gear, though a few must have possessed a copy. The Book belonged in the cabin, in the hands of the master, and nowhere else. It was for use on solemn occasions only, at Sunday services and in sea burials.

"It was Mrs. O'Brien's custom to come on deck each morning and stand between the knight-heads where she read the Bible aloud to her children. More especially the sailors disliked the grave matron herself, hooded in rusty black, and they had a bitter grudge against her book. To that, and the incantations muttered over it, they ascribed the head winds that haunted us; and Blunt, our Irish cockney, really believed that Mrs. O'Brien purposely came on deck every

* Thatcher, *Superstitions.*

morning in order to secure a foul wind for the ensuing twenty-four hours.

"At last, upon her coming forward one morning, Max the Dutchman accosted her, saying he was sorry for it, but if she went between the knight-heads again with her book, the crew would throw it overboard for her.

"Notwithstanding the rebuke and threat of the sailor, the widow silently occupied her old place; and with her children clustering around her, began her low muttered reading, standing right in the extreme bows of the ship and slightly leaning over them, as if addressing the multitudinous waves from a floating pulpit. Presently Max came behind her, snatched the book from her hands, and threw it overboard." *

As recently as 1915, when the tanker *Standard* caught fire in the Gulf of Mexico, the crew decided that a Bible, left after German possession of the vessel, was the cause of the trouble. The fire was a dangerous one, yet three of the crew took time out from fighting the flames to rush forward and give the Book to the deep six.

Old Gloucester was rich in Jonah legends. "A young man engaged in the haddock fishery, secured a berth with one of the smartest skippers who sails from Gloucester. But, notwithstanding the fact that every possible effort was put forth, poor results followed, and the months of November and December wore away, and the crew in the meantime not sharing more than $25 to a man. Everybody felt discouraged. At this time, however, the young man of whom I am speaking, and who, it was said, was one of the unlucky ones, left the vessel and shipped in another. On the next trip the vessel he had left shared $20 from only two days' fishing, and on succeeding trips did even better than that, making an excellent winter's work. But the second vessel in which the man shipped (though commanded by one of the most expert skippers) failed to get a share of the fish after he joined her, and the same result was met by this unfortunate individual in a third vessel which he joined during the winter. The mysterious part of it was that in each of the three cases the vessels which met with poor success while he was in them did much better than the average during the rest of the season.†

* Melville, *Redburn.*
† *The Fisherman's Own Book.*

*The Ship As a Jonah*   "I recall a singular circumstance of this kind, with the particulars of which I was familiar at the time they occurred. Several years ago a new vessel was brought to Gloucester from the port where she was built. She was of the largest class employed in the fisheries—a beauty in model and rig—and the skipper, who was a young man and part owner, naturally felt a commendable pride in the fine schooner which he commanded. One day, however, while this vessel was being fitted for her first trip, an acquaintance said to him, 'I'm sorry you have had this vessel built.' When asked for his reasons, he continued, 'I have known the man who built her to launch more than twenty schooners during the past few years, and none of them have ever made a dollar for their owners, while few of them have lived more than two or three years, being either wrecked on the shore or foundered at sea.' Strange to say, that, for the nineteen months the first skipper sailed in her, 'there was nae luck aboot the house.' This was exceedingly trying to one who had previously been fortunate and felt a pride in his profession. Finally, becoming disgusted and somewhat disheartened by his ill-success and unrequited labors, he sold out his share of the vessel and left her, almost convinced that what he had been told by his friend was not very far from the truth.

"The sad sequel remains to be told. The schooner—not yet two years old—was lost at sea on her next voyage. The captain and two of the crew were drowned, and the survivors, after enduring much suffering while lashed to the wreck, were finally taken off and returned home to tell the particulars of this ill-fated episode." *

## Davy Jones and His Locker

American sailors would rather not talk about Davy Jones and his infamous locker. They are ready enough to refer to him and his dwelling place, but just leave him an indefinite, unbodied character who keeps to his place at the bottom of the sea. Pressed, they will profess that they do not know what he looks like, his locker is to them something like an ordinary sea chest or a coffin, always open to catch any sailor unfortunate enough to find himself in the sea. Some

* *Ibid.*

English sailors incline to the belief that his name is a corruption of Duffer Jones, a clumsy fellow who frequently found himself overboard.

The only time Davy comes to life is in the ceremony of Crossing the Line. Then he is usually impersonated by the smallest sailor on board, given a hump, horns and a tail, and his features made as ugly as possible. He is swinish, dressed in rags and seaweed, and shambles along in the wake of the sea king, Neptune, playing evil tricks upon his fellow sailors.

Old sailors, rather than speak of the devil, called him Deva, Davy or Taffy, the thief of evil spirit; and Jones is from Jonah, whose locker was the whale's belly. Jonah was often called Jonas, and as Davy Jones, the enemy of all living sailors, he has become the mariners' evil angel.

To be cast into the sea and sink is to fall into his locker and have the lid popped down on one. It is generally agreed that the Christian sailor's body goes to Davy Jones's locker, but his soul, if he is a proper sailorman, goes to Fiddlers' Green.

## Kittle Cargoes

Lawyers usually carried little black bags, and these gentlemen of the bar were doubly hated by seaman, who usually only met the profession ashore and always to their own disadvantage. "Land sharks" was the sailors' term for them, and they were so glib, so cunning, that if they could not talk up trouble for a man or a ship, they could produce it from their black bags.

Women were considered kittle cargo * rather than actual Jonahs. Sailors were reluctant to sign on a vessel in which the captain's wife was carried. These were known as "hen-frigates," and the sailors' dislike stemmed from the tendency of the old man's wife to countermand orders and to find fault with the personal appearance of the crew. But most sailors looked askance at carrying women passengers. "It is always bad luck," said one, "to have either a woman or a minister on board. I never knew it to fail yet. It is either a long passage, or getting dismasted, or short of provisions, or there's a terrible row

* Kittle, anything hard to handle, a difficult or ticklish cargo.

in the camp. It's bad enough to carry one woman, as the *Eagle* is going to do, but when it comes to taking four or five of them and two missionaries besides, as the *Tempest* does, it's the very mischief. I don't believe she'll ever reach port." *

* Adams, *On Board the Rocket*.

# Omens and Superstitions

## Lucky and Unlucky Days

THE belief in lucky and unlucky days still prevails among seamen, though more widely among fishermen. There were supposed to be twenty-eight lucky and fifty-four unlucky days in a year, but most of these have been lost to the records.

*Sunday*. A lucky day for both seamen and fishermen.

*Monday*. Usually considered a lucky day, save for the first Monday in April (Cain's birthday) and the second Monday in August (anniversary of the destruction of Sodom and Gomorrah).

*Tuesday*. Not an auspicious day to commence a voyage. It seems to stem from the Spanish and Portuguese sailors: "El Martes, ne te casas, ne te embarques, ne de te mujer apartarse"—"On Tuesday don't marry, don't go to sea, and do not leave your wife."

*Wednesday*. This day, consecrated to Odin, the one-eyed, who, as Hnicker, was the Viking mariner's chief deity, was considered a lucky day.

*Thursday*. Dedicated to Thor, the eldest son of Odin and Frigga. He launched the thunder, presided over the air, winds, and seasons, and protected man from lightning and evil spirits. It was the seaman's lucky day.

*Friday.* Traditionally unlucky.
*Saturday.* Entirely without significance to the sailor.

*Friday*

> Friday's noon
> Come when it will,
> It comes too soon.

⚓

"There has been a singular superstition prevalent among seamen about sailing on Friday: and in former times, to sail on this day would have been regarded as a violation of the mysterious character of the day, which would have been visited with disaster upon the offender. Even now it is not entirely abandoned; so if a voyage commenced on Friday happens to be unfortunate all the ill-luck of the voyage is ascribed to having sailed on that day. An intelligent shipmaster told me that, although he had no faith in the superstition, yet so firmly were sailors impressed with superstitious notions respecting the day, that, until within a few years, he should never have ventured to sail on a Friday, for the men would be appalled by the dangers which they would think light of on common occasions." *

⚓

> Sunday sail, never fail,
> Friday sail, ill luck and gale.

Many folklorists attribute Friday's bad character to early Catholicism, when out of respect for the day of universal redemption, the day on which Christ was crucified, seamen and fishermen were told by the priests to await tomorrow's sun. Yet in pagan days and in non-Christian countries the day is also feared.

It was also known to sailors as "the hangman's day" and "the witches' sabbath," a day on which wizards and witches exert great powers over the winds and the seas.

⚓

* Olmsted, *Incidents of a Whaling Voyage.*

"On a Friday she was launched,
   On a Friday she set sail,
On a Friday met a storm,
   And was lost too in the gale."

⚓

In the days of sail many owners and officers made many attempts to break down the superstition, but with very little success. English, French, and Russian folklore, as well as American, have tales of these efforts, but in every case only failure was reported. In steam today, however, we find as many ships leaving port on Friday the thirteenth as the day before or the day after, or even ten days later.

When Wilmington, Delaware, was a great seaport, a Quaker shipmaster in an effort to destroy the superstition, had the keel of a new ship laid on a Friday, he caused her to be launched on Friday, giving her the name of Friday, and sent to sea upon a Friday under the command of a master named Friday. Just a week later she was seen foundering at sea. The shipmaster's wife, when she heard of it, said: "I told thee so, Isaiah! This is all thy sixth-day doings. Now thee sees the consequences. *Thee never had the vessel insured!*"

⚓

Columbus sailed on a Friday, August 3, 1492, and made his first landfall on a Friday.

*Lucky Dates*   The seventh of any month was good for fishing, the seventeenth and twenty-ninth for long voyages. According to Hesiod, the fourth was a good day for launching a ship.

*Unlucky Dates*   The thirteenth of any month was not a good day to begin a voyage. Cain's birthday and the anniversary of the destruction of Sodom and Gomorrah were also unlucky days, as was the thirty-first of December, the day on which Judas, who betrayed Christ, hanged himself.

St. Peter's Day, June 26, was not a good day for fishermen. Other saints who put their blight on fishermen who used their days for working were St. Blaise, St. George, and St. Martin.

⚓

"Upon St. Martin's eve, no net shall be let down;
No fisherman of Wexford shall, upon that holyday,
Set sail, or cast a line within the scope of Wexford Bay." *

⚓

Candlemas Day and Good Friday were considered particularly evil days for fishermen.

## Whalers' Superstitions

"Why is it that all merchant seamen, and also all pirates and man-o-war's men, and slave ship sailors, cherish such a scornful feeling toward whale ships?" †

⚓

After the blanket pieces had been taken off, the head removed, and the intestines searched for ambergris, the carcass of the whale was cut adrift, usually sinking. If it floated away with the drift of the tide it was a sign of good luck.

⚓

Whalers used to think it a lucky circumstance if they had a sperm whale head at the starboard yard-arm and a right whale's head on the port side, as the ship would then never capsize.‡

⚓

"A custom prevails among the seamen of these vessels, when traversing the polar seas, to fix, on the first day of May, a garland aloft, suspended midway on a rope leading from the main topgallant mast head to the first topmast head, ornamented with knots of ribbon, love tokens of the lads for their lassies, etc. This garland remains suspended until the ship returns to her port." § It was regarded as an ill omen to detach this garland or for it to suffer any accident.

* O'Reilly, *Songs from the Southern Seas.*
† Melville, *Moby Dick.*
‡ *Ibid.*
§ Hone, *Table Book.*

## Fishermen's Superstitions

"He will undertake nothing of consequence upon a Friday, and can prove by a hundred incidents how infallible are the signs and omens which he believes in. He thinks to die in his bed. True it is that he has been overset; that his boat, loaded with fish to the 'gunnel,' has sunk under him, and that a vessel has run him down, but he is still alive and was not born to be drowned. . . . He believes in witches and dreams." *

⚓

Some fishermen, operating along the New England coast, always throw the first fish taken back into the sea. They will never tell how many fish they have taken until they are through fishing. They also consider it unlucky for the fish to be counted while on board their vessel.

⚓

Fishermen believe the black spots on each side of a haddock, near the gills, is the impression of St. Peter's finger and thumb, when he took the tribute money from the fish's mouth.

⚓

Fishermen believe that a loaf of bread left lying upside down foretells a wreck, and leaving a knife sticking in a loaf of bread predicts a fight.

⚓

They believe that the fish they catch are infested with fleas. (So did Shakespeare—*Henry IV*, Part I, Act II, Scene 1.)

⚓

* M. H. Perley, *Reports on the Sea and River Fisheries of New Brunswick*.

"Some fishermen believe that a valise, when carried on board a vessel, is a Jonah. Probably this belief is largely due to the prejudice felt against carrying such an unseamanlike article on a fishing trip.

"Opinions differ as to whether certain other things are Jonahs or not. Among those believed to be such by a few persons may be mentioned violins, checkerboards, toy boats, a bucket sitting on deck partly filled with water, soaking mackerel in a bucket, etc.

"The accidents and actions of members of the crew that are supposed to bring ill success, or to be the forerunners of such, are, dropping a hatch cover in the hold, turning a hatch bottom up, breaking a looking-glass, driving nails on Sunday, and letting the splices of a cable stop in the hawse-pipe when the vessel is anchoring on the fishing ground.

"As to other beliefs, it may be said that all fishermen whistle for a breeze when it is calm, and some occasionally stick a knife in the after side of the mainmast to bring a fair wind. A bee, or a small land bird coming on board, it is supposed, will bring good luck, while ill-fortune will follow the lighting of a hawk, owl or crow on the rigging of a vessel. It is supposed that a smart blow on the head of a fish that has just been separated from the body, will kill the latter which still retains muscular motion. A hook which has been stuck in a hand, is immediately thrust into a piece of pine so that the wound will not be sore." *

"It is said he is credulous and superstitious. Admit that 'Kidd's money' has been dug for in every dark nook of the coast, or talked about in every cuddy, for a century and a half, and that horseshoes are nailed to the masts of fishing vessels to keep off witches, what then? Is he the only one who has been or still is, guilty of the same follies?" †

## Rats Leave a Doomed Ship

A rotten carcass of a boat, not rigg'd,
Nor tackle, sail, nor mast; the very rats
Instinctively have quit it.‡

---

* J. W. Collins, "Fishermen's Superstitions," in *The Fishermen's Own Book.*
† L. Sabine, *Report on the Principal Fisheries of the American Seas.*
‡ Shakespeare, *The Tempest*, Act I, Scene 2.

It is only natural for rats to leave a sinking ship; they, unlike most sailors, are able to swim. But most sailors believed that these rodents were psychic, that they could foretell a vessel's doom. A writer in the *Shipping Gazette*, in 1869, writes: "It is a well-authenticated fact that rats have often been known to leave ships in harbor previous to their being lost at sea. Some of those wise-acres who want to convince us against the evidence of our senses, will call this superstition." *

## Birds

From birds in sailing, men instruction take,
Now lie in port, now sail, and profit make.
Aristophanes

It was always considered an ill omen to kill any bird that follows ships at sea; the albatross, the gull, or the stormy petrel. The two latter were supposed to be the souls of seamen lost at sea. The albatross was the bringer of winds and of fogs and mists. The Ancient Mariner was at first condemned for killing the bird that brought the wind, and later he was praised for destroying the bringer of the fog.

* Bassett, *Sea Phantoms*.

Sailors believed it a good omen for their ship to pass through a flock of gulls sitting on the water without disturbing them.

⚓

In *Moby Dick* Melville says that it was an ill omen for ravens to perch on the masts of a ship at the Cape of Good Hope.

⚓

"Ah, well-a-day," the sailor said,
  "Some danger must impend,
Three ravens sit in yonder glade,
  And evil will happen, I'm sore afraid,
  Ere we reach our journey's end."

"And what have the ravens with us to do?
  Does their sight betoken evil?"
"To see one raven is lucky, 'tis true,
  But it's certain misfortune to light upon two,
  And meeting with three is the devil." *

⚓

One of the most curious instances of a belief in bird omens occurred in 1857. Captain Johnson, of the Norwegian bark *Ellen*, which fortunately picked up forty-nine of the passengers and crew of the steamship *Central America*, after that vessel had sunk, arrived in New York September 20 and made the following statement:

"Just before six o'clock in the afternoon of September 12th., I was standing on the quarter-deck, with two others of the crew, beside the man at the helm. Suddenly a bird flew around me, first grazing my right shoulder. Afterwards he flew around the vessel, then it again commenced to fly around my head. It soon flew at my face, when I caught hold of it and made it a prisoner. The bird was unlike any bird I ever saw, nor do I know its name. The color of its feathers were a dark iron-gray; its body was a foot and a half in length, with wings three and a half feet from tip to tip. It had a beak full

* M. G. Lewis, "Bill Jones."

eight inches long, and a set of teeth like a small hand-saw. In capturing the bird it gave me a good bite on my right thumb; two of the crew who assisted in tying its legs were also bitten. As it strove to bite everybody, I had its head cut off, and the body thrown overboard.

"When the bird flew to the ship, the bark was going a little north of north-east. *I regarded the appearance of the bird as an omen*, and an indication to me that I must change my course; I according headed to the eastward direct. I should not have deviated from my course had not the bird visited the ship; and had it not been for this change of course, I should not have fallen in with the forty-nine passengers, who I fortunately saved from certain death." *

⚓

During the summer the osprey, or fish hawk, is abundant along the coast of New England, and its early coming is hailed by fishermen as the omen of a good season.

> The osprey sails above the sound,
>   The geese are gone, the gulls are flying;
> The herring shoals swarm thick around,
>   The nets are launched, the boats are plying.
> Yo, ho, my hearts! Let's seek the deep,
>   Raise high the song, and cheerly wish her,
> Still as at the bending net we sweep,
>   God bless the fish-hawk, and the fisher!
> *Fisherman's Hymn*

## Cats

To sailors the cat is always feminine and is considered a breeder of bad weather. Her every act has deep significance. She carries 'a gale in her tail'; when she plays with a string or a lanyard she is provoking a storm; when she tears at carpets and furniture she is raising a wind; if she mews at night she is summoning a tempest, and if she howls or cries at any time she is calling for the witches to do their worst. Even licking her fur the wrong way bodes no good for the ship.

* Jones, *Credulities, Past and Present.*

Cats are said to smell a wind, while pigs see it.

They have always been considered unlucky, and cats were never made a ship's mascot: if one happened to be on board it was always someone's cat, never the ship's.

The malevolent character of the cat is shown in maritime nomenclature: the cat-o'-nine-tails was not a desirable acquaintance; nor do sailors have a love of the miscellaneous gear connected with the raising of the anchor, such as the cathead, catfall, cat block, cat davit. The meanest sailing craft afloat is a catboat, and the lubber's hole, which it was thought humiliating for an able seaman to use, is in French "trou de chat."

Weak drinks were called cat-lap and an unsatisfactory sleep was a cat nap.*

On Block Island there is a legend of a man who put a cat in a barrel and then headed the barrel up to prevent another man, against whom he bore a grudge, from sailing. No wind came until the cat was released.†

## Miscellaneous Omens and Superstitions

The boatmen, ere his sail he spreads,
Watched for an omen there.
*Basque legend*

*Dead Bodies* The carrying of dead bodies aboard ships has always been a sore point with sailors, who regard it as a disastrous omen. The ship, they say, cannot abide to be made a bier. And, 'the living make the ship go and the dead slow it down.'

⚓

*Sharks* To have a shark following a ship was always regarded an ill omen, especially if there were sick on board.

"A sailor always regards the presence of a shark about a ship a most fatal omen to the sick on board. The highest exultation I ever witnessed on board a man of war, was occasioned by the har-

* Bassett, *Sea Phantoms.*
† Livermore, *A History of Block Island.*

pooning a shark that was hanging about while a favorite was sick." *

It was also believed that a shark was able to scent a victim and would follow for miles a ship in which a dead body lay.

⚓

*Clothes* It was a bad omen to wear the clothes of a fellow seaman who has died, before the termination of the voyage.

Sailors never subscribed to the belief of landsmen that luck could be changed by turning the hat backward: they insist the hat or cap be worn in the proper manner lest it affect the wind. Some few believed the man at the wheel could influence the wind by pointing the peak of his cap in the direction from which the wind was wanted.

⚓

*Gear* To lose or tear the ship's colors was considered a bad omen for the ship; to pass a flag through the rungs of a ladder, or through a window, would bring ill luck to one or both engaged.

⚓

The loss of a bucket or swab overboard was unlucky. It truly was if observed by an officer, for such losses were charged against the seaman's account.

⚓

*Crowing Hen* Sailors believed that the crowing should be done by the cock; the crowing of a hen indicated approaching disaster.

"But the superstition of a seaman's mind is not easily subdued; and it was with some difficulty that I could preserve a hen who had been hatched and bred on board, and who at this time was accompanied by a small brood of chickens from being destroyed in order to quit

* Colton, *The Sea and the Sailor*. New York, 1860.

the ill-omen that had been occasioned by the unexpected crowing of the animal during the preceding night." *

⚓

*Ninth Wave*  The ninth, or sometimes the tenth, wave was called the mother wave, the avenging wave, and the death wave. It was believed that this wave was malevolent and that in its course to the shore it overtook and passed the preceding eight. Its power could be broken only by making the sign of the cross above it.

⚓

*Remora*  A fish of the sucker family. It was believed that giants of the species could stay the course of the ship to which it adhered.

⚓

*Sneezing*  "A potent omen since ancient days, had its portent for good or bad luck among seamen; a sneeze on the port side at the moment of embarking was too ominous a sign to be disregarded; while a sneeze on the starboard side betokened a favorable voyage." †

⚓

*Salt*  Salt spilling was regarded a bad omen, yet a pinch of salt in a sailor's pocket brought him good luck.

⚓

*Children*  Children were always considered omens of good luck, for they were not born to die at sea; and the more of them the better the luck.

⚓

* Leslie, *Old Sea Wings, Ways, and Words.*
† Jones, *Credulities, Past and Present.*

*Ship's Bell*   Many seamen believe that the ship's bell will toll just as she is sinking, even if it is securely lashed in place.

⚓

*Paring the Nails and Cutting Hair*   Paring the nails or cutting hair during a calm was believed to bring good winds; during a blow such acts were considered bad omens.

⚓

*Sewing Sails and Mending Clothes*   Any sewing, of sails or clothing, during a spell of bad weather was frowned upon; the bad weather, it was thought, was being sewed in for all time.

⚓

*Playing Cards*   Religious sailors called them the devil's prayer book. They believed that he sat in on every game and that with a run of luck he might win possession of the ship and all on board.

⚓

*Horseshoe*   A horseshoe nailed to the mainmast was believed by many to be not only a security against the evil one, but a protection against many dangers. The practice prevailed only in smaller ships and among fishermen.

⚓

*Hunchbacks*   A hunchback aboard a ship was a very good omen as long as he was not a member of the crew: a practical superstition, considering that such a sailor could not hold up his end with other members of his watch.

⚓

*Cross-eyed Persons*   Sailors called them "swivel-eyed" and often considered them Jonahs. They insisted that persons so handicapped could not hold a vessel to its course. Fishermen always passed a cross-eyed person with a counter charm. A cross-eyed Finn was considered a positive menace.

⚓

*Counter Charms Used by Seamen*   Many sailors follow the custom of crossing the first and second fingers to ward off ill-luck. Some spit into the palm of the left hand, or wet the middle finger of the right hand and press it against the palm of the left hand and then strike the left palm with the right fist. Others spit into their hats. Another counter charm was to break a small piece of wood with a snapping noise; it was called "the lucky break."

## Weather Lore

"THERE is but a plank between a sailor and eternity; and perhaps the occasional realization of that fact may have had something to do with the broad grain of superstition at one time undoubtedly lurking in his nature. But whatever the cause, certainly the legendary lore of the sea is as diversified and interesting as the myths and traditions which haunt the imagination of landsmen, and it is not surprising that sailors, who observe the phenomena of nature under such varied and impressive aspects, should be found to cling with tenacious obstinacy to their superstitious fancies. The winds, clouds, waves, sun, moon, and stars have ever been invested with propitious or unlucky signs; and within a score of years we have met seamen who had perfect faith in the weather lore and traditions acquired during their ocean wanderings.*

⚓

If the Bermudas let you pass,
   Oh, then beware of Hatteras;
If safely you get by Cape May
   You'll catch it sure in Boston Bay.

⚓

* Gibbons, *Boxing the Compass.*

Once clear of the land the old deepwaterman was more concerned with weather than he was with women or booze. He lived, and very often died, by the weather, and he trusted his own experience more than any science the captain might possess. His observations, sometimes cast into simple verse, to be more easily remembered, were frequently sound and just as often arrived at by jumped-at conclusions.

Some of his rules may be found to contradict others, but they are set down here, not as a weather guide, but as a guide to what the men in sail thought about the weather. A few, it may be claimed, belong to the farmer and landsmen, but most sailors were born ashore and took all they had learned with them when they signed on their first vessels. Others may be classified only as wisecracks: "the air is so clear you can see three days ahead." "You may look for six weeks of weather in March" is quite as true today as when it was first uttered.

⚓

"We're waitin' on the weather, sir," said the man at the wheel to the mate just coming on deck.

"Then we'll have to make it ourselves," said the officer, beginning to whistle.

### Sun

A red sun has water in its eye.

⚓

When the sun sets behind a bank,
  A westerly wind you shall not want.
When the sun sets clear as a bell—
  An easterly wind as sure as hell!

⚓

If red the sun begins his race,
Be sure the rain will fall apace.

⚓

Red sky in the morning
Is a sailor's sure warning;
Red sky at night
Is a sailor's delight.

or

When it is evening, ye say, it will be fair weather: for the sky is red. And in the morning, It will be foul weather today: for the sky is red and lowring.

Matthew 16:2, 3

When the sun's rays are visible, sailors say the sun is setting up his backstays and it is time to look out for foul weather.

### Moon

Circle around the moon,
Sailors go aloft full soon.

⚓

A dim or pale moon indicates rain, a red moon indicates wind.

⚓

The moon swallows the wind.

⚓

A fog and a small moon,
Bring an easterly wind soon.

⚓

Never a circle to the moon
   Should send your tops'ls down:
But when it is around the sun,
   With all the masts it must be done.

⚓

"I saw the new moon late yestere'en,
   Wi' the auld moon in her arms;
And if we gang to sea, maister,
   I fear we'll come to harm." *

⚓

For I fear a hurricane;
Last night the moon had a golden ring,
And tonight no moon we see.†

⚓

The moon and the weather
   May change together;
But change of the moon
   Does not change the weather.

## Stars

When the stars flicker in a dark background, rain or snow follows soon.

⚓

* *Ballad of Sir Patrick Spens.*
† Longfellow, *The Wreck of the Hesperus.*

If a big star is dogging the moon, wild weather may be expected.

⚓

The prudent mariner oft marks afar,
The coming tempest by Boötes' star.

⚓

One star ahead of the moon, towing her, and another astern, chasing her, is a sure sign of a storm.

## Winds

Winds at night are always bright,
But winds in the morning, sailors take warning.

⚓

Sailors believe that whistling will produce a wind, a soft whistle for a breeze, a loud one for a gale.

⚓

When the wind backs and the weather glass falls,
Then be on your guard against gales and squalls.

⚓

When the wind's in the south,
The rain's in its mouth.

⚓

A nor'wester is not long in debt to a sou'wester.

⚓

With an east wind, changing to southward, heave to on the starboard tack.

With an east wind, changing to northward, run west-northwest or heave to on the port tack.

With an east-southeast wind, changing to southward, heave to on the starboard tack.

With an east-southeast wind, changing to eastward, run to the northwest or heave to on the port tack.

With a southeasterly wind, changing to southward, heave to on the starboard tack.

With a southeasterly wind, changing to eastward, run north-northwest or heave to on the port tack.

With a south-southeasterly wind, changing to southward, or heave to on the starboard tack.

With a south-southeasterly wind, changing to eastward, run north or heave to on the port tack.

And so on around the compass.

⚓

A northwest wind brings a short storm,
A northeast wind brings a long storm.

⚓

Easterly wind and fog,
Southerly wind, all snug.

⚓

No weather is ill,
If the wind be still.

⚓

The sharper the blast,
The sooner it's past.

⚓

When freshly blow the northern gales,
  Then under courses snug we fly;
When lighter breezes swell the sails,
  Then royals proudly sweep the sky.

## Clouds

A sunset with a cloud so black,
A westerly wind you shall not lack.

⚓

It will not rain much so long as the sky is clear before the wind,
but when the clouds fall in against the wind, rain will soon follow.

⚓

If clouds be bright,
'Twill clear tonight:
If clouds be dark,
'Twill rain—do you hark?

⚓

If you see clouds going across the wind, there is a storm coming up.

⚓

*Cirrus:*  curl clouds, mares' tails, goat's hair.

⚓

Mares' tails,
Leave short sails.

*Cirro-stratus*

If clouds look as if scratched by a hen,
Get ready to reef your topsails then.

⚓

*Cirro-cumulus:* mackerel sky.
> Mackerel sky, mackerel sky,
> Never long wet and never long dry.

⚓

A mackerel sky denotes fair weather for that day, but rain a day or two later.

⚓

> Mackerel sky *and* mares' tails,
> Make lofty ships carry low sails.

⚓

A dappled sky, like a painted woman, soon changes its face.

*Cumulus:* rain balls, wool pack.

> A round-topped cloud, with flattened base,
> Carries rainfall in its face.

⚓

> When mountains and cliffs in the clouds appear,
> Some sudden and violent showers are near.

*Cumulo-stratus*

When at sea, if cumulo-stratus clouds appear on the horizon, it is a sign that the weather is going to break up.

⚓

*Nimbus:* shaggy head.

*Stratus*

> When the mist comes from the hill,
> Then the weather it doth spill;

When the mist comes from the sea,
Then good weather will it be.

## Sky
Open and shet,
'S a sign of wet.

⚓

When as much blue is seen in the sky as will make a Dutchman a
pair of pants the weather will clear.

## Rain
The more rain, the more rest,
Fine weather's not always best.

⚓

With the rain before the wind,
Your tops'l halliards you must mind:
With the wind before the rain,
Your tops'ls you can hoist again.

⚓

Marry the rain to the wind and you have a calm.

⚓

No one so surely pays his debt,
As wet to dry and dry to wet.

## Barometer
Glass high, heave short and away;
Glass low, let your anchor stay.

⚓

Long foretold, long past;
Short warning, soon past.

⚓

When the glass falls low,
   Then prepare for a blow.
When it rises high,
   Let all your kites fly.

⚓

First rise after a low,
Squalls expect and more blow.

⚓

If the barometer and the thermometer both rise together,
It is a very sure sign of coming fine weather.

## Birds

When sea-birds fly out early and far to seaward, moderate winds and fair weather may be expected. When they hang about the land or over it, sometimes flying inland, expect a strong wind with stormy weather.

⚓

Sea gull, sea gull, sit on the sand,
It's never fair weather while you're on the land.

⚓

When sea-birds fly to land,
   A storm is at hand.

⚓

Stormy petrels gathering under the stern of a ship indicate the coming of foul weather; the greater the number, the more severe the storm.

## Denizens of the Deep

When porpoises and whales spout about ships at sea, storms may be expected.

⚓

Dolphins, as well as porpoises, when they come about a ship and sport on the surface, betoken a storm.

⚓

"It was blowing a pleasant westerly breeze this day; but at noon a school of porpoises came dashing along, passed the ship's bow without stopping to play around it, as they are so fond of doing, and made away towards the northwest. The captain said it was a sure sign that the wind was coming from that quarter; for sailors regard it as an established fact that porpoises either go 'head to the wind' or else towards the quarter of a coming breeze." *

⚓

Sharks go out to sea at the approach of a cold wave.

⚓

When codfish bite ravenously it is a sign of a coming storm.

⚓

If the codfish run early, in October or November, instead of December, fishermen insist that it means an early and severe winter.

* Adams, *On Board the "Rocket."*

## *Miscellaneous*

At mealtime when every last morsel is eaten it indicates clear weather.

⚓

The good sailor notes the tightening of the cordage of the ship as a sign of coming rain.

⚓

Evening gray and morning red
Shorten all spare sails ahead;
Evening red and morning gray,
You're sure to have a fishing day.

⚓

Murphy has a weather eye,
He can tell whene'er he pleases,
Whether it's wet or whether it's dry,
Whether it's hot or whether it freezes.
*Murphy's Almanac, 1836.*

# II

# The Ship and the Company
# She Keeps

## *Customs, Traditions, Legends, and Yarns*

When a land forgets its legends,
Sees but falsehoods in the past,
When a nation views its sires
In the light of fools and liars—
'Tis a sign of its decline,
And its glories cannot last.
Branches that but blight their roots
Yield no sap for lasting fruits.

*Anonymous*

NOTHING a man builds or creates with his own hands becomes a living thing save a ship. A beautiful ship may be a work of art, yet it is infinitely more, for even an ugly vessel has the quality of life. Nothing save a beautiful woman can excite a man as a fine ship under full sail.

Quite probably it was the early Greeks who decreed that ships should be feminine, for they dedicated all their vessels to their goddesses and placed them under their divine protection. A ship is far more like a woman than like a man: like a woman she inspires love and desire, she has enchantment; like a woman she will respond to loving treatment by her men; and when she is old and tired, even though she becomes a crank, a grumbling old hulk, there will be many who can recall her in her prime. As long as she has life and vitality and keeps her good name she will always find men to love her, to serve her, and to see that she arrives home safely.

Sailors are ever ready to ascribe consciousness and even sympathy to their ships; she walks the waters; she can do anything but talk, and sometimes she will do that too. The man at the wheel often speaks to his ship, and he knows when she answers him. There is an old yarn of a master who urged his ship to greater speed by promising her a new coat of paint or a new set of sails.

Ships no longer seaworthy have been known to give forth moaning sounds. None of her men can tell how the noise is made or whence it comes, but they know its import full well, and their hearts fail. Cooper, in *Red Rover*, has Fid say: "A ship which is about to sink makes her lamentations just like any other human being."

# The Ship

## The Personality of a Ship

"A SHIP is born when she is launched, and lives so long as her identity is preserved. Prior to her launching she is a mere congeries of wood and iron—an ordinary piece of personal property—as distinctly a land structure as a house, and subject only to mechanics' liens created by a state law and enforceable in the state courts. In the baptism of launching she receives her name, and from the moment her keel touches the water she is transformed, and becomes a subject of admiralty jurisdiction. She acquires a personality of her own; becomes competent to contract, and is individually liable for her obligations, upon which she may sue in the name of her owner, and be sued in her own name. Her owner's agents may not be her agents, and her agents may not be her owner's agents. She is capable, too, of committing a tort, and is responsible for damages therefor. She may also become a quasi-bankrupt; may be sold for the payment of her debts, and thereby receive a complete discharge from all prior liens, with liberty to begin a new life, contract further obligations, and perhaps be subjected to a second sale." *

\* *Tucker v. Alexandroff, 183 U.S. 424, 438.*

## Launching

Frae rocks and saands
An' barren lands,
An' ill men's hands,
Keep's free.
Weel oot, weel in
Wi' a guid shot.

*Scottish Launch Chant*

⚓

The custom of christening a ship can be traced to antiquity. In pagan days the vessel was decked with flowers and wreaths and placed under the protection of a particular goddess, and a libation was offered as the vessel struck the water. In medieval times the flowers were still used and the ship was cleansed and purified by a priest, anointed with wine, and consecrated in the name of some saint. Early sailors all believed that a ship that had not been christened would be much more exposed to danger than one that had been.

All that is left of the old ceremony is the breaking of wine and the actual naming, but to the sailors these are of tremendous importance. Accidents, especially when anyone is killed at the launch, give the ship a bad name, and the use of anything but wine or ardent spirits is sure to bring later ill luck, possibly to the sailors. Among fishermen it is still believed that a ship that has not been properly christened will catch no fish, and it is held by some that the owner is sure to be drowned.

*Old Ironsides*   A Navy legend has it that the U.S.S. *Constitution* twice refused to leave the ways when doused with water at her christening ceremony, and it was only upon the third attempt, when Commodore James Sever broke a bottle of old Madeira over her bowsprit, that she consented to report for duty.

*The Great Republic*   In 1853 the greatest crowd in Boston history gathered to witness and celebrate the launch of the *Great Republic*, the largest sailing vessel built up to that time. Schools and shops closed and business was suspended, so that all could journey to East

Boston to join in the christening of Donald McKay's masterpiece. It was reported that 30,000 crossed by ferry and that many more thousands came by other routes; the harbor shipping was decorated, bands played, and speeches were delivered.

It had long been East and South Boston's boast that they had more grogshops than public water pumps. Just before the launch the mains bringing the new Cochituate water were completed, and it became the aim of temperance advocates to see that water got an even break with whiskey. Mr. McKay was pressed to permit his great vessel to be baptized in water from this new source as an aid to temperance. He consented, and on October 4 Capt. Alden Gifford broke a bottle of the water over her bow, naming her *Great Republic*.

So greatly did the ship resent this treatment that she literally leaped from the ways, and it was only through the use of two heavy anchors and a powerful jug-eared tug that she was kept from venting her wrath on the Chelsea Bridge. After receiving her masts and spars at the Navy Yard shears, she was towed to New York.

Before her royals were bent she was burned at her wharf in South Street and was turned over to the underwriters. No one has ever heard the charge that the tragedy was due to the water baptism, but it must be remembered that she had not yet shipped her first crew, being still in the hands of the riggers when she burned. There can be little doubt that when it came to signing on her crew many sailors would have preferred other berths to sailing in a vessel that had been humiliated in such a manner.

*Excursion Steamer*   In 1878 a large excursion steamer was launched at Norfolk, Virginia, in the presence of many invited guests. The ceremony of wine breaking was dispensed with at the launch, and many predicted disaster for the vessel. The omen was verified when she was lost while being towed to New York.*

## A Ship Loses Her Name and Luck

"The steamer with the pretty name of *Ianthe*, was formerly the *Rose*, and before she was the *Rose* she was that most ill-fated ship which, if 'not built in the eclipse,' was certainly attended with curses

* Bassett, *Sea Phantoms*.

dark, the *Daphne*, whose launch on the Clyde, it will be recollected, caused the drowning of an appalling number of men. She sank in the Clyde as the *Daphne;* she was raised, and then sank in Portrush Harbor as the *Rose;* she was raised again, and still as the *Rose*, she ran ashore on Big Cumbrae. Then she was got off and lost sight of for a little, and now reappears as the *Ianthe*, comfortably lodged on the mud which she seems to love so well, and to which her instincts regularly direct her, after having threatened to go down in deep water, and then changing her mind and plumping on a rock. She is evidently an unlucky ship. Common sense must yield to superstition, and partake of the sailor's view of such a vessel as this." *

## On Deck

"Like most merchant ships, we had but two boats, the long-boat and the jolly-boat. The long-boat, by far the largest and stoutest of the two, was permanently bolted down to the deck, by iron bars attached to its sides. It was almost as much of a fixture as the vessel's keel. It was filled with pigs, fowls, firewood, and coals. Over this the jolly-boat was capsized without a thole-pin in the gunwales; its bottom bleaching and cracking in the sun." †

"In those happy Board-of-Tradeless days, the heavy long-boat of even a fast 'line-of-packet ship' bound only for a short trip of five or six weeks between London and New York, looked more like a working model of Noah's Ark than anything likely to save life at sea, or even to live upon it. Always securely stowed amidships, well lashed down and housed over, the boat, as she lay upon the ship's deck, was full of live provender; being divided as to her lower hold into pens for sheep and pigs; while upon the first floor, or main-deck, quacked ducks and geese, and above them (literally in the cock-loft) were coops for another kind of poultry.

"This great central depot was closely surrounded by other small farm-buildings, the most important being the cow-house, where, after a short run ashore on the marshes at the end of each voyage, a well-seasoned animal of the snug-made Alderney breed, chewed the cud in sweet content.

* "Sketches of Foreign Travel, 1847," quoted in Bassett, *Sea Phantoms.*
† Melville, *Redburn.*

"In fact, when in the old days a passenger-ship began her voyage, the hull of her clumsy long-boat was nearly hidden by the number of temporary sheds and pens required to house the live stock for the supply of her cabin-table; and with its many farmyard and homelike sounds, a ship was then even more like a small bit of the world afloat than it is now. Various forms of life appeared and passed away during the voyage—expended, so to say, like the marline spun on board—in the narrow world it began in.

"In smaller vessels, carrying no passengers, the skipper's live stock was not always home-fed—pigs and goats being often turned loose to cater for themselves among the odds and ends in the waist, or deck, between the poop and the forecastle. Some of the poultry soon became tame enough to be allowed the run of this part of the ship; the ducks and geese finding a particular delight in paddling in the wash about the lee-scuppers." *

* Leslie, *Old Sea Wings, Ways, and Words.*

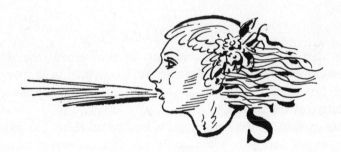

## Her People

### The Afterguard

THIS term, taken over from the old Navy, applies to those who have their quarters aft, the location of which is often called "the officers' country." These include the captain, his mates, and, if there is one aboard, the supercargo.

### The Captain

The Master, the Old Man, and, only in small vessels, the Skipper. He is in complete control of the ship and its navigation and working, of all other officers, the crew, passengers, and cargo, and is the representative of the owner.*

"The captain, in the first place, is lord paramount. He stands no watch, comes and goes when he pleases, is accountable to no one, and must be obeyed in everything, without a question even from his

---

* In their convention at West Palm Beach, December, 1947, the American Association of Port Authorities approved a resolution urging the Congress to adopt a statute "clearly providing that the master of a merchant vessel shall be in command of that vessel, and all of the officers and crew therefore shall be subordinate to the lawful orders of the master." The resolution declared that the assumption that the master of an American vessel of the merchant marine is commander of the vessel is supported generally by tradition, custom, and ruling of the courts, rather than by any statute.—*The New York Times*, December 7, 1947.

chief officer. He has the power to turn his officers off duty, and even to break them and make them do duty as sailors in the forecastle.* Where there are no passengers and no supercargo, as in our vessel, he has no companion but his own dignity, and few pleasures, unless he differs from most of his kind, beyond the consciousness of possessing supreme power, and, occasionally, the exercise of it." †

⚓

He is not only the ruler in his own ship, he is also the father, the physician, the preacher, and, upon occasion, the judge to both crew and passengers.

⚓

When he is on deck, the weather side of the quarter-deck belongs to him, and as soon as he appears the officer of the watch will leave it and go over to the leeward.

⚓

Where the safety of his ship is concerned, in the eyes of the law his authority is supreme.

⚓

Custom has it that the captain is always the last into a small boat and the first out of it.

⚓

In time of peril he is the last to leave his ship.

⚓

He is the only one on board who in death rates the half-staffing of the ensign as the ship enters her home port.

⚓

* Even Dana questions his power to do this in the case of the first mate.
† Dana, *Two Years before the Mast.*

"He has a power and influence, both direct and indirect, which may be the means of much good or much evil. If he is profane, passionate, tyrannical, indecent, or intemperate, more or less of the same qualities will spread themselves or break out among officers and men, which, perhaps would have been checked, if not in some degree removed, had the head of the ship been a man of high personal character. He may make his ship almost anything he chooses, and may render the lives and duties of his officers and men pleasant and profitable to them, or may introduce disagreements, discontent, tyranny, resistance, and, in fact, make the situation of all on board as uncomfortable as that in which any human being can well be placed." *

"Every day, a few minutes before noon, if there is any prospect of being able to get the sun, the master comes upon deck with his quadrant or sextant, and the chief mate usually takes his. The second mate does not, except upon a Sunday, or when there is no work going forward. As soon as the sun crosses the meridian, eight bells are struck and a new sea day begins. The reckoning is then corrected by the observation, under the master's superintendence." †

In the old Navy there was more ritual:

"For a ship is a bit of terra firma cut off from the main; it is a state in itself; and the captain is its king.

"It is no limited monarchy, where a sturdy Commons have a right to petition, and snarl if they please; but almost a despotism, like the Grand Turk's. The captain's word is law; he never speaks but in the imperative mood. When he stands on his quarterdeck at sea, he absolutely commands as far as the eye can reach. Only the moon and stars are beyond his jurisdiction. He is lord and master of the sun.

"It is not twelve o'clock till he says so. For when the sailing-master, whose duty it is to take the regular observation at noon, touches his hat, and reports twelve o'clock to the officer of the deck, that functionary orders a midshipman to repair to the captain's cabin, and humbly inform him of the respectful suggestion of the sailing-master.

" 'Twelve o'clock reported, sir,' says the middy.

" '*Make* it so,' replies the captain.

* Dana, *The Seaman's Friend.*
† *Ibid.*

"And the bell is struck eight by the messenger boy, and twelve o'clock it is." *

"The master also takes the lunar observations, usually with the assistance of both his officers; in which case the master takes the angle of the moon with the star or sun, the chief mate takes the altitude of the sun or star, and the second mate the altitude of the moon." †

## The Chief Mate

Sometimes the first officer, or, as he was called on deck, *the mate*, was the active superintending officer. In the day's work the mate was the only man who appeared to be in command. It was his task to carry on the work, to find every man something to do, and to see that it was done. He received, stowed, broke out, and discharged all cargo. He kept the ship's log.

He was also in charge of all the rigging, and he was supposed to report anything of importance to the captain and take his orders, save in a small or common matter, when he would order changes or repairs as required.

In working the ship, when all hands had been called and the master was on the quarter-deck, the mate's place was on the forecastle, where, under the direction of the master, who never left the quarter-deck, he commanded the forward part of the ship and was the organ of communication with the men aloft.

When all hands were on deck, with the master below, the first mate was in complete command; in case the second mate's watch alone was on deck, the first mate yielded the weather side of the quarter-deck to the inferior officer. Regardless of the other officers or crew, in the case of death or incapacity of the master the mate automatically became captain.

He was entitled to many courtesies, among them that of being addressed as Mister by the master. In the matter of the master's ability to turn an officer back to the forecastle and a sailor's rating, it could not have been done, if, as was the custom, the mate had been placed on board by the owners.

* Melville, *White Jacket*.
† Dana, *The Seaman's Friend*.

A competent master made it a practice never to reprimand or find fault with a mate before the crew, doing it if necessary in the privacy of the cabin. He issued all orders directly to the mate, who in turn passed them on to the men. This rule applied not only to the captain, but to pilots and dockmasters as well; the mate usually spoke the language understood by the seaman.

"The dock-master, for instance, would say, 'That'll do, Mr. Stork, with your head-line; if you will be good enough to shift your starn-line to your port-quarter, and get a small pull upon it.' Which, through the mate's trumpet, comes to the crew as 'Vast 'eaving there for'ard; lay aft, som' of ye, an' tail on to that quarter-line. Lay aft! G-d d—n ye, lay aft there! Jump out quick, one of ye, and take it clear of the main-brace. In with it! smart now! run away with it, boys. Hurrah! hurrah! boys! there she slews." *

## Second Mate

While known on board as "the sailor's waiter," he must be addressed as Mister and answered with the traditional Sir. He heads the starboard watch when the captain is not on deck. At best he is but a watch officer, to have an eye to the helm and the weather, keep a bright lookout, and see to the trimming of the yards, the making and taking in of light sails, heaving the log, and keeping an account of the winds, courses, and the rate of sailing. In case anything important occurs, he calls the captain.

"His titles are the only dignities he enjoys; for, upon the whole, he leads a puppyish life, indeed. He is not deemed company at any time for the captain, though the chief mate occasionally is, at least deck company, though not in the cabin; and beside this, the second mate has to breakfast, lunch, dine, and sup off the leavings of the cabin table; and even the steward, who is accountable to nobody but the captain, sometimes treats him cavalierly; and he has to run aloft when topsails are reefed; and put his hand a good way down into the tar-bucket; and keep the key of the boatswain's locker, and fetch and carry balls of marline and seizing-stuff for the sailors when at work in the rigging, besides doing many other things which a

* Leslie, *Old Sea Wings, Ways, and Words.*

true-born baronet of any spirit would rather die and give up his title than to stand." *

## Third Mate

He was even smaller potatoes than the second, entitled to all the dignities of rank and the indignities of a lackey. He was a member of the larboard watch and acted as a straw boss when the mate was engaged in more important tasks. In the later days of sail, when three mates was the rule, each standing four hours' watch with eight hours below, his was the four-to-eight watch. He was then replaced as a task boss by the boatswain.

## Supercargo

The supercargo, or owner's representative aboard a trading vessel, was not a member of the ship's company, had no authority save in disposing of the cargo, and was not, unless he had experience, subject to call when all hands were turned out. Various nicknames were applied to him, among them "the ship's cousin" and many others entirely unprintable.

## The Idlers

Certain members of the ship's company, such as the carpenter, sailmaker, cooper, steward, and cook, were called "idlers" by the seamen because they stood no regular watch, "slept in" at night, and were called upon to perform their regular duties only in the daylight hours. They took no part in the inferior duties of the crew, such as sweeping or flushing decks, slushing, tarring, and such, but in cases of shorthandedness or when all hands were called they took their places with either watch. Their quarters were in the steerage, but they messed with the forecastle hands.

⚓

* Melville, *Redburn*.

*The Carpenter*   Known as Chips, he works at his trade under the direction of the master. He is stationed with either watch as he may be needed, but if there is no third mate aboard usually with the larboard. If he does not expressly ship for a seaman as well as a carpenter, no nautical skill can be required of him, but he must, when all hands are called, or if ordered by the master, pull and haul about decks, and go aloft in the work usual upon such occasions, as reefing and furling.

He is not an officer and cannot give an order even to the greenest boy. The chief mate has no authority over the carpenter in his trade, except in the case of the master's absence or illness. Yet when he is working in the capacity of seaman he must obey orders from any or all mates. Sometimes, usually in the case of illness, the carpenter takes the wheel to relieve a more active seaman for other tasks.

On packet ships in the emigrant trade he was possibly the busiest man aboard. He had to erect the bunks in which the steerage passengers slept; it was his job to stow them and their goods and to check the food they brought with them and the equipment with which to prepare it. He issued the water to his charges, he was their physician, and his most serious duty was to prevent fire. When he got rid of his passengers it was time for him to fumigate their quarters.

The carpenter had charge of all the farm animals on deck, though the feeding and cleaning was handled by Jimmy Ducks. He had no place on the quarter-deck unless summoned by the master: his place was on the forecastle with the seamen.

⚓

*The Sailmaker*   Called Sails. On large, well-manned ships the sailmaker was kept busy at his own trade, and then he was under the sole direction of the master, under the same conditions as the carpenter. When he was shipped as an able seaman, he was a sailmaker only upon occasion and at such time was withdrawn from his watch and allowed to "sleep in." Much of the training of the boys and green hands was his responsibility.

⚓

*Cooper*   Known as Hoops. A cooper was usually carried only in whale ships. In addition to coopering, he took his tricks according to his ability.

⚓

*The Steward*   In the passenger-carrying packets this factotum held the rank of a superintendent, having cooks, under-stewards, and waiters under him. His was a rather indefinite standing, for he was neither an officer nor a member of the working crew; he was directly under the master and stood no watch nor came on deck when all hands were called.

In vessels which were not passenger ships, he cleaned the cabin and staterooms, made the beds, set, tended, and cleared the table, provided everything for the cook, and had charge of the pantry, where all the table furniture and the small stores were kept.

He was also the body servant of the master, and his most important duty was to see that the old man got the choicest tidbits from the galley. His relation to the chief mate was somewhat doubtful; but the general understanding was that, although he waited upon the mate when at table and must obey him in all matters relating to ship's work, yet he was not in any respect his servant. If the mate wished any personal service done, he would ask it, or make some compensation.

⚓

*The Cook*   Called the Doctor. He spends his time mostly in the cookhouse, which is called the galley, where he cooks for both the cabin and forecastle. This, with keeping the galley, boilers, pans, kids, etc., clean and in order, occupies him during the day. He is called with all hands and, in tacking and wearing, worked the fore sheet.

## The Men Before the Mast *

Those serving before the mast are divided into three classes—able seamen, ordinary seamen, and boys or green hands. The crews are

* The material in this section not otherwise credited is condensed from Dana's *The Seaman's Friend*, edition of 1869.

not rated by the officers after they get to sea, but, both in the merchant service and in the navy, each man rates himself when he ships. The shipping articles, in the merchant service, are prepared for so many of each class, and a man puts his name down and contracts for the wages and duty of a seaman, ordinary seaman, or boy, at his pleasure. Notwithstanding this license, they are very few instances of its being abused; for every man knows that if he is found incompetent to perform the duty he contracts for, not only can his wages be reduced to the grade for which he is fitted, but something additional will be deducted for the deception practiced upon all concerned, and for the loss of service and the numerous difficulties incurred, in case the fraud is not discovered until the vessel has got to sea. But, still more than this, the rest of the crew consider it a fraud upon themselves, as they are thus deprived of a man of the class the vessel required, which makes her short-handed for the voyage, and increases the duty put upon themselves. If, for instance, the articles provide for six able seamen, the men expect as many, and if one of the six turns out not to be a seaman, and is put upon inferior work, the duties which would commonly be done by six will fall upon the five. The difficulty is felt still more in the watches; as, in the case supposed, there would be in one watch only two able seamen instead of three, and if the delinquent was not a capable helmsman, the increased duty at the wheel alone would be, of itself, a serious evil. The officers also feel at liberty to punish a man who has so imposed upon all hands, and accordingly every kind of inferior and disagreeable duty is put upon him; and, as he finds no sympathy from the crew, his situation on board is made very unpleasant. Indeed, there is nothing a man can be guilty of, short of a felony, to which so little mercy is shown on board ship; for it is a deliberate act of deception, and one to which there is no temptation, except the gain of a few dollars.

⚓

"A chest that is neither too large nor too small
Is the first thing to which your attention I'd call;
The things to put in it are the next to be named,
And if some I omit, I am not to be blamed.

Stow first in the bottom a blanket and quilt,
To be used on the voyage whenever thou wilt;
Thick trowsers and shirts, woolen stockings and shoes,
Next your papers and books to tell you the news;
Good, substantial tarpaulins to cover your head.
Just to say, keep a journal, "N.C., nuff sed,"
Carry paper and ink, pens, wafers and wax.
A shoemaker's last, awls, pegs, and small tacks;
Some cotton and thread, silk, needles, and palm,
And a paper of pins as long as your arm.
Two vests and a thimble, a large lot of matches,
A lot of good cloth that will answer for patches.
A Bible and hymn-book, of course, you must carry,
If you expect at the end of the first voyage to marry.
Don't forget to take essences, pipes and cigars;
Of the sweetest of butter, a couple of jars.
A razor you'll want, a pencil and slate;

A comb and a hairbrush you'll need for your pate;
A brush and some shaving-soap, plenty of quills;
A box of those excellent Richardson's pills:
Opodeldoc and pain-killer surely you'll need,
And something to stop the red stream, should you bleed.
Some things I've omitted, but never mind that;
Eat salt-junk and hard bread, laugh and grow fat." *

⚓

"A sailor has a peculiar cut to his clothes, and a way of wearing them which a green hand can never get. The trousers, tight round the hips, and thence hanging long and loose round the feet, a superabundance of checked shirt, a low-crowned, well-varnished black hat, worn on the back of the head, with half a fathom of black ribbon hanging over the left eye, and a slip-tie to the black silk neckerchief, with sundry other minutiae, are signs, the want of which betrays the beginner at once. Besides the points in my dress which were out of the way, doubtless my complexion and hands were quite enough to distinguish me from the regular *salt*, who, with a sunburnt cheek, wide step, and rolling gait, swings his bronzed and toughened hands athwartships, half opened, as though just ready to grasp a rope." †

"It is often observable, that, in vessels of all kinds, the men who talk the most sailor lingo are the least sailor-like in reality. . . . On the other hand, when not actively engaged in his vocation, you would take the best specimen of a seaman for a landsman. When you see a fellow yawing about the docks like a homeward-bound Indiaman, a long Commodore's pennant of black ribbon flying from his mast-head, and fetching up at a grog-shop with a slew of his hull, as if an Admiral were coming alongside a three-decker in his barge; you may put that man down for what man-of-war's-men call a *damn-my-eyes-tar*, that is, a humbug. And many damn-my-eyes humbugs there are in this man-of-war world of ours." ‡

*Able Seamen*    There is, of course, a great deal of difference in the

* By Joseph B. Gow; quoted in Cheever, *The Whale and His Captors.*
† Dana, *Two Years before the Mast.*
‡ Melville, *White Jacket.*

skill and neatness of the work of different men. No man will pass for an able seaman in a square-rigged vessel who cannot make a long and short splice in a large rope, fit a block strap, pass seizings to lower rigging, and make the ordinary knots in a fair, workmanlike manner.

"A thorough sailor must understand much of other vocations. He must be a bit of an embroiderer, to work fanciful collars of hempen lace about the shrouds; he must be something of a weaver, to weave mats of rope-yarns for lashings to the boats; he must have a touch of millinery, so as to tie graceful bows and knots, such as *Matthew Walker's roses*, and *Turk's heads;* he must be a bit of a musician, in order to sing out at the halyards; he must be a sort of a jeweler, to set dead-eyes in the standing rigging; he must be a carpenter, to enable him to make a jury-mast out of a yard in case of emergency; he must be a sempstress, to darn and mend the sails; a ropemaker, to twist *marline* and *Spanish foxes;* a blacksmith, to make hooks and thimbles for the blocks: in short, he must be a sort of Jack of all trades, in order to be master of his own. And this, perhaps, in a greater or less degree, is pretty much the case with all things else; for you know nothing until you know all; which is the reason we never know anything.

"A sailor, also, in working at the rigging, uses special tools peculiar to his calling—*fids, serving-mallets, toggles, prickers, marling-spikes, palms, heavers* and many more. The smaller sort he generally carries with him from ship to ship in a sort of canvas reticule.

"The estimation in which a ship's crew hold the knowledge of such accomplishments as these is expressed in a phrase they apply to one who is a clever practitioner. To distinguish such a mariner from those who merely '*hand, reef, and steer*'—that is, run aloft, furl sails, haul ropes, and stand at the wheel—they say he is '*a sailorman*'; which means that he not only knows how to reef a topsail, but is an artist in the rigging." *

⚓

In allotting the jobs among the crew, reference is always had to a man's rate and capacity; and it is considered a decided imputation

* Melville, *Redburn.*

upon a man to put him upon inferior work. The most difficult jobs, and those requiring the neatest work, will be given to the older and more experienced among the seamen; and of this none will complain; but to single out an able seaman and keep him at turning the spunyarn winch, knotting yarns, or picking oakum, while there are boys on board, and other proper seaman's work going forward at the same time, would be looked upon as punishment, unless it were temporarily, or from necessity, or while other seamen were employed in the same manner.

Also, in consideration of the superior grade of an able seaman, he is not required to sweep down the decks at night, slush the masts, etc., if there are boys on board and at hand. Not that a seaman is not obliged to do these things. There is no question but that he is, just as much as he is obliged to do any other ship's work; and if there are no boys on board or at hand at the time, or from any other cause it is reasonably required of him, no good seaman would object, and it would be a refusal of duty to do so. Yet if an officer were deliberately, and without necessity for it, when there were boys about decks at the time, who could do the work as well, to order an able seaman to leave his work and sweep down the decks, or slush a mast, it would be considered as punishment.

⚓

*Ordinary Seamen*  An ordinary seaman is one who, from not being of sufficient age and strength, or from want of sufficient experience, is not quite competent to perform all the duties of an able seaman, and accordingly receives a little less than full wages, and does not contract for the complete qualities of an able seaman.

An ordinary seaman is expected to hand, reef, and steer (including "boxing the compass") under common circumstances; to be well acquainted with all the running and standing rigging of a ship; to be able to reeve all the studdingsail gear, and set a topgallant or royal studdingsail out of the top; to loose and furl a royal and a small topgallant sail or flying jib; and perhaps, also, to send down or cross a royal yard. He need not be a complete helmsman, and if an able seaman should be put in his place at the wheel in very bad weather, or when the ship steered with difficulty, it would be no imputation upon him, provided he could steer his trick creditably under ordinary circumstances.

It is commonly understood that an ordinary seaman need not be a workman upon rigging. Yet there are probably few men capable of performing the duties of ordinary seamen who would not be somewhat acquainted with work upon the rigging, and who could not do the simpler parts of it, such as servicing and splicing small ropes, passing a common seizing, or the like; and it is always expected that an o.s. shall be able to make all the hitches, bends, and knots in common use, such as two half-hitches, a rolling hitch, timber hitch, clove hitch, common bend, and bowline knot. He would also be thought deficient if he could not draw, knot, and ball up yarns, and make spunyarn, foxes, and common sennit. Yet it is said that if he can steer his trick, and do his duty creditably in working ship and taking in and making sail, he is entitled to the rate and wages of an ordinary seaman, though he cannot handle a marlinspike or serving board.

⚓

*Boys*  A boy does not ship to know anything.

"But you must not think from this that persons called *boys* aboard merchant ships are all youngsters. In merchant ships, a *boy* means a green-hand, a landsman on his first voyage. And never mind if he is old enough to be a grandfather, he is still called a *boy*; and boy's work is put upon him." *

In the ordinary day's work, the boys are taught to draw and knot yarns, make spunyarns, foxes, sennit, etc., and are employed in passing a ball or otherwise assisting the able seamen in their jobs. Slushing masts, sweeping and clearing up decks, holding the log reel, coiling up rigging, and loosing and furling the light sails, are duties that are invariably put upon the boys and green hands. They stand their watches like the rest, are called with all hands, go aloft to reef and furl, and work whenever and wherever the men do, the only difference being in the kind of work upon which they are put.

* Melville, *Redburn.*

# The Work of a Ship

## The Watches

A WATCH is a term both for the division of the crew, and for the period of time allotted to such division. The crew is divided into two watches, larboard, or port, and starboard; the larboard is commanded by the first mate, and the starboard by the second mate. If there is no second mate, the starboard watch is the captain's watch. These watches divide the time between them, being on and off duty, or, as it is termed, on deck and below, every other four hours. If, for instance, the chief mate with the larboard watch has the first night watch, from eight to twelve, at the end of the four hours the starboard watch is called, and the second mate takes the deck, while the chief mate and the larboard watch go below until four in the morning. At four they come on deck again and remain until eight.*

Where this alternation of watches is kept up throughout the twenty-four hours, it is called "watch and watch" or "toe and heel watches."

The watches are named:

    12 noon to 4  P.M.  afternoon watch
    4 P.M. to 6  P.M.  first dog watch

* Dana, *The Seaman's Friend.*

338

6 P.M. to 8 P.M.   second dog watch
8 P.M. to 12 mid.   first watch
12 mid. to 4 A.M.   middle or churchyard watch
4 A.M. to 8 A.M.   morning watch
8 A.M. to 12 noon   forenoon watch.

*Dog Watches* The watch from 4 to 8 P.M. is divided into two half-watches of two hours each, called dog watches. The object of this is to make an uneven number of watches, seven instead of six; otherwise the same watch would stand the same hours for the whole voyage, and those who had two watches on deck the first night out would have the same throughout the passage. But the uneven number shifts the watches. The dog watches, coming about sundown, or twilight, and between the end of the day's work and the setting of the night watch, are usually the time given for recreation, for smoking, telling yarns, etc., on the forecastle head, things which are not permitted during the day.

*Calling the Watch* "Do you hear the news there, sleepers?"

> Larbowlins stout,
> You must turn out
>   And sleep no more within.
> For if you do,
> We'll cut your clew
>   And let starbowlins in.

"Eight bells would at last be struck, and the men on deck, exhilarated by the prospect of changing places with us, would call the watch in a most provokingly mirthful and facetious style.

"As thus:—

"Larbord watch, ahoy! eight bells there, below! Tumble up, my lively hearties; steamboat alongside waiting for your trunks: bear a hand, bear a hand with your knee-buckles, my sweet and pleasant fellows! fine shower-bath here on deck. Hurrah! hurrah! your ice-cream is getting cold.

"Whereupon some of the old croakers who were getting into their trowsers would reply with 'Oh, stop your gabble, will you? don't be in such a hurry, now. You feel sweet, don't you?' with other exclamations, some of which were full of fury.

"And it was not a little curious to remark, that at the expiration of the ensuing watch, the tables would be turned; and we on deck became the wits and jokers, and those below the grizzly bears and growlers." *

⚓

Rouse and shine
For the Black Ball Line.

*The Helmsman*   At the summoning of the new watch the man whose turn it is to take the helm goes immediately aft, and ought to be the first on deck. The relieving of the helm is a sign that the watch has been changed, and no man is permitted to go below until that has been done. It is a man's watch on deck so long as a member of his watch is at the wheel.

The watch on deck supplies the helmsman, even when all hands have been called. Each man stands at the helm for two hours, which is called his trick. At night, the alternate helmsman is lookout with his station at the bow; in daytime, when a lookout is not required, his is the duty of polishing the brightwork on the quarter-deck.

The new helmsman goes to the wheel and takes hold of the spokes over the body of the man he is relieving, so as to have the wheel in control when the other lets go. Before releasing his hold, the retiring helmsman gives the course in an audible voice and the new helmsman repeats it before the old helmsman removes his hands.

Sometimes in very cold weather the tricks are reduced to one hour, with the alternate hour below to warm up; and if the ship steers badly in a gale, two men are sent to the wheel at once. In this case the man who stands on the weather side is the responsible helmsman, the man to the lee merely assisting him by heaving the wheel when necessary.

When a man is at the wheel he has nothing to attend to but steering the vessel, and he is allowed no conversation, save with an officer. If he wishes to be relieved during his trick it cannot be done without the permission of an officer, and all the formalities must be gone through even if he is to be absent but a minute or two.

* Melville, *Redburn.*

## The Ship's Bell

Time on shipboard was originally estimated by the glass, a sand-glass, running half an hour; it was the only clock by which sea time was kept. The chimes of this clock were the ship's bell, struck by the man at the wheel or the quartermaster, who eight times in each watch turned his half-hour glass, marking at the same time, by strokes upon the bell, the number of half hours that had passed since his watch came on deck.

Though the old sea clock is now superseded by a ship's clock or the big watch in the binnacle, the term "flog the clock" remains among sailors when putting it forward or back when sailing east or west; and is evidently derived from the much older one of flogging the glass—that is, turning it before all the sand has run through, in order to shorten the watch on deck.*

The ship's bell is always struck, never rung.

A sailor inquires the time by asking, "How many bells have gone?"

During a storm, especially when the ship was rolling, the bell rope was made fast to keep it from tolling what to the sailors sounded like their death knell.

| One bell   | 12.30 | 4.30 | 8.30  |
|------------|-------|------|-------|
| Two bells  | 1.00  | 5.00 | 9.00  |
| Three "    | 1.30  | 5.30 | 9.30  |
| Four  "    | 2.00  | 6.00 | 10.00 |
| Five  "    | 2.30  | 6.30 | 10.30 |
| Six   "    | 3.00  | 7.00 | 11.00 |
| Seven "    | 3.30  | 7.30 | 11.30 |
| Eight "    | 4.00  | 8.00 | 12.00 |

In British ships, during the dog watch, the bells from four to six follow the usual course; but at half-past six, instead of five bells only one is struck, two at 7 P.M., and three at 7.30, and the full eight bells at eight o'clock. The reason for this deviation from custom is that five bells in the second dog watch was the signal for the Mutiny at

* Leslie, *Old Sea Wings, Ways, and Words.*

the Nore,* and since that occasion it has never been struck on a British ship.†

*Sixteen Bells*   In the Royal Navy it has long been the custom of having the oldest man in the ship, be he an admiral or a matelow, strike eight bells at midnight, December thirty-first. This was immediately followed by eight bells for the new year struck by the youngest boy on board.

Bells are sounded by two quick strokes and then after an interval two more, and so on. If it is an odd number, always on the half hour, the odd stroke is struck alone. Five bells would be: Ding-ding! Ding-ding! Ding!

## Rules of the Road

### Day

Two close-hauled ships upon the sea,
　　To one safe rule must each agree;
The starboard tack must keep his luff,
　　The port—bear off!

### Night

When both side lights you see ahead
　　You port your helm and show your red.
For green to green, or red to red—
　　Is perfect safety, go ahead.
And when upon your port is seen
　　Another's starboard light of green,
There's nothing much for you to do,
　　For green to port, keeps clear of you.

### At All Times

When in safety and in doubt
　　Always keep a sharp lookout;
Strive to keep a level head,
　　Mind your lights and heave your lead.

* The Mutiny at the Nore (1797) was the most serious of all affecting the Royal Navy. The official explanations that it was inspired by the French Revolution, or by agents of Irish discontent, do not cover the real fact that the British sailor was protesting against intolerable abuses. His condition and treatment were considerably improved thereafter.

† Clements, *A Gypsy of the Horn.*

*P.S.*
When a dozen lights you see ahead,
You're surely drunk, so off to bed.

## Heaving the Lead

There are two types of lead, both known as the sailor's third eye: the hand lead, called the blue pigeon and used in shallow waters, weighing up to fifteen pounds, and the deep-sea lead, called the dipsey lead, weighing above fifty pounds.

The markings on the lead line are: at two fathoms, two strips of leather; at three fathoms, three strips of leather; at five fathoms, a white rag; at seven fathoms, a red rag; at ten fathoms, a piece of leather with a hole in it; at thirteen, the same as three; at fifteen, the same as five; at seventeen, the same as seven; at twenty fathoms, two knots.

Deep-sea lead lines are marked the same as far as twenty fathoms, then add a strip of leather for every five fathoms, and a knot for every ten fathoms.

Heaving the lead is generally performed by a man who stands in the main chains to the windward. Having the line all ready to run out, without interruption, he holds it at a distance of nearly a fathom from the lead, and having swung it backward and forward three or four times in order to acquire greater velocity with the swing, he then swings it over his head, and thence as far forward as is necessary; so that by the lead sinking while the ship advances, the line may be almost perpendicular when it reaches the bottom. The seaman sounding then proclaims the depth of the water in a kind of singing manner. Thus: if the mark of five fathoms is close to the surface, he sings out, "By the mark five!" and, as there are no marks at 4, 6, 8, etc., he estimates those numbers and sings out, "By the deep four!" etc. If he considers it to be a quarter or a half more than a particular mark, he sings out, "And a quarter five!" or, "And a half four!" etc. If he conceives the depth to be three-quarters more than a particular mark, he calls it a quarter less than the next; thus, at four fathoms and three-quarters, he calls, "A quarter less five!" and so on, according to the depth of the water.*

* Brady, *Kedge Anchor.*

## The Points of the Compass

| The compass says: | The helmsman answers: |
| --- | --- |
| North | Nothe * |
| North by east | Nothe by east |
| North-northeast | No'-nothe-east |
| Northeast by north | Nothe-east by nothe |
| Northeast | Nothe-east |
| Northeast by east | Nothe-east by east |
| East-northeast | East-nothe-east; east-no'-east |
| East by north | East by nothe |
| East | East |
| East by south | East by southe † |
| East-southeast | East-southe-east; east-suth-east |
| Southeast by east | Southe-east by east |
| Southeast | Southe-east |
| Southeast by south | Southe-east by southe |
| South-southeast | Sou'-sou'-east |
| South by east | Southe by east |
| South | Southe |
| South by west | Southe by west |
| South-southwest | Sou'-sou'-west |
| Southwest by south | Sou'-west by southe |
| Southwest | Sou'-west |
| Southwest by west | Sou'-west by west |
| West-southwest | West-sou'-west |
| West by south | West by southe |
| West | West |
| West by north | West by nothe |
| West-northwest | West-nor'-west |
| Northwest by west | Nor'-west by west |
| Northwest | Nor'-west |
| Northwest by north | Nor'-west by nothe |
| North-northwest | Nor'-nor'-west |
| North by west | Nothe by west |
| North | Nothe |

\* Pronounced to rhyme with "loathe."
† Pronounced to rhyme with the verb "to mouth."

## Leisure

IN the hard-driven packets in the fast North Atlantic passage there was no time for anything but work and sleep. On longer voyages the men were given a little time for themselves, apart from the dog watches and Sunday afternoon. They had to supply their own entertainment. On the forecastle head in pleasant weather, below when it was bad, they swapped yarns and experiences, sang songs, and relaxed. If there was a joker, practical or otherwise, among the crew, or a butt for japes and jokes, so much the better.

There were times, on good ships, when the captain, sensing boredom in his men, would give them time off for skylarking, a good sea term that has come ashore to stay. He might send a couple of bottles of liquor forward, give the order to "splice the main brace," and leave the sailors to their own devices. Men raced each other through the rigging, boxed, or fought and cut up generally. They were rough men and were content with only rough fun: sometimes men were hurt, but they returned to duty feeling better and with something to talk about.

At times in foreign ports, where shore leave could not be granted, the captain sometimes permitted a "tarpaulin muster," wherein the men pooled their finances and sent ashore for liquor. The mates wisely refrained from interfering, standing their usual watches, but always on the alert for real trouble.

## Folk Art in the Fo'c'sle

In every crew there were serious and industrious men: some spent their time reading, studying, or writing letters. A few turned their hands to the arts and crafts. With the general run of seamen ship-model building seems to have been the favorite avocation. Using scraps of hardwood from the carpenter's cuddy, they whittled each piece to scale with their pocket knives. Often the hull, the spars, and the yards were completed but were not assembled until all were ready. Many of these models were crude, a few were excellent.

In the museum of the Old Dartmouth Historical Society, at New Bedford, Mass., there is an exquisite model of a full-rigged 74-gun frigate, made entirely of beef bones, save for the small cannon, which are of brass. It was the work of Cape Cod sailors who were held as prisoners in Dartmoor Prison during the War of 1812. They were allowed to bring the model home only on condition that they mount a British ensign on it.

Some seamen were competent artists, using oils and water colors, but these for the most part were officers. Today these works are eagerly sought as "primitives."

This writer has seen several hooked rugs said to have been made at sea. While it is quite possible they were made by male hands, it is equally probable they were made by "the old men's wives."

Scrimshaw is the sole folk art that evolved from the work of seamanship, and it belongs entirely to the whalemen. The word "scrimshaw" is used to describe both the process and the result. When a whaleman took a piece of bone or ivory, or even hardwood, and began to shape it and decorate it with his knife, he was engaged in scrimshaw. The finished object—ditty box, busk, or jagging wheel—was scrimshaw. Melville called it *skrimshander*, and to Cheever it was *mux*, and the process *muxing*.

The art lay in shaping the material and scratching upon it a design which might or might not be filled in with black or colored inks. Any material handsome enough and hard enough would serve: you can find scrimshaw made of teakwood, mahogany, tortoiseshell, and even silver, or a combination of several. What the craftsman liked best and always used when he could get it was the tooth of a sperm whale or a piece of the panbone.

He could carve the teeth into small images and statues, or etch on them the portrait of a loved one, a home scene, a patriotic design, or a view of his ship at sea. From the panbones he could fashion busks, to be worn in ladies' corsets; swifts, revolving reels on which yarn or knitting wool was to be wound; jagging wheels, for crimping the edges of pie crust. Canes, chessmen, dominoes, paper knives, bodkins, crochet hooks, shuttles, and a host of other small and useful articles were also made.

The tools he used were those at hand—sailmaker's needles, the point of his knife, saws, and files. The finishing was done with wood ashes and the final polish given by rubbing with the palm of the hand.

# Customs and Traditions

## Death at Sea

"IF harm comes to me, why, put it in the log, with a word or two about the manner in which I played my part. That is the most proper epitaph for a sailor." *

"Death is at all times solemn, but never so much so as at sea. A man dies on shore; his body remains with his friends, and 'the mourners go about the streets'; but when a man falls overboard at sea and is lost, there is a suddenness in the event, and a difficulty in realizing it, which gives to it an air of awful mystery. A man dies on shore—you follow his body to the grave, and a stone marks the spot. You are often prepared for the event. There is always something which helps you to realize it when it happens, and to recall it when it has passed. A man is shot down by your side in battle, and the mangled body remains an object and a real evidence; but at sea, the man is near you— at your side—you hear his voice, and in an instant he is gone, and nothing but a vacancy shows his loss. Then, too, at sea—to use a homely but expressive phrase—you *miss* a man so much. A dozen men are shut up together in a little bark upon the wide, wide sea, and for months and months see no forms and hear no voices but their own, and one is taken suddenly from among them, and they miss

* Cooper, *The Red Rover*.

him at every turn. It is like losing a limb. There are no new faces or new scenes to fill up the gap. There is always an empty berth in the forecastle, and one man wanting when the small night watch is mustered. There is one less to take the wheel, and one less to lay out with you upon the yard. You miss his form and the sound of his voice, for habit had made them almost a necessity to you, and each of your senses feels the loss.

"All of these things make such a death peculiarly solemn, and the effect of it remains upon the crew for some time. There is more kindness shown by the officers to the crew, and by the crew to one another. There is more quietness and seriousness. The oath and the loud laugh are gone. The officers are more watchful, the crew go more carefully aloft. The lost man is seldom mentioned, or is dismissed with a sailor's rude eulogy—'Well, poor George is gone! His cruise is up soon! He knew his work, and he did his duty, and was a good shipmate.' Then usually follows some allusion to another world, for sailors are almost all believers in their way; though their notions and opinions are unfixed and at loose ends. They say, 'God won't be hard upon the poor fellow,' and seldom get beyond the common phrase which seems to imply that their sufferings and hard treatment here will be passed to their credit in the books of the Great Captain hereafter—'*To work hard, live hard, die hard and go to hell after all, would be hard indeed!*' " *

*Sea Burial* "All hands to bury the dead!" The body of a deceased seaman was given over to the sailmaker; a heavy weight, usually a broken or worn holystone, was placed at the feet and the body wrapped in old canvas and sewed, the last stitch in the shroud being taken through the nose of the deceased. Sometimes a coin was placed in the body's mouth. When ready for burial, the wrapped body was placed on a plank laid across the rail; the captain read the service, and at the words "we commit this body to the deep," the inner end of the plank was raised and the body slipped quietly into the sea.

⚓

Almost immediately after burial or loss at sea, an auction is held of the deceased's effects, to be bid in by his late fellows, the money

* Dana, *Two Years before the Mast.*

to be deducted from their wages at the end of the voyage. Sentiment often caused these to bring higher than shore prices. But the dead man's clothes would not be worn, or his tools used, during the same voyage.

⚓

The stormy petrels, Mother Carey's chickens, that follow all vessels were believed to be the souls of sailors drowned at sea.

⚓

"For concerning the peculiar reptile inhabitants of these wilds— whose presence gives the group its second Spanish name, Gallipagoes —concerning the tortoises found here, most mariners have long cherished a superstition, not more frightful than grotesque. They earnestly believe that all wrecked sea-officers, more especially commodores and captains, are at death (and in some cases before death) transformed into tortoises; thenceforth dwelling upon these hot aridities, sole solitary Lords of Asphaltum." *

⚓

The bodies of humans were always buried from the starboard side, those of animals from the port side.

## The Dead Horse

American seamen frequently received a month's wage in advance upon signing the ship's articles, to pay their shore debts, to purchase clothing and gear, or for a last binge. They then thought they were working for nothing the first thirty days at sea, and this debt, hung about their necks, was called "the dead horse." When the debt was worked out, the dead horse had died. It was the custom on a contented ship to celebrate the event by making a horse of canvas stuffed with waste material saturated with oil. This was ignited and cast overboard, while the crew sang:

* Melville, *The Encantadas.*

They say, old man, your horse will die,
*And they say so, and they hope so.*
For thirty days I've ridden him,
*Oh, poor old man!*

And if he lives, I'll ride him again,
*And they say so, and they hope so.*
We'll hoist him up and bury him low,
*Oh, poor old horse!*

## Flogging

The earliest sea laws of which records remain, the codes of Rhodes, Oleron, Wisby, and Amalfi, provided severe punishments for all breaches of the peace on board a ship while at sea. A man guilty of killing another was to be tied to the body and both cast overboard; if a man drew the blood of an opponent with a knife he was to lose a hand; and one guilty of theft was to have his head shaved, covered with boiling pitch and decorated with feathers and was to be put ashore at the first land the ship touched.

The Royal Navy in the time of Elizabeth had a rule that a man on watch "being taken asleep, he shall be hanged to the bowsprit in a basket, with a can of beer, a loaf of bread, and a sharp knife, and choose to hang there until he starve or cut himself into the sea."

Custom and tradition made the master a law unto himself while his ship was at sea, and he believed he could mete out any punishment he cared to, whether in anger or otherwise. The laws were explicit—a master could do this or that to preserve order and discipline—but many captains cared as little for the law as they did for the seamen themselves. Invariably the punishment ordered was flogging, and men have been given as many as five hundred lashes on the bared back. In the Royal Navy one punishment was "being whipped about the fleet," in which an offender was ordered to receive so many lashes before the eyes of the crew of each warship.

"You see a human being," says Melville, "stripped like a slave; scourged worse than a hound. And for what? For things not essentially criminal, but only made so by arbitrary laws."

The flogged man knew that once ashore he could proceed against the master, but he also knew from experience that the lawyer, whom he called "a land shark" would sell him out—that is, come to some settlement with the captain and then defraud the seaman of his due. As a rule he accepted his punishment, squarely facing the fact that justice was not for him. On a merchant ship he was far better off than he would be in the navy.

"It is one of the evils of the naval service, that a sailor must submit to every species of insult and abuse that officers may feel disposed to heap upon him, without the power of resenting it, and without hope of redress. If an officer strike a man, and the matter be reported to the commander, a reprimand may follow, or it may not, but happen the worst punishment than can to the offender, it will never exceed a reprimand. But the reprimand is often avoided by the offender pleading passion in extenuation of his offence. If Mr. Whittle knocks me down, and I report his violence to the captain, Mr. Whittle tells the captain he did it in a passion, and the plea of passion covers the whole difficulty. But put the ship on the other tack, and see how she will sail then: Suppose, when I recover from Mr. Whittle's knockdown, I jump up and give him a good knock over the nose, what follows then? Will the plea of passion excuse me? According to municipal law, he is guilty of an assault and battery on me, and I am acting only in self-defence; but the naval regulations that screen him under a plea of passion, designate my proper punishment for resisting him to be that of hanging. A court-martial will immediately be convened on my offence for striking a superior officer, at which Mr. Whittle will himself sit as a judge, and sentence me, if not to hanging, to a punishment at least equally as intolerable." *

## Crossing the Line

This is a survival of the early Dutch custom of ducking lubbers upon crossing the thirty-sixth parallel, approximately off the Straits of Gibraltar, then considered a long way from home by the Hollanders. The victims, men who had not passed that point before, were hailed before a kangaroo court by the Lords of Misrule, invariably found guilty and sentenced to pay a fine, called ducking

* Hazen, *Five Years before the Mast.*

money, or to be dipped into the sea from the bowsprit. Dana says that in his time "this ancient custom is now seldom allowed, unless there are passengers on board, in which case there is always a good deal of sport." *

Passing through the doldrums, that belt of calms between the northern and southern trades, was a difficult time for all, officers, crew, and passengers, and the skylarking relieved the tedium. During the night before crossing the equator a voice, coming, it would seem, from the sea, announced that King Neptune and his court would board the vessel the next day to initiate all lubbers, those who had not yet crossed the line. On the day of the visit the victims were kept below decks until His Majesty boarded the vessel; then they were brought up one by one, blindfolded.

The court consisted of Triton, with his horn, as master of ceremonies, King Neptune and Queen Amphitrite (usually Hampertight), Davy Jones, complete with horns, humped back, and a tail, usually carrying a trident of wood. Davy was the court jester. Other characters were often added, especially a sea lawyer, who was assigned to defend the victim but served only to get him into deeper trouble.

* Dana, *Two Years before the Mast.*

At times the treatment given the novice was pretty rugged: the blindfolded man was seated on a plank thrown across a tank of sea water and interrogated, either by Triton or Davy Jones. He was asked his name, age, and origin and accused of being a lubber, a soger, and other terms offensive to seamen. Whether he answered politely or otherwise meant nothing to the court, for each time he opened his mouth a swab soaked in soogy-moogy was thrust into it, and if he refused to answer he was pricked by the trident or a bucket of water was dashed into his face. Neptune would then order him shaved and more soogy-moogy was swabbed on his face and scraped off with a wooden razor.

Neptune would then address the victim:

"You have now the right to become an able seaman, boatswain, mate and so upward to captain, if you are not killed, worked to death, or drowned. In the latter event you will be turned into a sea-horse, and forever be my subject. You may now do your duty, eat salt junk, sour mush, and weevily bread, without grumbling. Sir Triton, engross this seaman's name on the royal rolls."

The lubber, believing his ordeal over, suddenly found the plank on which he was seated overturned and himself floundering blindfolded in the water. When he finally regained the deck he was usually permitted to watch the others go through the ceremony.

The custom is still practiced in the Navy, both in crossing the equator and in crossing the international date line, and in cruise ships, where it is a tepid affair, a part of the long program in the hands of the cruise director.

## Hazing a Boy

Sometimes called *running*. In a good ship the advent of a boy or a green hand was a signal for skylarking. If the lubber was seasick, and he usually was, he was offered antidotes, among them chewing tobacco or munching on a piece of salt junk, either of which only added to the victim's misery.

When he eventually appeared on deck he was greeted with mock sympathy and some very unsound advice. Redburn tells of his shipmates "advising me as soon as I ever got home to pin my ears back, so as not to hold the wind, and sail straight away into the interior of the country, and never stop until deep in the bush, far from the least running brook, never mind how shallow, and out of sight of the smallest puddle of rainwater." *

His first days on duty were further made miserable by being given orders by his shipmates.

"Go to the bosun's locker and get some red oil for the larboard light and green oil for the starboard light."

"Go to the man at the wheel and get the key to the starboard watch and then go and wind it."

"Go find Charley Noble and and tell him to report to the first mate."

"Go down the lazaret and break out the galley down haul."

"Go to the galley and ask the cook for a pailful of fresh steam to prime the donkey engine."

"Go and fetch me the key to the keelson."

## A Wife in Every Port

This is at best a woman's petulant accusation. Sailors were known to be the heaviest patrons of the waterside brothels, but it is doubtful if any woman of a port town would have married an itinerant seaman unless it was to pinch his purse or for some other ulterior purpose.

Melville spins a yarn about Max the Dutchman.

"Not long after anchoring several boats came off; and from one of them stepped a neatly-dressed and very respectable-looking woman, some thirty years of age, I should think, carrying a bundle. Coming forward among the sailors, she inquired for Max the Dutchman, who immediately was forthcoming, and saluted her by the mellifluous appellation of *Sally*.

"Now during the passage, Max in discoursing to me of Liverpool, had often assured me that that city had the honor of containing a spouse of his; and that in all probability, I would have the pleasure of seeing her. But having heard a good many stories about the bigamies of seamen, and their having wives and sweethearts in every port, the round world over; and having been an eye-witness to a nuptial parting between this very Max and a lady in New York, I

* Melville, *Redburn*.

put down this relation of his for what I thought it might reasonably be worth. What was my astonishment, therefore, to see this really decent, civil woman coming with a neat parcel of Max's shore clothes, all washed, plaited, and ironed, and ready to put on at a moment's warning.

"They stood apart a few minutes giving loose to those transports of pleasure which always take place, I suppose, between man and wife after long separations.

"At last, after many earnest inquiries as to how he had behaved himself in New York; and concerning the state of his wardrobe; and going down into the forecastle, and inspecting it in person, Sally departed, having exchanged her bundle of clean clothes for a bundle of soiled ones: and this was precisely what the New York wife had done for Max, not thirty days previous.

"So long as we laid in port, Sally visited the *Highlander* daily; and approved herself a neat and expeditious getter-up of duck frocks and trowsers, a capital tailoress, and so far as I could see, a very well-behaved, discreet, and reputable woman.

"But from all I had seen of her, I should suppose Meg, the New York wife, to have been equally well-behaved, discreet, and reputable; and equally devoted to keeping in good order Max's wardrobe.

"And when we left England at last, Sally bade Max good-bye, just as Meg had done; and when we arrived in New York, Meg greeted Max precisely as Sally had greeted him in Liverpool. Indeed, a pair of more amiable wives never belonged to one man; they never quarreled, or had so much as a difference of any kind; the whole broad Atlantic being between them; and Max was equally polite and civil to both. For many years he had been going Liverpool and New York voyages, plying between wife and wife with great regularity, and sure of receiving a hearty domestic welcome on either side of the ocean." *

## Tattooing

Sailors adopted this primitive practice of marking the skin in a desire to assure identity in case of death by shipwreck or drowning. It seems to have originated among the natives of the South Pacific

* Melville, *Redburn.*

and spread as far north as Japan, where it was brought to high artistic development until prohibited by law. Roman Catholic sailors were the first to adopt it, having a crucifix tattooed on their bodies so that in case of serious injury or illness they might receive the last rites of their church and burial in consecrated ground.

"And many sailors not Catholics were anxious to have the crucifix painted on them, owing to a curious superstition of theirs. They affirm—some of them—that if you have that mark tattooed upon all four limbs, you might fall overboard among seven hundred and seventy-five thousand white sharks, all dinnerless, and not one of them would so much as dare to smell at your little finger." *

⚓

A pig tattooed on a sailor's foot was a charm against drowning.

## Coins at the Step of the Mast

The custom of placing a coin or coins at the heel of the masts seems to have a double purpose. In antiquity it was to pay the fares of the crew across the River Styx if the ship should be lost at sea; more latterly it was done to assure good fortune. The coins must be placed face up, for to have them face down would be to invite disaster.

Even to this day the owner of a small craft will secrete a coin aboard, the location, value, and date of which are known to him alone—the knowledge enabling him to prove his ownership should it ever be questioned.

## Miscellaneous Customs

A seaman leaving the forecastle to go aft, either for his trick at the wheel or other work, goes aft along the lee side of the vessel, unless his immediate duty lies to the windward.

⚓

* Melville, *White Jacket.*

A seaman summoned to the captain's cabin removed his cap and dropped it to the deck just outside the door.

⚓

A mariner entering a new ship, or even an old ship, for the first time makes certain that his right foot is the first to touch the deck.

⚓

It was a breach of etiquette for a seaman to lock his sea chest while on board his ship. Offenders often found, when they returned to the forecastle from their watch on deck, that the cover had been nailed down.

⚓

In the British and United States navies a scarf of black silk is worn, originally as a mark of mourning for the death of Lord Nelson.

⚓

In the Royal Navy, officers who have been round either the Cape of Good Hope or Cape Horn may put one foot on the wardroom table; both Capes carry the right to put both feet on the table.

⚓

By naval custom the senior officer present is always the last into a boat and the first out of it.

# Forecastle Yarns

## A Living Corpse *

IT was destined that our departure from the English strand should be marked by a tragical event, akin to the sudden end of the suicide which had so strongly impressed me on quitting the American shore.

Of the three newly shipped men, who in a state of intoxication had been brought on board at the dock gates, two were able to be engaged at their duties in four or five hours after quitting the pier. But the third man yet lay in his bunk, in the self-same posture in which his limbs had been adjusted by the crimp, who had deposited him there.

His name was down on the ship's papers as Miguel Saveda, and for Miguel Saveda the chief mate at last came forward, shouting down the forecastle scuttle, and commanding his instant presence on deck. But the sailors answered for their new comrade; giving the mate to understand that Miguel was still fast locked in his trance, and could not obey him; when, muttering his usual imprecation, the mate retired to the quarter-deck.

This was in the first dog-watch, from four to six in the evening.

* Melville, *Redburn*.

359

At about three bells, in the next watch, Max the Dutchman, who, like most old seamen, was something of a physician in cases of drunkenness, recommended that Miguel's clothing should be removed, in order that he should lie more comfortably. But Jackson, who would seldom let anything be done in the forecastle that was not proposed by himself, capriciously forbade this proceeding.

So the sailor still lay out of sight in his bunk, which was in the extreme angle of the forecastle, behind the *bowsprit-bitts*—two stout timbers rooted in the ship's keel. An hour or two afterward, some of the men observed a strange odor in the forecastle, which was attributed to the presence of some dead rat among the hollow spaces in the side planks; for some days before, the forecastle had been smoked out, to extirpate the vermin overrunning her. At midnight, the larboard watch, to which I belonged, turned out; and instantly as every man waked, he exclaimed at the now intolerable smell, supposed to be heightened by the shaking up of the bilge-water from the ship's rolling.

"Blast that rat!" cried the Greenlander.

"He's blasted already," said Jackson, who in his drawers had crossed over to the bunk of Miguel. "It's a water-rat, shipmates, that's dead; and here he is,"—and with that he dragged forth the sailor's arm, exclaiming, "dead as a timber-head!"

Upon this the men rushed toward the bunk, Max with the light, which he held to the man's face.

"No, he's not dead," he cried, as the yellow flame wavered for a moment at the seaman's motionless mouth. But hardly had the words escaped, when, to the silent horror of all, two threads of greenish fire, like a forked tongue, darted out between the lips: and in a moment, the cadaverous face was crawled over by a swarm of worm-like flames.

The lamp dropped from the hand of Max, and went out; while covered all over with spires and sparkles of flame, that faintly crackled in the silence, the uncovered parts of the body burned before us, precisely like a phosphorescent shark in a midnight sea.

The eyes were open and fixed; the mouth was curled like a scroll, and every lean feature firm as in life; while the whole face, now wound in curls of soft blue flame, wore an aspect of grim defiance and eternal death. Prometheus, blasted by fire on the rock.

One arm, its red shirt-sleeve rolled up, exposed the man's name, tattooed in vermilion, near the hollow of the middle joint; and as if there was something peculiar in the painted flesh, every vibrating letter burned so white, that you might read the flaming name in the flickering ground of blue.

"Where's that d——d Miguel?" was now shouted down among us from the scuttle by the mate, who had just come on deck, and was determined to have every man up that belonged to his watch.

"He's gone to the harbor where they never weigh anchor," coughed Jackson. "Come you down, sir, and look."

Thinking that Jackson intended to beard him, the mate sprang down in a rage; but recoiled at the burning body as if he had been shot by a bullet. "My God!" he cried, and stood holding fast to the ladder.

"Take hold of it," said Jackson at last, to the Greenlander; "it must go overboard. Don't stand shaking there, like a dog; take hold of it, I say! But stop"—and smothering it all in the blankets, he pulled it partly out of the bunk.

A few minutes more, and it fell with a bubble among the phosphorescent sparkles of the damp night sea, leaving a coruscating wake as it sank.

This event thrilled me through and through with unspeakable horror; nor did the conversation of the watch during the next four hours on deck at all serve to soothe me.

But what most astonished me, and seemed most incredible, was the infernal opinion of Jackson, that the man had been actually dead when brought on board the ship; and that knowingly, and merely for the sake of the month's advance, paid into his hand upon strength of the bill he presented, the body-snatching crimp had knowingly shipped a corpse on board of the *Highlander*, under the pretence of its being a live body in a drunken trance. And I heard Jackson say, that he had known of such things having been done before. But that a really dead body ever burned in that manner I cannot even yet believe. But the sailors seemed familiar with such things; or at least with the stories of such things having happened to others.

For me, who at that age had never so much as happened to hear of a case like this, of animal combustion, in the horrid mood that came over me, I almost thought the burning body was a premonition of the hell of the Calvinists, and that Miguel's earthly end was a foretaste of his eternal condemnation.

Immediately after the burial, an iron pot of red coals was placed in the bunk, and in it two handfuls of coffee were roasted. This done, the bunk was nailed up, and was never opened again during the voyage; and strict orders were given the crew not to divulge what had taken place to the emigrants: but to this, they needed no commands.

After the event, no one sailor but Jackson would stay alone in the forecastle, by night or by noon; and no more would they laugh or sing, or in any way make merry there, but kept all their pleasantries for the watches on deck. All but Jackson: who, while the rest would be sitting silently smoking on their chests, or in their bunks, would look toward the fatal spot, and cough, and laugh, and invoke the dead man with incredible scoffs and jeers. He froze my blood, and made my soul stand still.

## *Little Short of a Miracle* *

"I once made a voyage in the ship *Laguna* from Boston to Cadiz and back with a cargo of salt. Coming home we had a Cuban planter and his son, a boy of nineteen, as passengers. The boy was always whistling, and our mate, who was a regular old sea-dog, who hated to hear whistling, except in a calm when it would help to raise the wind, kept prophesying that the Nightingale, as he called the boy, would be sure to bring some bad luck. One day, when a heavy swell was running, but the wind had nearly died away, a large shark came up in our wake and followed the ship. The boy was leaning over the taffrail watching the shark, and his father was walking up and down the poop deck with his pocket-knife in his hand, whittling a stick. The ship suddenly gave a heavy pitch and the boy lost his balance and tumbled overboard. He screamed as he fell, and the father gave another yell and jumped overboard after him. There was a pretty kettle of fish. The main yard was thrown aback, though the ship wasn't making much headway, and everything handy about decks was tossed overboard—gratings, life-buoys, and planks. Most everybody threw something, and the carpenter, who was a stupid muff of

* Adams, *On Board the "Rocket."*

a fellow, wanted to do his share towards the rescue, so he picked up his grindstone and threw that overboard. The passengers disappeared immediately, and as nothing could be seen of them from aloft it was useless to get out a boat. We filled away again with sad feelings, and the old mate said Nightingale might whistle the whole passage if he would only come back. In a little while the captain spied a shark under the stern. He got the shark-hook and put a big junk of salt pork on it, and soon the shark took hold. We slipped a running bowline around his tail and hauled him on deck. After we had smashed his head with handspikes we cut him open, and there we found the man, the boy and the grindstone. The boy was turning the grindstone and his father was sharpening his knife in order to cut a hole in the shark to get out of. They were greatly astonished to find themselves on our deck again, and the father said it was little short of a miracle."

## *Thar She Blows!* *

We was cruising down the Mozambique channel under reefed tops'ls and the wind blowin' mor'n half a gale, two years out er New Bedford an' no ile. An' the masthead lookout shouts, "Thar she blows!"

An' I goes aft.

"Cap'n Simmons," sez I (his being the same name as mine, but no

* Zephaniah W. Pease, *History of New Bedford*. Reprinted by courtesy of Mr. William H. Tripp.

kith or kin, thank God!) "the man at the masthead sez, 'Thar she blows!' Shall I lower?"

"Mr. Simmons," sez the cap'n, "it's blowin' a little too peart an' I don't see fittin' for to lower."

An' I goes forrard.

An' the man at the masthead sings out, "Thar she blows an' breaches!"

An' I goes aft.

"Cap'n Simmons," sez I, "the lookout at the masthead sez, 'Thar she blows an' breaches!' Shall I lower?"

"Mr. Simmons," sez the cap'n, "it's blowin' too peart an' I don't see fittin' fer to lower."

An' I goes forrard.

An' the lookout at the masthead sings out, "Thar she blows an' breaches, an' sparm at that!"

An' I goes aft.

"Cap'n Simmons," sez I, "the lookout sez, 'Thar she blows an' breaches, an' sparm at that!' Shall I lower?"

"Mr. Simmons," sez he, "it's blowin' too peart an' I don't see fittin' fer to lower, but so be you sees fittin' fer to lower, Mr. Simmons, why lower an' be good an' damned to ye."

An' I lowers an' goes on the whale, an' when I comes within seventy-five foot of her I sez, "Put me jest three seas nearer, fer I'm hell with the long harpoon." An' I darted the iron an' it tuk.

When I comes alongside the ship Cap'n Simmons stands in the gangway. "Mr. Simmons," sez he, "you are the finest mate that ever sailed in this ship. Below in the locker on the port side there's rum and seegars at your sarvice."

"Cap'n Simmons," sez I, "I don't want your rum, no more your seegars. All I want of you, Cap'n Simmons, is plain seevility, an' that of the commonest, God-damndest kind."

An' I goes forrard.

## A St. Brandon Yarn

While they were sailing it came Christmas Day and the monks in the coracle said their matins and sang special thanks for the birth of their Savior. Shortly before noon they came upon an iceberg, a small iceberg upon which a man was reclining. They sailed close to the berg and hailed him, asking who he was and what he was doing there.

"I," said the man, "am Judas, Judas Iscariot."

The good monks recoiled in horror. Had they miscalculated their bearings? Were they on the road to perdition instead of sailing for the Islands of the Blest?

"What do you here?" demanded St. Brandon.

"It is Christmas," said Judas, "and for one hour I am free of the tormenting fires. Just one hour." He sighed. "When I died, by mine own hand, I was cast into the flames, which was my just fate. But on the first Christmas an angel came to me and said that for one hour I might be free to go and to cool my body. I asked from whence came this mercy. He recalled to me that once in Joppa, a leper had appealed for help in his misery, and I, Judas, had thrown him my cloak to cover his sores from the sun. For this, the angel said to me, I was to be given one hour's respite from torment each year, each Christmas, the day of Him whom I had betrayed."

The holy men in the coracle fell to their knees and bowed their heads in prayer and when they looked up Judas was gone, his hour had passed and he had already been returned to his torments.

## The Captain Who Could Taste His Ship's Position

There are many yarns extant of masters of sailing vessels who believed they could, by tasting the ground matter brought up by the dipsey lead, tell the exact position of their vessel.

One of these was the captain of a small brigantine trading among Central American ports. He had but a single mate aboard, which meant he had to stand watch himself, in fact, had to share command of his vessel with his only officer.

In one of the flash storms in the Gulf the old man was injured by a falling yard, a broken hip that confined him to his berth and put the mate on watch-and-watch with himself. The mate stuck to his post, catching cat naps whenever he could, especially when one of the better seamen was at the wheel.

The old man was not a good patient: demanding almost hourly reports on position, course, wind and everything else. He began to believe he could tell where his vessel was by the smell of the air, the color of water in which the vessel sailed, and by tasting the ground matter brought up by the lead when it was sounded. This last became a conviction and he ordered that at each sounding it be brought to his berth.

There came a spell of dirty weather, three days of it, and the old man was especially restive. There were, he insisted, hidden shoals in these waters and he was forever ordering the heaving of the lead. The officer and men tired of this and resolved to put an end to it.

They heaved the lead and brought it in. Carefully drying it they dipped it in water from the scuttle butt and sprinkled a little salt from the forecastle table over it. Then it was taken to the cabin.

"Thirty-seven fathoms, sir," said one of the men.

The captain applied the lead to his taster, his eyes sparkled a bit and smiling, he said: "Men, if I didn't know we were in the Gulf I'd swear we were in the Great Salt Lake." His voice and expression changed. "Now," he roared, "you sogers go and sound that lead good and proper and bring it back to me. *Jump!*"

## Real Tall *

Old Stormie's dead and gone to rest,
*To my way, hay, Stormalong, John!*
Of all the sailors he was the best,
*To my way, aye, way, Mister Stormalong!*

Only three voices carried the closing lines of the chantey: the oil lamp in the forecastle of the *Bride of the Sea* burned gloomily on its gimbals, barely lighting the faces of the singers. Outside there was a cold, icy drizzle on a flat sea, an Irishman's hurricane, and we were farming our watch out below. Seven bells was struck, three-thirty in the churchyard watch.

A man in an upper bunk, a quartermaster who had turned in all standing, raised himself on one elbow and looked down at the singers.

"Sing it again," he asked. Then, as though forgetting, he continued: " You know, bullies, I sailed with Old Stormie. There was a

* Based on the legend "Old Stormalong, the Sailorman," copyright 1930 by Frank Shay.

sailorman for you. Every hair a rope yarn and every drop of blood pure Stockholm tar. He was a big man, well set up, and tall, real tall. On his chest he had three letters tattooed, A.B.S. and once the Old Man asked him what they stood for.

" 'My initials, sir,' said Stormie in his quiet voice. 'Alfred Bulltop Stormalong. But everybody calls me John, sir.'

" 'Well, John,' says the Old Man in his homeward bound voice, 'to me they mean able-bodied seaman and I think that from now on we'll measure all sailormen by your standards.'

"That was on the *Courser*. You all heard of her. Biggest clipper ever built. Some say that she was one of Donald McKay's dreams come to life.

"I was eighteen at the time, but I was already shaving so you couldn't call me a boy. We were signed on by a boarding-house master in Cherry Street; he said she was a sharp ship, not an all-hands-tub, that there would be plenty of work, plenty to eat and good pay. It was enough for me. I signed on and was told to report to Coenties Slip, East River, next morning.

"There was no *Courser* at Coenties Slip, only a jug-shaped steam tender. The *Courser*, we were told, was anchored off Sandy Hook, she was too big to pass the Narrows. When I saw her, bullies, I was pure amazed. The first thing that caught my eye as I hit the deck was a lot of horses. 'Horse Boat,' I said and I'd a made a pierhead jump right then if there was a pier in sight.

" 'Horse boat nothing,' said a bosun's mate. 'Those horses are for the men on watch.'

"That's a fact, bullies, that packet was so big they had to have a double set of mates forward and another double set aft. She had an aftc'sle as well as a fo'c'sle, and she carried a crew of over six hundred, and many of us sailormen never did get to see all our shipmates. The Old Man gave his orders through a megaphone to signal men who couldn't keep their codes straight, and times we'd find the bow on one tack and the stern on another. A man couldn't ask for a finer ship, yet she sailed like a haystack.

"As I said, *Courser* was a tall ship. When you got to the skysail-yards you weren't halfway up. She had banks of sails atop those, sails you never saw or heard of: sky kites, moon-rakers, cloud-dusters, heaven-tormentors, and atop all, angels' footstools, the last being made of the finest silk. Atop the foremast was rigged a three-way sail, shaped like a ploughshare, called the cloud-separator, and it was manned by six men who wore oilskins all the time. The *Courser's* sails were so high that sometimes a cloud would stop her dead in her tracks. Well, the cloud-separator helped with the smaller clouds, but the men were supplied with Turkish swords and when they came up against a real heavy cloud they had to hack their way through. Naturally this caused rain but it didn't worry the men on deck, the ship was already well out of it and the rain fell three miles behind.

"Many a time I was sent aloft clean-shaven only to have a full beard by the time I made the deck again. Oh, she was a tall ship, real tall.

"She yawed badly. Her wake looked like a dog wetting in the snow. I used to say that she was all legs and wings, but the truth was, we didn't know how to handle her. Even with thirty-two men to man the wheel, sixteen to a watch, four on duty. Once I heard the Old Man talking to the forward mates: 'She isn't too big,' he said, 'we just haven't men big enough to handle her.'

"It seems now that the very next morning one of the after look-outs cried that a grampus was following us. The Old Man put his glass on it and said: 'That ain't no grampus, but I can't say what it is. Put her about and we'll have a look.'

"About two hours later we could see that it was a man, coming along at an eighteen-knot clip, and we wondered how he got out there. Couldn't be a sailorman, because none of us ever learned to swim and this fellow could. The Old Man ordered a boat lowered, but before we could put it in the water the man had rounded our stern and reaching up grabbed the larboard gunnel and pulled himself on board. The Old Man was waiting for him.

" 'Where you from and what are you doing in the middle of the South Atlantic?' he demanded.

"The big fellow shook the water out of his hair and beard. 'I was bosun on the *Queen's Dream* until midnight, sir,' he said to the Old Man. 'Last evening we passed you astern and as soon as I saw you I knew this was my ship. Sir, it took me until midnight to convince the captain I should have my release.' He dug into his wet trousers and brought out a paper and some banknotes. 'The captain gave me my discharge and due pay and then asked me what good they were, the big ship was out of sight. Well, sir, I took my bearings and left my shirt and shoes on deck, and here I be, sir.'

"The Old Man looked at the paper. 'What are you able to do?' he asked.

" 'Able to hand, reef and steer, sir,' he said modestly in his quiet voice.

" 'Then take the wheel and hold her sou'-sou'-east by east, three points south.' That was the way Stormalong joined the *Courser*. He went to the helm and that was the end of the yawing. He gentled her. It was there and then she got the name of a dream ship, but I can tell you it was ten per cent dream and ninety per cent Stormalong.

"I made the Double Triangle with him, round Cape Stiff to Frisco and on to China, then to London and back to New York. In every port he drove the women crazy; just as soon as they saw him they forgot their errands. At New York Swivel Eye Sue came down to welcome me and my pay, but once she put her roving eye on Stormie she forgot me.

"Stormalong took over the *Courser's* wheel on a twenty-four-hour watch, and a good thing too, for while he was at the helm the old ship was bung up and bilge free. When he needed a rest he looked at the weather and then lashed the wheel where he wanted it. If the weather changed he always woke up with the mate's first shout.

"Everything was sailor's weather with the *Courser* until the big blow of Umpty-Seven; that was in September, and we were for Liverpool with a cargo of cotton. The weather closed in on us and held for three weeks. We were under bare poles all the time, we'd lost our patent log and our chronometer went out, and there was no sun or stars to take a reckoning. For the first two weeks Stormie could tell about where we were, but on the fifteenth day he snoozed off without lashing the wheel, and the Old Man says to let him sleep. When he woke up he looked about and said: 'Guess I've lost my bearings, sir.'

" 'Hell,' said the mate on watch. 'We all have. But we're afloat, and that's as much as we can ask for.'

"There was another week of weather, of not knowing where we were, when a day dawned full and bright. The Old Man summoned all sixteen mates to help him shoot the sun, and, naturally, he got seventeen different positions, most of them saying we were in the North Sea. We heaved the dipsey lead and the Old Man shrugged his shoulders. Then the weather closed in again and we were driving before a nor'-nutheaster, still under bare poles. The Old Man and the mates crouched over their charts and decided that Stormie should hold her steady and try to make the English Channel and get back into the Atlantic.

"In those days the Channel wasn't as wide as it is now, and then the Old Man came up with the bad news that the *Courser* couldn't make it, her beam was only six inches under the width of the Straits of Dover. There was a lot of stomping around, the mates and look-outs on their horses, the signalmen fanning themselves with their flags; only Stormie was calm. 'Room enough, sir,' he said. 'I'll hold her to the starboard and then if I see we can't make it I'll throw her over and slide her on to Calais beach.' Then in a low voice he said to the Old Man:

" 'Better send men over the sides and smear a lot of soap, sir, and put an extra heavy coat on the starboard.'

"The Old Man put all hands and the cook to plastering the sides with sougie-mougie, and Stormie eased the packet through slick as honey. Our head-booms dispersed a regiment of soldiers on top of Dover cliffs and the spanker boom destroyed the fortifications at Calais, so you see it was a tight fit. The cliffs of Dover scraped every bit of soap off'n the starboard, and ever since then the cliffs have been white. That was from the *Courser's* soap and the action of the waves. Last time I was in the Straits the water was still foamy."

The bosun's mate stuck his head into the fo'c'sle and shouted: "Larbowlins, do you hear the news? Rise and shine, for the Black Ball Line!" On the quarterdeck eight bells was being struck.

> Stormie's gone, that good old man,
> *To my way, hay, Stormalong, John!*
> We shall not see his like again—
> *To my aye, way, aye, Mister Stormalong!*

## *This Ship—A Sailor's Opinion* *

I've followed the sea over thirty-two years,
In the Navy, hard packets and wild privateers;
But of all the old vessels that ever I cursed,
Just shiver my timbers if this ain't the worst.

The bloody old wall-sided cranky concern—
I think every squall she is sure to o'erturn,
And the way that she rolls and goes pitching about
Would have made all the patience of Job fizzle out.

It's enough to provoke a good parson to swear,
To see the bad way her old rotten sails tear,
And I never go higher aloft than the top
Without fear that the foot-ropes will give me a drop.

I wonder those owners are suffered to live
Who send out a ship that will leak like a sieve,
Which every time that she gives a bad jump
Makes fifty more strokes to be worked at the pump.

We ought to arrest the old man as a cheat
For bringing us here where there's nothing to eat;
It's a terrible shame for an old Yankee tub
To feed her good men with such horrible grub.

To be sure, he now and then gives us some flour;
But the mean dirty rat, it's because it's gone sour,
And as for his pies and the dried apple sauce,
I'd a precious deal rather have good old salt horse.

We slave every week day on board of the craft,
But on Sunday the hypocrite makes us come aft—
He preaches an hour about Christian hopes,
Then sends us on deck to give swigs at the ropes.

* Adams, *On Board the "Rocket."*

There's a heap of good sense in the famous old rule
Always choose a big rascal before a darned fool,
And one thing I promise, whatever may happen,
I'll not sail again with a psalm-singing Cap'n.

The ship must have been in amazing great straits
When she took such poor things as these men are for mates.
It worries one's temper beyond all its bounds
To be bossed round the decks by such humbugging hounds.

Now! shipmates, you know I'm not one given to growl,
And I hate a bad temper with all of my soul;
But worked and most starved till one scarcely can crawl,
A man that won't growl is just no man at all.

> Confound the bloody hooker,
> Builder and owner too,
> Blast this "old man" who took her
> To impose on me and you.
>
> Soon as we get relief,
> I should be pleased right well
> To hear she'd struck a reef,
> And gone right —
> There's one bell!

## The Charnel Ship, a Whaling Legend *

One serene evening in the middle of August, 1775, Captain Warrens, the master of a Greenland whale ship, found himself becalmed among an immense number of icebergs, in about seventy-seven degrees of north latitude. On one side and within a mile of the vessel, these were of immense height, and closely wedged together, and a succession of snow-covered peaks appeared behind each other as far as the eye could reach, showing that the ocean was completely blocked up in that quarter, and that it had probably been so for a long period of time. Captain Warrens did not feel altogether sat-

* Cheever, *The Whale and His Captors.*

isfied with the situation; but, there being no wind, he could not move one way or the other, and he therefore kept a strict watch, knowing that he would be safe as long as the icebergs continued in their respective places. About midnight the wind rose to a gale, accompanied by thick showers of snow, while a succession of thundering, grinding, and crashing noises gave fearful evidence that the ice was in motion.

The vessel received violent shocks every moment, for the haziness of the atmosphere prevented those on board from discovering in what direction the open water lay, or if there was actually any at all on either side of them. The night was spent in tacking as often as any case of danger happened to present itself, and in the morning the storm had abated, and Captain Warrens found, to his great joy, that his ship had not sustained any serious injury. He remarked with surprise that the accumulated icebergs, which had the preceding evening formed an impenetrable barrier, had been separated and disengaged by the wind, and that in one place a canal of open sea wound its course among them as far as the eye could discern.

It was two miles beyond the entrance of this canal that a ship made its appearance about noon. The sun shone brightly at the time, and a gentle breeze blew from the north. At first some intervening icebergs prevented Captain Warrens from distinctly seeing anything but her mast; but he was struck with the strange manner in which her sails were disposed, and with the dismantled aspect of her yards and rigging. She continued to go before the wind for a few furlongs, and then, grounding upon low icebergs, remained motionless. Captain Warrens's curiosity was so much excited that he immediately leaped into his boat with several seamen and rowed toward her.

On approaching, he observed that her hull was miserably weather-beaten, and not a soul appeared on the deck, which was covered with snow to a considerable depth. He hailed her crew several times, but no answer was returned. Previous to stepping on board, an open port-hole near the main chains caught his eye, and on looking into it, he perceived a man reclining back in a chair, with writing materials on a table before him, but the feebleness of the light made everything very indistinct. The party went up on deck, and having removed the hatchway, which they found closed, they descended to the cabin.

They first came upon the cabin which Captain Warrens had viewed through the port-hole. A tremor seized him as he entered it. Its inmate retained its former position, and seemed to be insensible to strangers. He was found to be a corpse, and a green damp mold had covered his cheeks and forehead, and veiled his eye-balls. He had a pen in his hand, and a log-book lay before him, the last sentence in whose unfinished page ran thus: "November 11th, 1762. We have now been enclosed in the ice seventeen days. The fire went out yesterday, and our master has been trying ever since to kindle it again without success. His wife died this morning. There is no relief."

Captain Warrens and his seamen hurried from the spot without uttering a word. On entering the principal cabin, the first object that attracted their attention was the dead body of a female, reclining on a bed in an attitude of deep interest and attention. Her countenance retained the freshness of life, and a contraction of the limbs alone showed that her form was inanimate. Seated on the floor was the corpse of an apparently young man, holding a steel in one hand and a flint in the other, as if in the act of striking fire upon some tinder which lay beside him. In the forepart of the vessel several sailors were found lying dead in their berths, and the body of a boy was crouched at the bottom of the gangway stairs.

Neither provisions nor fuel could be discovered anywhere; but Captain Warrens was prevented, by the superstitious prejudices of his seamen, from examining the vessel as minutely as he wished to have done. He therefore carried away the log-book already mentioned, and returning to his own ship, immediately steered to the southward, deeply impressed with the awful example which he had just witnessed of the danger of navigating the polar seas in high northern latitudes.

On returning to England, he made various inquiries respecting vessels that had disappeared in an unknown way, and by comparing these results with the information which was afforded by the written documents in his possession, he ascertained the name and history of the imprisoned ship and her unfortunate master, and found that she had been frozen in thirteen years previous to the time of his discovering her imprisoned in the ice.

# III

# Salty Speech

## *Cries, Epithets, Gripes, and Maxims*

"Of all the fabricks, a ship is the most excellent, requiring more art in building, rigging, sayling, trimming, defending, and mooring, with such a number of severall termes and names in continual motion, not understood of any landsman, as none would think of, but some few that know them."

*Captain John Smith*

THIS is not an attempt at a marine dictionary, nor will the reader find definitions of strictly technical terms. The main effort has been to give as many examples as possible of the mariner's way of saying things that are said differently by shore birds. There is slang and cant and a little profanity taken from all branches of the calling. If a term or a phrase belongs exclusively to one group, it has been given a distinguishing mark: (*f*) fishermen; (*l*) Great Lakesmen; (*n*) navy; (*s*) shellfishermen and (*w*) whalers.

A.B.  Short for *able-bodied seaman*, the official rating of a first-class sailor.

ABACK  Pressed backward; said of a square sail when the wind is directed against the front part of it, tending to force the vessel astern. To be taken aback means to be shocked or surprised.

ABAFT  Behind. Used in conjunction with some object; for instance, "abaft the foremast" = "behind the foremast."

ABEAM  On a line at right angles to a ship's side.

ACCOUNT, ON THE ACCOUNT  Pirates were said to be "on the account," or "on the main chance."

ADRIFT  Broken from its moorings or fasts. Said of any object

that has been mislaid or is found missing, even to a member of the crew who has failed to show up at sailing time.

**AFT** In the direction of the stern.

**AFTERGUARD, THE** The officers. In the navy, the men assigned to duty on the quarter-deck.

**AGAINST THE SUN** Counterclockwise.

**AHOLD** Close-hauled.

**AHOY** The conventional hail.

**AHULL** Hove to under bare poles.

**ALEE** On or toward the lee side, the side opposite that from which the wind blows. The helm is alee when the tiller is moved to the lee side.

**ALL A-TAUNTO** Every spar in place and properly rigged. All tight.

ALL GONE, SIR! The sailor's reply after obeying an order to cast off.

ALL HANDS AND THE COOK Just what it implies; the second and third mates, the sailmaker, the carpenter, and the steward were included in the order.

ALL-HANDS SHIP Practically an undermanned vessel, using only "as many cats as catch a mouse."

ALL HANDS FORWARD TO SPLICE THE MAIN BRACE A British order to come forward for an extra ration of grog as a reward for difficult or unusual service. American masters did not share their liquor with their crews.

ALL IN THE WIND With all sails shaking.

ALL LEGS AND WINGS Said of a vessel that is thought to be carrying too much sail. Also, *all arms and legs*.

*Alow* has given way to *below*, and the current phrase is "aloft, alow and below."

ALOW FROM ALOFT! (*w*) An order to the men in the hoops to descend to the deck, to give up looking.

AMAIN Suddenly; quick; at once.

ANCHOR The hook, mudhook, killick; the bowers, left and right or port and starboard. The hooks are called the *flukes* or *palms*, the shaft is the *shank*, and the transverse bar is the *stock;* the anchor chain is the *cable*, and the holes in the bows through which the cable passes are the *hawse-pipes*. When not in use the anchors are lashed to the deck of the forecastle, ready for instant use; when they are wanted they are *unstowed*, swung out, and lowered until the slack in the cable has been taken up, and are then *let go*. When an anchor has reached the ground it is *bitted*—that is, the cable is made fast within the ship. The anchor is *weighed* when the slack in the cable has been taken in by means of the windlass, and as it leaves the bottom it is *apeak* and, yielding to the strain, is *riding home;* as it breaks the surface it is *awash*, and when brought to the bows it is *catted*, swung into place, and *stowed*.

ALL SHIPSHAPE AND BRISTOL FASHION Everything in proper order and in its proper place.

ALL STANDING  A vessel brought to a quick stop is brought up "all standing." To turn in all standing means to turn in for sleep with one's work clothes on.

ALOFT AND ALOW  Formerly, any place above or below the deck.

ANTI-GALLICAN HITCH  A knot that cannot be untied and has to be cut.

APEAK  Vertical. When the cable is hove taut so as to bring the bow of the vessel directly above the anchor, the anchor is apeak. Dana writes: "The yards are *a-peek* when they are topped by contrary lifts."

APOISE  A well-trimmed ship under full sail is apoise.

APOSTLES  Another name for the bollards and bitts of a sailing vessel.

ARM THE LEAD  To fill the cavity of the lead with grease or tallow to bring up a sample of the bottom.

ARTICLES, SHIP'S  The contract signed by a seaman in joining a ship.

ASLEEP  A sail is asleep when there is just enough wind to keep her full and not flapping.

ASTERN  Behind the vessel; also in or toward the after part of a ship.

ATHWART  Across, at right angles.

ATHWARTHAWSE  Across a vessel's bow or cable.

ATHWARTSHIPS  Across the line of a vessel's keel.

ATRIP  Just clear of the bottom; said of the anchor.

AVAST  Usually *'vast*. An order to stop; as, " 'Vast heaving!" or " 'Vast hauling!"

AWASH  Level with the surface of the water, as when the seas wash over the deck of a vessel.

AWEATHER  On or toward the weather or windward side, the side from which the wind blows. The helm is aweather when it is moved to the windward side.

**Aye** Usually "Aye, aye, sir!" used by all ranks to a superior in acknowledging an order.

**Bald-headed** Of a schooner, without topmasts; of a square-rigged ship, with no sails above her topgallants.

**Baleen** (*w*) Whalebone.

**Ballyhoo of blazes** Confusion.

**Banian day** Sometimes *banyan day*. A meatless day aboard a vessel, usually Thursday. From the Banians, a sect in India, who eat no animal food.

**Banker** (*f*) A fishing vessel on the Grand Banks of Newfoundland.

**Bare poles** A vessel with no sails set is under bare poles. Sometimes *bare poles under*.

**Bark** A vessel with three or more masts, square-rigged on all save the aftermost, which is fore-and-aft rigged.

**Barkentine** A vessel with three or more masts, square-rigged on the foremast and fore-and-aft rigged on all others.

**Barnacle backs** Old sailors.

**Beach, on the** Said of a sailor ashore, usually without a ship or the hope of getting a berth in one.

**Beam** The width of the ship.

**Beam-ends, on her** Of a vessel, listing to such an extent that her beams are almost vertical.

**Bear** To be in a certain direction from the person looking; as, "The headland bore west-southwest." To bear down is to approach from the windward; to bear up is to run off to the leeward; to bear off is to clear an object.

**Bear a hand** To lend a hand.

**Beating** Making to the windward by tacking.

**Becket** Anything used to confine loose ropes. A handle made of rope in the form of a circle is called a becket.

**Before the mast** To ship before the mast is to ship as a sailor as distinguished from an officer—from the fact that sailors are quartered in the forecastle.

BELAY   To make a rope fast; to stop.

BELAYING PIN   A bar of metal or wood set in rails for securing the running rigging.

BELAYING PIN HASH (SOUP)   Brutal treatment of sailors by officers.

BELLS   The ship's bell is struck once for every half-hour elapsed in a watch. Thus 12:30 is marked by one bell, 1 o'clock by two bells, and so on until 4 o'clock, which is indicated by eight bells. At 4:30 one bell is again struck. "How many bells have gone?" is a sailor's way of asking the time.

BEND   To make fast. A bend is a knot by which one rope is made fast to another.

BERTH   The place where a vessel lies; also the bunk in which a person sleeps aboard a vessel. To give a person or a ship a wide berth is to keep clear of him or her.

BETWEEN WIND AND WATER   At a level the side of the vessel just above the waterline. Sometimes said of a sick seaman hovering between life and death.

BIBLES AND PRAYER BOOKS   The larger holystones are called bibles; the smaller, hand stones, are prayer books.

BIBLE BACKS (f)   Fishermen who will not fish on Sundays.

BIBLE LEAVES (w)   Blubber cut in thin strips for trying out.

BIG FISH, THE   Sometimes *big codfish*. The leader in the forecastle.

BIGHT   Literally any part of a rope except the ends, usually one of the flakes of a rope folded on deck. Also a break in the shore that makes a small inlet.

BIG IRON DOLLAR, THE (w)   The five-dollar bill which was given as a matter of custom to a whaleman with no money due him at the end of the voyage.

BILGE   The inside part of the vessel upon which she would rest were she aground. The greatest circumference of a cask.

BILGE, TO   To beef, complain, or grouse. Also to talk boastfully.

BILGED   A vessel stove in at the bilge or keel. Drunken. Flunked out in an examination.

BILGER (*n*)   An Annapolis midshipman who has been demoted.

BINNACLE   Formerly *bittacle*, from the Spanish *bittacole*. The housing for the ship's compass. "The old binnacle," writes Leslie, "besides containing the ship's compasses and a light between them, was used as a place to stow the log-reel, line and clip, with its half-minute glass, the log-board, and traverse-board, also charts in immediate use."

BITTS   Strong timbers framed together upright in the fore part of a vessel's main deck, around which the cable had a turn when the ship rode at anchor.

BLACKSTRAP (*n*)   Molasses; also the dark wines of the Mediterranean.

BLACKWALL HITCH   A turn of a rope about a hook in such a way that it binds itself.

BLANKET (*w*)   The first cutting of blubber from a whale. It is cut into horse pieces for storing on the blubber deck.

BLOOD SHIP   A vessel officered by cruel and exacting men.

BLOW-ALONG, ROLL-ALONG TUB   Any heavy going, ungainly vessel.

BLUBBER HUNTER   A whaler.

BLUENOSER   A Nova Scotiaman.

BLUE PETER   The international code signal for the letter P, which is blue with a white square. When this is hoisted to the fore, it signifies that the ship is about to sail.

BLUE PIGEON   The hand lead. See *Dipsey lead*.

BLUE-WATER MAN   Sometimes *deepwater man*. A deep-sea sailor.

BOARD HO! (*w*)   Warning shouted when a blanket piece is about to be swung inboard.

BOATSWAIN   (Pronounced bosun.) An unlicensed officer in charge of the crew, a straw boss. He is a member of the first mate's watch and usually takes charge of deck work while that officer is on watch.

BOATSWAIN'S MATE    The alternate of the above, a member of the captain's or second mate's watch.

BOATSWAIN'S CHAIR    A seat suspended by a bridle and used to take a man aloft in working on the rigging, or over the side of a vessel. Used ashore by riggers and steeplejacks.

BOATSWAIN'S LOCKER    A cuddy given over to the boatswain's stores but often a catchall for anything that might come in handy in an emergency.

BODGO! (f)    "It was the custom for Marblehead men to hail vessels passing in a fog, at night, or in the distance within hearing, with the cry of 'Bodgo!' If the reply came back 'Molly Waldo,' it was known the vessel hailed was a Marblehead fishing schooner." *

BONE IN HER TEETH (MOUTH)    The white foam of the bow waves.

BOOT-TOPPING    Originally the act of scraping grass, slime, and barnacles from a vessel's bottom and paying it over with a coating of tallow and sulphur, or lime and resin, designed to discourage the elements that had been scraped off. Now a composition used to paint above and below the waterline.

BOWER    An anchor carried forward. The best bower is the heavier of the two forward anchors.

BOWGRACE    Old junk or chain hung over the bow at the waterline to defend the vessel against the cutting, sawlike action of drift ice.

BOWHEAD (w)    The right whale.

BOWSE    To haul upon a tackle. To put back into a task. Also (n) to drink immoderately.

BREAM    To clean a ship's bottom by burning.

BREAKER (w)    The small cask of drinking water carried in a whaleboat.

BRIG    A vessel with two masts, square-rigged on both. Also (n) the ship's prison.

BRIGANTINE    A vessel with two masts, square-rigged on the foremast and fore-and-aft rigged on the mainmast. Formerly called a hermaphrodite brig.

* Roads, *The History and Traditions of Marblehead.*

BRIGHT LOOKOUT, A   An alert and wakeful lookout.

BRIGHT SIDE   The polished and varnished band around an American ship.

BRIGHTWORK.   The brasswork that must be polished.

BRISTOW   Bristol, England.

BROACH TO   A vessel broaches to when, sailing before the wind, she comes to the windward and lies in a trough of the sea. This may be the result of bad steering, a very high sea, or from some accident to the rudder or sails.

BROKEN-BACKED   Also *hogged*. Said of a ship when, from age or mistreatment, her frame is so loosened as to allow her to droop at either or both ends.

BROUGHT UP TO THE MAST (*n*)   Often also *masted*. Brought before the captain on charges of misbehavior.

BROW   The gangway.

BULGINE, BULLGINE   The Negro stevedores' name for the donkey engine.

BULL   A small keg, one holding but a gallon or two.

BUMBOAT   The small boat used by shore peddlers who visit ships selling native fruits, souvenirs, etc.

BUNG UP AND BILGE-FREE   Slang for "I'm all right!" When casks are properly stowed, bungs are up and the casks rest on racks to keep them clear of the water in the bilge.

BUNGS (*w*)   The ship's cooper.

BUNT   The middle of a square sail.

BURGEE   A small tapered or swallow-tail pennant.

BURGOO   A porridge made of oatmeal or mush.

BY THE HEAD, BY THE STERN   Said of a vessel when one end is lower in the water than the other.

BY THE WIND   Short of cash.

CABLE   The heavy rope, wire, or chain used on anchors and in towing.

CABLE'S LENGTH   Variously from 100 to 120 fathoms.

CABLE TIER   The place in the hold where cables are stowed.

CABLE, TO SLIP ONE'S   To die.

CABOOSE   A house on a vessel's deck, usually the galley.

CACHALOT (w)   A sperm whale.

CALLYO   (Pronounced cal-eye'oh.) Callao, Peru.

CALL AWAY (w)   The ready signal for a whaleboat to leave. The final order is "away!"

CAMEL   A buoyant device for assisting vessels over a shoal or a bar. Any heavy, bluff-bowed vessel.

C AND S (n)   Clean and sober, in describing the condition in which a sailor returned from liberty; the opposite of *D and D*, drunk and dirty.

CANT   To turn, especially a vessel in a river or harbor.

CANVASBACK   A steam sailor's term for a sailing-vessel sailor.

CAPE HORN CURRENT   Easterly current in the vicinity of the Cape.

CAPE HORN FEVER   A feigned illness.

CAPE HORN SNORTER   A heavy gale.

CAPE STIFF   Sailor's name for Cape Horn.

CAREEN   To lie over when sailing on the wind. Also, to heave a vessel down on her side for the purpose of cleaning her bottom.

CARRICK BEND   The real sailor's knot, used to bend two ropes together. There are single, double, and open carrick bends.

CARRY AWAY   To break, to be lost or washed overboard.

CARRY ON OR CARRY UNDER   The creed of the packet captains— crowd on all sail and to hell with the risk.

CAST   To throw. To turn by throwing a vessel's head to port or starboard in getting under way.

CAT   The tackle used to hoist the anchor to the cathead.

CAT BLOCK   The block of the same tackle.

**CATHEAD**  Large timbers projecting from the vessel's sides to which the anchor is raised and secured.

**CAT THE ANCHOR**  The act of bringing the anchor to the cathead.

**CAT, THE**  The cat-o'-nine-tails. Nine pieces of leather or cord eighteen inches in length, fastened to a handle of rope; each tail had three knots near the end.

**CAT, THIEVES**  The same as above with metal balls instead of knots. Affectionately called "the gunner's daughter."

**CATCH A TURN**  To make a rope temporarily fast around a bitt.

**CAT'S-PAW**  A light current of air that disturbs the surface of the water during a calm. Also a kind of hitch made in a rope by which two eyes are formed.

**CHAPELING**  "A ship was said to build a chapel when, without headway, she turned completely around in a light or baffling wind" (Leslie). Now used for the act of wearing a ship around without bracing the head yards.

**CHARLEY NOBLE** (*n*)  The pipe of the galley stove. To shoot Charley Noble is to discharge a pistol into the pipe to clear it of soot.

**CHARLIES**  Officers of the law seeking smugglers among sailors.

**CHEWING HER OAKUM** (*f*)  Said of a vessel that is losing the oakum in her seams.

**CHRONOMETER**  The ship's clock.

**CHECK**  To slack off a bit on a rope or a brace, usually following the order to belay.

**CHEERLY, MEN!**  Sometimes *cherrily;* quickly and with a will.

**CHINSE**  To caulk with oakum with a small iron.

**CHIPS**  Nickname for the ship's carpenter.

**CHOKE THE LUFF**  To jam the sheave of a block with an end of rope. "I choked his luff" means "I told him just where he got off."

**CHOW RAG** (*n*)  The mess pennant.

**CHURCHYARD WATCH**  The watch between midnight and four in the morning, sometimes called the graveyard watch.

CLAP ON To put on more sail, sometimes an order to seize hold of a rope or other object.

CLAP A STOPPER ON YOUR TONGUE Mind what you are saying, there are officers present.

CLEAN SHIP (w) A whaler that has returned to port without oil.

CLOSE-HAULED Applied to a vessel with sails trimmed to sail as close to the wind as possible.

CLUBBING Drifting with the current with an anchor dragging the bottom.

CLUBHAULING Bringing a vessel's head around on the other tack by letting go the lee anchor as soon as the wind is out of her sails, after which, the moment her headsails are aback, the helm is put amidships, the cable slipped or cut, and the sails trimmed on the other tack.

COBBING Corporal punishment—"the application of a barrel stave to the rear end of a seaman."

COCKBILL The yards are acockbill when they are hauled at different angles, the lower mainyards inclining to the starboard, the fore and mizzen to port, while the upper yards on each mast take a direction opposite to that of the lower ones; a sign of mourning. The anchor is acockbill when it hangs by its ring at the cathead, ready for dropping.

COCKPIT (n) The well or small compartment near the after hatch of a man-of-war, used by the surgeon during an action.

COLD AS BLUE FLUGIN (FLUJIN) So cold, according to sailors, that fire freezes.

COLT, A TOUCH OF THE The colt was a short length of rope or hose carried by the boatswain and used as a persuader on slow-moving sailors.

COME DOWN UPON (n) To attack from the windward.

COME UP, TO To slacken off on a rope or cable.

COME HOME The anchor comes home when it breaks from the ground.

COMPASS, TO BOX THE To recite the thirty-two points in order.

COMPOSITE SHIP   A vessel with a wooden hull upon a steel frame.

CON (CONN)   To exercise control of the steering of a vessel; an officer cons the ship by directing the movements of the helmsman.

COURSES   Sails hanging from a ship's lower yards. The foresail is called the forecourse and the mainsail the main course.

COXSWAIN   (Pronounced cox'n.) The man who steers the small boat and has charge of it.

CRANG (*w*)   The remains of the whale after the blubber has been flensed off.

CRANK   Said of a vessel that is inclined to lean over and that cannot bear much sail, due to faulty construction, strains, or bad stowage.

CRIMP   The agent or runner for a sailors' boardinghouse keeper.

CRINKUM-CRANKUM (*w*)   A whale too smart to be caught.

CROSSJACK YARD (CROJACK, CROJICK)   The lower yard on the mizzenmast. "The lateen mizzen-yard, about the year 1800, became a gaff; but the lower yard upon the mizzen-mast, which should have succeeded to the title, never did so but remained a crojack, or cross-jack yard and rarely had a sail upon it, until some fifty years ago, about 1840, when a Yankee captain set what he called a crojack, or mizzen-course upon it. But old English skippers only shook their heads when they saw one, and knew the ship ten miles off for a damned Yankee" (Leslie). Whalers called it the crotchet.

CROWD   To put on all sail possible.

CRUMB BOSUN   Any boy or poor seaman who was detailed to help the cook or the steward.

CUDDY   Usually a small cabin aboard a small vessel. On large ships the carpenter's cabin was usually called his cuddy.

CUN (*n*)   Same as *con*.

CUT AND COME AGAIN   Food, usually hard bread or a dish of beans, left on the mess table at all times for the convenience of the crew.

CUT AND RUN   To cut the cable and run off before the wind to escape an enemy or danger. "He cut and run the moment he saw us."

**CUT ONE'S PAINTER**   To die or desert. Also to get going, be on one's way.

**D AND D** (*n*)   Drunk and dirty. See *C and S*.

**DANSKER**   A Dane or Danish vessel.

**DANDY FUNK**   A pudding made of crumbled ships' biscuits, fat, and molasses and baked. Also *dunderfunk*.

**DARBIES** (*n*)   Handcuffs. In the merchant marine all such constrainers were called irons.

**DART** (*w*)   The harpoon; it is darted, never thrown.

**DAY**   The nautical day is reckoned as beginning and ending at noon, in distinction from the civil day, which begins and ends at midnight. In the United States Navy, the day the eagle screams is payday.

**DEADEYES**   The three-holed wooden blocks through which the lanyards that connect the shrouds with the ship's side pass. Originally *deadman's eyes,* from their resemblance to a skull.

**DEADEYES UNDER**   Listing.

**DEAD HORSE**   The time a sailor has to work to pay off his advance.

**DEADLIGHTS**   Originally heavy port lights placed in the cabin windows in bad weather. In modern ships they are the metal plates that protect the port light in the same instances.

**DEAD MARINE** (**DEAD SOLDIER**) (*n*)   An empty bottle. Qualified in the presence of marines or soldiers by the addition of "He has done his duty and is ready to do it again."

**DEAD MEN**   Reef or gasket ends hanging free. See *Irish pennants*.

**DEAD RECKONING**   Literally deduced reckoning. A reckoning kept to show the theoretical position of the ship, without referring to objects on land or the taking of the sun, but relying on the courses steered and the distances run.

**DEAD WHALE OR A STOVE BOAT, A**   A whaler's boast.

**DEEP SIX** (**DEEP EIGHT**)   The deep sea. Anything thrown overboard that will sink is said to have been given to deep six.

DEEPWATER MAN    An all-round sailor, not one who confines himself to fishing, whaling, or coastwise vessels.

DEVIL TO PAY AND NO PITCH HOT    A lost opportunity. The devil is a seam between the garboard and the keel and one difficult to calk. Often when the ship was listed and the opportunity offered, it came when there was no pitch ready for use.

DEVIL'S HOLE, OR DEVIL'S BLOWHOLE    According to Captain S. Samuels, this storm center of the Atlantic is about latitude 45°, longitude 45°.

DIFFERENT SHIPS, DIFFERENT LONG SPLICES    Procedures differ according to vessels and officers.

DIPSEY LEAD    The deep-sea lead.

DIRTY WORK FOR CLEAN MONEY    Service on a whaleship.

DITTY BAG (BOX)    Sailor's receptacle for holding sewing kit, buttons, etc.

DIVE THE TWINE (f)    Of a fish, to escape a purse-seine before it can be closed.

DOCTOR    Nickname for the ship's cook.

DOG-BARKING NAVIGATOR    The deepwater man's term for a coastal navigator. It was supposed that he determined the ship's position by recognizing the barks of the dogs along shore.

DOG BEFORE ITS MASTER    The swell that precedes a gale.

DOG WATCHES    Half watches of two hours each, from 4 to 6, and from 6 to 8 P.M. The watches are changed (dogged) at 6 P.M.

DONKEY    Sailors' name for a duffel bag.

DONKEY'S BREAKFAST    A straw-filled mattress.

DOWN THE WIND    To leeward.

DO YOU HEAR THE NEWS?    A call used to turn out the new watch. See *Rise and shine*.

DREENER (s)    A drainer.

DRY NURSE    See *Paper jack*.

DROGHER    A West Indian coasting vessel. The term is applied to one-cargo vessels: lumber droghers, guano droghers, hide droghers, etc.

DRUDGE (s)  A dredge.

DUFF  A corruption of dough, a mixture of flour and water, with raisins or prunes added (plum duff) and baked, a delicacy. Sometimes called figgy duff, lum duff. The day, usually Thursday, when duff was served instead of meat was known as duff day.

DYING MAN'S DINNER  The food, usually cold and eaten out of hand, served during an emergency.

FAKE  A single complete turn of a rope in a coil. A French fake is a rope coiled flat and concentrically to form a mat.

FAKE DOWN  To lay a rope so that it will pay out freely.

FANG  To prime—as, "to fang the pumps."

FARE (f)  The haul or catch of a vessel.

FARMING  At sea, any work not strictly nautical. Also, loafing.

FAST  To make secure, to tie. In New England they say, "A woman ties a horse, a man hitches him, but a sailor makes him fast."

FAST HO! (w)  Cry of the harpooner, and the signal to the ship that the whale has been harpooned.

FAVOR  To ease.

FEASE (FEAZE)  To unravel a rope's end.

FID  A hardwood pin similar to a marlinspike used in splicing and for other duties.

FIDDLERS' GREEN  Originally any shore resort where there were women, music, dancing, and drinking. Latterly it became the name for the sailors' paradise. Also *Lubber Land*.

FIELD DAY (n)  The day, usually Friday, given over to cleaning ship.

FIRST LUFF (n)  A first lieutenant.

FISHERMAN'S PHILOSOPHY  Sometimes you think you are going to make a fortune, but you never do; sometimes you think you are going to starve to death, but you never do.

FISHERMAN'S WALK   Any restricted place; from the size of a fishing boat, where it would be "three steps and overboard."

FISHY MAN, A (*f*)   One who knows where the fish are biting.

FIVE AND FORTY MORE! (*w*)   The happy cry when the last piece of blubber has been brought aboard. "Five and forty m-o-r-e!"

FLASH PACKET   A fine-appearing vessel. Also, a woman of the port towns.

FLAT ABACK   See *Aback*.

FLEMISH COIL   According to Dana, a rope coiled so that each fake rides the fake beneath. Nowadays *Flemished down*.

FLOGGING THE BOOBY   Warming oneself by beating the arms against the body.

FLOGGING THE CLOCK   Changing the time when sailing east or west.

FLOGGING THE GLASS   Trying to hurry the sand through the glass to shorten the watch.

FLURRY (*w*)   The whale's dying struggle.

FLYING-FISH SAILOR   A term applied to sailors who took shore jobs during the cold winter months.

FOREBITTER   Old name for a sea song or ballad.

FOREIGN PORTS   Asked what he had seen in such and such a port, the old sailor dismissed it with: "Like any other place, filled with Yankee ships, Limejuice skippers, Bluenose mates, Norwegian sailors, Swedish matches, and German women."

FOUL   Opposite of clear.

FOUR-POSTER   A four-masted vessel.

FRESH HAND AT THE BELLOWS   A phrase used when a gale increases.

FRAP   To bring together with ropes; to pass ropes round a sail to keep it from blowing loose.

FULL AND BY   Sailing close-hauled on a wind. As an order given to the man at the helm it means to keep the sails full and at the same time close to the wind. Also said of a person who has had more than enough to drink.

FULL AND PLENTY  Describing the usual rations on an American ship.

GAM (w)  "A social gathering of two (or more) Whale-ships, generally on a cruising-ground; when, after exchanging hails, they exchange visits by boats' crews; the two captains remaining for a time, on board of one ship, and the two chief mates on the other" (Melville, *Moby Dick*).

GEAR  The sailor's term for the tools of his trade, or for his personal possessions. Ship's gear would be the appurtenances of the vessel.

GHOSTING ALONG  Of a vessel, making headway when there is no apparent wind.

GIBS (f)  Gurry, entrails of fish, waste.

GIRLS HAVE HOLD OF THE TOW-ROPE  Said when a vessel is making good headway on the homeward voyage.

GLORY HOLE  The lazarette or other place where specie and treasure were kept.

GO ABOUT  To take the opposite tack.

GO BELOW THE WATCH  The usual form for dismissing the watch.

GOING BOARD AND BOARD (f)  Visiting other boats on the Grand Banks.

GONEY  The albatross.

GOOSEWINGED  Of a sail, furled on one side only.

GRANNY  Any unseamanlike knot or hitch.

GRAVEYARD WATCH  The middle or 12 midnight to 4 A.M. watch. The lookout on the graveyard watch is often called "gravy-eye."

GREGO (n)  Greatcoat, the sailor's heavy outer coat worn while on watch in the colder zones.

GREASY LUCK (w)  A phrase used to wish a whaler good fortune.

GROG  Diluted rum. Named for Admiral Vernon, Royal Navy, who first served it in place of neat rum, and who was called "Old Grog" from his grogram greatcoat. Sailors said, "I would rather have my wind stopped than my grog."

GROUNDING ON HER BEEF-BONES   Said of a ship that has been long anchored in the same spot—referring to the amount of garbage dumped overboard over a long period.

GUNNER'S DAUGHTER (*n*)   The cat-o'-nine-tails.

GUNNER'S DAUGHTER, MARRYING THE (*n*)   Being flogged over a gun.

HAIRLEGGER   New England fishermen's term for a farmer.

HALF-SEAS OVER   Half drunk.

HAND   To hand a sail is to furl it; hand-over-hand, hauling rapidly on a rope; bear a hand, make haste; lend a hand, assist.

HAND GEAR   Any device using manpower.

HAND, REEF, AND STEER   Abilities required of an ordinary seaman.

HAND LEAD   The small lead used in sounding in shallow waters. Also known as the blue pigeon.

HANDSOMELY   Slowly, carefully; little by little, as in easing off.

HANDSPIKE   A bar for lifting heavy weights. When used at the windlass, it is called a capstan bar.

HANDSPIKE HASH   A blow with a handspike; a harsh method of enforcing discipline.

HANDY BILLY   A watch tackle; a small hand pump.

HARNESS CASK   The receptacle in which were kept the daily rations of salt meat. The name may have been derived from the bright bands of metal secured with gilt screws surrounding the cask, or from the toughness of the meat, sailors often insisting that instead of a piece of meat they had been served the harness of the horse.

HARD AWEATHER   To put the helm hard over toward the weather side.

HARD OVER   As far over as the helm will go.

HARDTACK   Hard bread, ship's biscuit.

HARD AND FAST   Completely aground.

HARD FISH   Fish that has been salted and dried.

**HARRIET LANE** Canned meat. Taken over from the Royal Navy, from the girl whose murdered body was cut up and hidden in a box.

**HAT MONEY** A bonus given a shipmaster for the safe delivery of cargo. Formerly *hatch money*.

**HARD ALEE** To put the helm hard over toward the lee side.

**HAUL** The sailor's word for *pull*. "Haul away" is the order to pull on a rope.

**HAUL HER WIND** A vessel when she comes up close upon the wind is said to haul her wind.

**HAZE** "A word of frequent use on board ship. It is very expressive to a sailor, and means to punish by hard work" (Dana).

**HEAVE** The sailor's word for *throw*.

**HEAVE AHEAD** To move forward.

**HEAVE AND AWEIGH** The order to man the windlass and break out the anchor.

**HEAVE AND PAWL** To exert pressure on the windlass or capstan until a pawl drops.

**HEAVE DOWN** To careen for cleaning or repairing the hull.

**HEAVE SHORT** To heave in on the cable until the bow of the vessel is over her anchor.

**HEAVE TO** To put the vessel in the position of lying to.

**HEAVE UP ANCHOR** To die.

**HELL BOX** The galley stove.

**HELL SHIP** A ship officered by hard cases.

**HEN FRIGATE** A ship with the captain's wife aboard. The men always believe the wife is the real captain.

**HIGH LINE** (*f*) The man on board who catches the most fish.

**HIT THE BEACH** (*n*) To go on shore leave.

**HIT THE DECK** (*n*) The phrase used to summon the watch; the same as "Do you hear the news?"

HERMAPHRODITE BRIG  Former name for a brigantine.

HERRING CHOKER  New England term for a fisherman.

HOGGED  See *Broken-backed*.

HOIST  (Invariably pronounced h'ist.)  "H'ist away!"

HOLDERS (*n*)  The men whose duties confine them to the holds of vessels. "They may circumnavigate the world fifty times, and they see about as much of it as Jonah did in the whale's belly" (Melville).

HOLIDAY  An unpainted or unwashed spot on any part of a vessel.

HOMEWARD-BOUND STITCHES  Careless or clumsy sewing, usually with sail twine, just enough to keep a sailor's clothes going until he reaches port.

HOLYSTONES  Blocks of sandstone used in whitening wooden decks. The large stones, operated with a handle, were called bibles; the smaller hand stones were called prayer books.

HOOKER  An old vessel, from the Dutch *hoeker*. Also a woman of the town.

HOODLUMS  Usually men shipped by crimps as able-bodied seamen and found to be lubbers after the vessel had left port.

HOOSIERS  Same as *hoodlums*.

HORSE LATITUDES  The belt of calms at the northern edge of the northeast trade winds.

HORSE SALTS  Glauber salts or other purgatives prescribed for sailors.

HUG A BIGHT AND SHUN A POINT  A pilot's maxim. In working a ship against a tide, a pilot avoids the swift currents off points and takes advantage of every tidal eddy in the bights.

HURRAH'S NEST (HOORAH'S NEST)  Confusion.

IDLER  Any one on board a vessel who, being at work all day, does not keep watch at night, but who is nevertheless expected to answer when all hands are called.

IF I HADN'T BEEN BORN A BLOODY FOOL I WOULDN'T HAVE JOINED THE NAVY. FIRE! (*n*)   Chant used for timing salutes.

IN A VESSEL   A mariner sails or ships in a vessel, never on her.

IN EVERYBODY'S MESS AND NOBODY'S WATCH   Said of a malingerer, or a busybody.

IRISH FITOUT   The sailor's meager wardrobe; "a put-on, a take-off, and a go-naked."

IRISH HURRICANE   Drizzling rain in a calm.

IRISH MAN-OF-WAR   A large unwieldy vessel, usually a barge that has to be towed.

IRISH PENNANT   Loose end of a rope or sail blowing free.

IRON MEN AND WOODEN SHIPS   "When I went to sea they had iron men and wooden ships, now they have iron ships and wooden men." A shellback's appraisal of modern sailors.

IRONS   Handcuffs and leg manacles. Also, the tools of the whaler's trade. A ship is said to be in irons when she fails to come about.


JACOB'S LADDER   A rope ladder with wooden rungs used over a vessel's side. Named for the ladder which Jacob dreamed reached from earth to heaven.

JAVA (JAMOCHA, JAMOKE) (*n*)   Coffee.

JEWING   Sewing clothes.

JEWING BAG   Another term for *ditty bag*.

JIB, THE CUT OF ONE'S   One's general appearance. "I didn't like the cut of his jib."

JIBBER THE KIBBER   To decoy ships ashore by false lights.

JIGGER   A small tackle used about decks or aloft.

JIMMY LEGS (*n*)   The master-at-arms.

JIMMY SQUAREFOOT   The devil.

JOHN COMPANY, THE   The Honorable East India Company. Probably the officers' nickname; the sailors had harsher words for the company.

JOHNNY CRAPPO   A Frenchman, from Jean Crapaud.

JOLLY BOAT   The most frequently used of the ship's boats; it was usually hoisted at the ship's stern.

JOLLY ROGER   The pirates' ensign.

JONAH   Anyone or anything supposed to bring or to be responsible for bad luck.

JUNK   Originally condemned rope set aside for making mats, swabs, oakum, etc. Latterly, any condemned gear.

JUNK, SALT   Salt meat, either pork or beef.

JUMP SHIP   To desert.

JURY   A term applied to any makeshift used in an emergency, as "jury anchor," "jury mast," etc. From the French *jour*, for the day.

KEELHAULING   Originally a Dutch form of punishment, in which the culprit was hauled under the ship's keel from one side to the other by a rope passing under the ship's bottom.

KEDGE ANCHOR   A light anchor used in warping.

KID   The wooden tub or trough in which the sailors' rations are carried from the galley. Kids were used for wet or liquid foods; barges were used for bread.

KEEP YOUR LUFF   Keep her close to the wind.

KILLICK   A small grapnel, sometimes the anchor.

KITTLE CARGO   A ticklish or hard-to-handle cargo.

KNOCK DOWN AND DRAG OUT   The bucko mate's method of getting a watch to turn out promptly.

KNOCK OFF   An order to stop working.

LABOR   A vessel is said to labor when she rolls or pitches heavily.

LANDFALL   The first land made after being at sea; when a vessel makes the land intended she has made a good landfall.

LAND HO!   The cry used when land is first seen.

LARBOARD  Formerly the left side, now called *port*.

LARBOWLINS (LARBOLINS)  The men of the port watch.

LARGE  Said of a vessel when she has the wind free.

LAUNCH HO!  High enough.

LAY  To come or go: "Lay aft!" "Lay aloft!"

LAY (f, w)  The individual's share in the takings of a fishing or whaling voyage.

LEAD  A cone of lead with a cavity in the base for holding tallow or grease, and used in sounding.

LEAD, ARM THE  To fill the cavity of the lead with soap or tallow.

LEAVE THE SEA AND GO INTO STEAM, TO  A sailor's expression for deserting sail.

LEE  The side opposite to that from which the wind blows.

LEEWARD  (Pronounced lu-ard.) The lee side.

LEEWAY  The distance a vessel is carried to the leeward.

LIFT  The weather lifts when it improves.

LIKE A DOG WETTING THE SNOW  The wake of a vessel when an awkward or lubberly hand is at the helm. Or, "An eel would break his back if he tried to follow our wake."

LIME-BURNER'S TWIST  A drink taken straight from the bottle.

LIMEJUICER  A British sailor or vessel.

LINE GALE  An equinoctial storm.

LOBLOLLY BOY  A boy at the beginning of his first voyage.

LOBSCOUSE ('SCOUSE)  A hashed and baked mixture of sea biscuit, chopped salt meat, potatoes, and onions.

LOG  (1) A mechanical device for measuring the distance a vessel has traveled or the speed at which she is traveling. There are patent or taffrail, harpoon, and chip Logs. (2) Also *Logbook*. A record kept by the chief officer in which the course, situation of the vessel, winds, weather, distances and matters to do with the vessel and its company are included. (3) To record in the log. To log a seaman is to punish him and record it in the log.

LONGBOAT  The largest boat in a merchant vessel, used only in emergencies. When at sea it was carried between the fore and main masts.

LONG SEA  A sea with the crests of waves far apart.

LONG SHIP (*n*)  Sometimes a dry ship, in which "it's a long time between drinks."

LONG TOGS  The sailor's shore clothes.

LORD OF THE PLANK  The officer on watch.

LORD RODNEY  The old sailor's name for his pigtail.

LUBBER  From land lover, an awkward or green hand.

LUBBER LAND  Another name for Fiddler's Green.

LUCKY BAG (*n*)  The receptacle in which are placed all unclaimed articles found on deck, later to be redeemed or auctioned.

LUFF  To bring a vessel up toward the wind.

LUFF (*n*)  A lieutenant.

LUFF AND TOUCH HER  To sail as close to the wind as possible.

MAKE  To attain an objective. To make land is to see it; to make sail is to set it; to make water is to leak; the tide makes, that is, comes in; a storm makes or comes up.

MAKE AND MEND DAY (*n*)  Usually Wednesday afternoon, given over to making and mending clothes. See *Rope yarn Sunday*.

MAKE BAD WEATHER OF IT  To do a disagreeable job in a disagreeable manner. To take umbrage at another's remark.

MAKE SAIL ON THE SLY (*n*)  To desert.

MAN, TO (*n*)  To take station, as in "man the capstan."

MAN, EVERY INCH OF HIM A  The highest praise a sailor could bestow upon an officer.

MANAVALINS  A term with various meanings, all relating to food. "At sea, the monotonous round of salt pork and beef at the messes of the sailors—where but very few of the varieties of the season are to be found—induces them to adopt many contrivances in order to diversify their meals. Hence the various sea-rolls, made dishes, and Mediterranean pies, well known by men-of-war's men—*Scouse, Lobscouse, Soft-tack, Soft-Tommy, Skillagalee, Burgoo, Dough-boys, Lob-Dominion, Dog's-Body,* and lastly, and least known, *Dunderfunk;* all of which come under the general denomination of *Manavalins*" (Melville).

MANIFEST　Actually the ship's passport. It contains all the documents necessary to enter or clear a port, the names of the owners, charterers, together with the nationalities of all members of the crew, the contents or cargo, consignee and origin, destination and all marks and symbols.

MARINE　Formerly, a man who was ignorant or clumsy about a seaman's work. A greenhorn. Also one who was reluctant to soil his hands or his clothes in dirty work. See *Soger.*

MARINE DUTY　"To make a sailor shoulder a handspike, and walk fore and aft the deck, like a sentry, is as ignominious a punishment as can be put upon him. Such a punishment inflicted upon an able seaman in a vessel of war might break down his spirit more than a flogging" (Dana).

MARLINSPIKE　An iron or steel tool used in making splices.

MARLINSPIKE SAILOR　One competent in the use of the tool.

MARRY　To bring two ropes together with a seizing.

MASTER TAKES HER OUT BUT THE MATE BRINGS HER HOME, THE Based upon the old rule that the starboard, or captain's watch, takes eight hours on deck the first night outward bound, and the port, or mate's watch, does the same the first night of the homeward-bound voyage.

MATELOW, MATLOW, MATTALOW　English slang for *sailor,* often applied to an old-timer.

MERRY MEN OF MAY　Currents caused by an ebbing tide.

MIDSHIPMEN'S NUTS　Broken pieces of sea-biscuit.

MITTEN MONEY　Extra pay for winter service.

MOLLY HAWK　The small albatross found in southern seas.

MOLLY WALDO!　See *Bodgo!*

MONKEY (*n*)  The wooden container in which grog was served.

MONKEY BAG (*n*)  The purse sailors wore tied about their necks to hold their money and valuables.

MOSES BOAT (*f*)  In the days of deck fishing only one boat was carried by the vessel; it corresponded to a ship's longboat.

MOTHER CAREY'S CHICKENS  The stormy petrel.

MUDHOOK  The anchor.

MUD PILOT  The pilot who takes a sea-going vessel into fresh water streams. One who pilots a ship by eye, studying the bottom and the changes of the color of the water.

MUG UP (*f*)  To go below for a cup of coffee.

MUX, MUXING  Another term for scrimshaw.

NANTUCKET SLEIGH RIDE (*w*)  This term refers to the wild ride experienced when a harpooned whale goes off with the whaleboat in tow. It has a literary sound.

NAVIGATOR *vs.* PILOT  A navigator gets frightened when he sees land and a pilot gets frightened when he can't see land.

NAVY CHEST  Sometimes Coast Guard chest. Too much fat around a man's waistline from living the easy life.

NEAP TIDES  The tides which occur at the time of the moon's first and last quarters, when the range between high and low tide is least.

NEAPED  A ship is said to be neaped when she has gone aground or is within a bar harbor during a spring tide and has not enough water to take her off the ground or over the bar until the next spring tide.

NIP  A short turn in a rope.

NIP AT THE CABLE (*n*)  A surreptitious drink.

NIPCHEESE (*n*)  A purser.

NO MORE CATS THAN CAN CATCH MICE  A crew just large enough to handle the necessary work aboard a ship; no extra hands.

NORSKER  A Norwegian ship or sailor.

NORWEGIAN STEAM    Human muscle.

NO SUNDAYS OFF SOUNDINGS    The seven-day work week while at sea.

NO SUNDAYS IN TEN FATHOMS (w)    The same.

NOVA SCOTIA PUMP    A bucket used in bailing.

OAR ON MY SHOULDER    "I'm going to put an oar over my shoulder and start walking inland until someone asks me what that stick I'm carrying is, and right there I'm going to settle down." The sailor hates the sea.

OFF AND ON    First on one tack and then on the other. An unmoored vessel waiting for the tide is standing off and on.

OFFICERS' COUNTRY    That part of any vessel reserved for the use of the officers.

OFFING    Distance from the shore.

OFF SOUNDINGS    Literally beyond the reach of land.

OFF THE WIND    Sailing with the sheets slacked off.

OLD MAN, THE    Regardless of his age, the captain.

ON THE BONES OF HIS BACK (NECK)    Broke and hungry.

ON THE WIND    Close-hauled.

OPEN AND SHUT    Alternating spells of clear and overcast weather.

ORLOP    The lowest deck, often the one on which the cables are stored.

O.S.    Ordinary seaman, one required to hand, reef and steer.

OVERRAKE    A ship is overraked when she takes water over her bows while at anchor in a head sea.

PACKET    A fast sailing vessel carrying passengers, mail, and freight and keeping to a schedule.

PACKET RATS    The tough and hardy men who manned the packet ships.

PAID BY THE LAY (w, f)    Sharing in the results of a voyage.

PAID OFF BY THE BOOM   Said of a man who had a big pay due and was conveniently knocked overboard by an officer.

PALM   The sailmaker's thimble. Also the flat of the fluke on an anchor.

PAPER JACK   A captain who knows nothing of navigation and is dependent upon his mate or mates, who are known as dry nurses.

PAPERS   The ship's manifest.

PARCEL   To wind tarred canvas about a rope. Also, to service.

PART   Ashore a rope breaks, at sea it parts.

PASSED FROM ONE END OF THE SHIP TO THE OTHER   Said of a man who has won promotion from the forecastle to the quarter-deck.

PATCH UPON PATCH AND A PATCH OVER ALL   The condition of a sailor's work clothes at the end of a long voyage. Variants: *patch upon patch like a sand-barge's mainsail; patched like a whaleman's shirt.*

PATENT   As in "patent log," is pronounced pay-tent. A "patent tackle" would be pay-tent tay-kel.

PAY   To pay is to cover with tar or pitch; to pay out is to slack up on a rope or cable and let it run out. Pay-off is when a vessel's head falls off from the wind.

PAY THE SHOT   To pay for something you did not ask for. From the old custom of a man-of-war's demand that the merchantman pay for the shot across his bows to stop, especially irksome when the merchantman's papers were found to be in good order.

PAY WITH A FLYING FORE-TOPSAIL (*n*)   To sail without paying one's shore debts. Also, *pay with the topsail sheet.*

P.D.L. (*n*)   Pass down the line.

PHILADELPHIA CATECHISM   It has one all-inclusive commandment: "Six days shalt thou labor and do all thou art able, and on the seventh holystone the deck and polish up the cable."

PIERHEAD JUMP OR LEAP   To desert just as the vessel is about to sail.

PIPE DOWN (*n*)   The call for silence.

**Pod** (*w*)   A group of whales, often miscalled a herd, or school.

**Pole**   A mast. In the old days it applied only to the tallest mast.

**Polish the Cape**   Of a vessel, to have difficulty in rounding either of the Capes.

**Poop**   The raised deck and after structure of a vessel.

**Pooped**   When the sea breaks over a vessel's stern, she is said to be pooped.

**Porchmouth**   Portsmouth.

**Port**   The left side of a vessel. Formerly *larboard*.

**Port your helm**   Put your helm to the larboard.

**Portingale**   A Portuguese.

**Portuguese man-of-war**   A floating jellyfish found in the warmer waters of the tropics.

**Portuguese parliament**   A gathering where everyone talks and no one seems to be listening.

**Pound and pint ships**   Poor feeders, from the British who are fed the Board of Trade schedule of a pound of food and a pint of liquid. See *Full and plenty*.

**Powder rag** (*n*)   Flag "B" flown when a vessel was loading ammunition. Used in the merchant marine when loading or carrying inflammables.

**Prayer book**   A small holystone.

**Pricker**   A small marlinspike used in sail making.

**Primage**   A percentage, usually 5 per cent, given the captain as a bonus. Later the term covered all the little grafts of the master, his percentage of money spent for supplies, repairs, etc., in foreign ports, carrying passengers between ports of call, etc.

**Privilege of boring, with**   A phrase usually included in offering a ship for inspection to a prospective purchaser to enable him to ascertain whether or not the vessel was sound.

**Purser rigged and parish damned**   From the English, said of a sailor who enlisted in the Navy because of poverty.

**Put**   To go, as in "put to sea," "put about."

QUARTER The part of a vessel's side between the after part of the main chains and the stern. The quarter of a yard is between the slings and the yardarm.

QUARTER-DECK That part of the upper deck abaft the mizzen. Usually reserved for the exclusive use of the officers.

QUARTERMASTER (*n*) A petty officer. In the merchant marine, the helmsman and lookout.

QUEER FELLOWS Shore birds, usually lubbers, who have official authority over ships in port.

QUINTAL (*f*) (Pronounced kentle.) A hundredweight (of fish).

RAISE To come within sight of: "raise the land," "raise Highland Light," etc.

RAISE THE WIND To obtain ready money by some expedient. See *Tarpaulin muster*.

RAM-CAT (*f*) The cabin stove.

RAMMEREES, THE The Diego Ramirez Rocks off Cape Horn.

RAP-FULL A little off the wind, with all sails drawing well.

RATTLING DOWN Fitting new ratlines to a vessel's shrouds.

RAVELINGS (*n*) Stingy or miserly sailors.

RAZEE To reduce a ship's height by removing her upper deck.

READY TO RIG HIS YARN TACKLE, ALWAYS Always ready with a yarn.

REEF To reduce a sail by taking it in upon its head.

REEFER (*n*) A midshipman.

REEVE To pass the end of a rope through a block, or through any aperture.

RENDERING Easing off or free passing of a rope through a block.

RIDE To lie at anchor. A vessel rides out a storm; she rides the waves, a rope rides when it passes easily. "Let her (it) ride!" indicates that conditions are good enough.

RIDE YOU DOWN AS I WOULD THE MAIN TACK, I'LL An officer's threat to break a man's spirit.

RIDING LIGHT   The anchor light.

RIG   The cut of a vessel, her sail and mast arrangements. To rig a vessel is to send aloft her spars and the rigging required, to ready her for her sails.

RIGGING   The ropes of a vessel. Also a common term for the shrouds with their ratlines. The running rigging is the running gear—the ropes that reeve through blocks and are hauled. Standing rigging is that part of a vessel's rigging which is made fast and not hauled upon.

RIGHT   To right the helm is to put it amidships.

RISE AND SHINE!   Used to summon the new watch.

> Rise and shine,
> For the Collins' Line.

ROARING FORTIES   The turbulent winds prevailing between the 40° and 50° South parallels.

ROBANDS   Originally rope-bands, small pieces of plaited line by which a sail was made fast to its yard.

ROGUE'S YARN   Originally *the King's yarn*. A rope yarn differing in color from the strands of the rope, and twisted in the reverse way. Used in the Royal Navy to mark the king's cordage and cables to discourage stealing.

ROLLING DOWN TO ST. HELENA   (Pronounced aleena.) Pleasant sailing.

ROPE-YARN SUNDAY (*n*)   Any day, save Sunday, set aside for washing, mending and making clothes.

ROPE'S END   Punishment administered with a piece of rope.

ROPE-YARN TEA   Keeping sailors constantly occupied in small tasks.

ROUND IN   To haul in quickly.

ROUND UP   To haul on a tackle.

RUN   The after part of a vessel's bottom, which rises and narrows as it approaches the sternpost; the distance a vessel has covered in a period of time. To scud before a gale is to run. To let go by the run is to let go altogether, instead of slacking off.

SAG   To drift; to sag to the leeward is to drift off bodily to the lee-ward. Also, a vessel that has settled amidships is said to have sagged —the opposite of *hogged*.

SAIL HO!   The lookout's cry when a sail is discovered at sea.

SAILING ON HER OWN BOTTOM   This phrase means that the vessel has already paid for herself.

SAILOR'S BLESSING   A curse, a bawling out.

SAILORS' FRIEND   The moon.

SAILOR'S PLEASURE   The privacy necessary to go over one's pos-sessions.

SAILORS' WAITER   The second mate.

SAILORS' WEATHER   A fair wind and plenty of it.

SAILS   Nickname for the sailmaker.

SALT HORSE   Beef or pork pickled in brine.

> "Old horse! old horse! what brought you here?"
> "From Sacarap to Portland Pier
> I've carted stone for many a year;
> Till, killed by blows and sore abuse,
> They salted me down for sailors' use.
> The sailors they do me despise,
> They turn me over and damn my eyes;
> Cut off my meat, and scrape my bones
> And heave the rest to Davy Jones."

(Sacarap has been identified by Mr. Storer B. Lunt in *The American Neptune*, 1945, as a part of Westbrook, Maine, located near Portland.)

There was an English version.

> "Old horse, old horse, what brought you here,
> After carrying sand for many a year,
> From Bantry Bay to Ballywhack,
> Where you fell down and broke your back?"
> "Now after years of such abuse,
> They salted me down for sailors' use,
> They tanned my hide and burned my bones,
> And sent me off to Davy Jones."

SAND IN YOUR EARS BEFORE MORNING, YOU'LL HAVE   A sailor expects to be wrecked.

SATURDAY NIGHT BOTTLES (*w*)   The rum issued by the captain after a whale has been taken.

SAVE-ALL   Sometimes *water sail*. Usually a sail set under other sails to catch all the wind.

SCOFF (*n*)   To eat.

SCHOONER   A vessel with two or more masts, fore-and-aft rigged. A topsail schooner is a vessel carrying square topsails. On the Great Lakes some lumber schooners were given auxiliary engines and were derisively called "teem kooners." *Schooner-rigged*, of unknown origin, indicates that a man is destitute.

'SCOUSE   See *Lobscouse*.

SCRIMSHAW, SCRIMSHANDER, SCRIMSHONT (*w*)   Carved work done by sailors out of the bones and teeth of the whale.

SCUD   To run before a squall or a gale.

SCUTTLE BUTT   Originally *scuttled butt*.   A cask with a hole cut in the head and holding water for drinking purposes. (*n*) Slang for a rumor.

SEA-CUNNY (CONNY)   A Lascar steersman.

SEA DOG   An old-time sailor.

SEA LAWYER   A sailor who knows his rights and is ready day and night to argue.

SEAMAN'S DISGRACE   A fouled anchor.

SEA PIE   The sailors' festive dish, made of meat or fish and vegetables, each in layers with pastry between.

SEA PIG   Porpoise meat.

SEE YOU IN LIVERPOOL   Parting hail of old sailors.

SEIZE   To tie up, bind, or make fast with rope yarn.

SEND   A ship sends when her head or stern pitches suddenly and violently out of the trough of the sea.

SHAKE A LEG (*n*)   Hurry up.

SHANGHAI   To kidnap a sailor while he is drunk or doped and place him aboard an outgoing vessel, originally one bound for Shanghai or other Chinese ports.

SHARK (LAND SHARK)   A lawyer or any sharp dealer ashore.

SHEET   A rope used in setting a sail.

SHEET ANCHOR   A vessel's largest anchor, carried in the waist and always ready in an emergency.

SHE SUCKS!   The happy cry set up when a pump sucked air, indicating that the ship was again dry.

SHELLBACK   An old sailor.

SHIP   A vessel with three or more masts, square-rigged on all. Regardless of the rig, a sailor always speaks of his vessel as his ship.

SHIPPED   Taken aboard: a sailor is shipped, so is the cargo. When a sea comes aboard it is said to be shipped.

SHIP BREAKER   One who breaks up old and decommissioned vessels.

SHIP'S COUSIN   Any one aboard who is neither a member of the crew or of the afterguard or a regular passenger. Sometimes a friend of the owner, or of the captain.

SHIP'S HUSBAND   The agent of the owner who takes charge of the vessel while she is in port and the officers and crew have gone ashore.

SHIPKEEPERS (w)   Men who remain on board when all boats are chasing whales.

SHIPPED THEIR QUARTER-DECK FACES (n)   The sailors' description of the stern expressions assumed by officers while on duty.

SHIPPED THEIR HOMEWARD-BOUND FACES   Said of officers of the merchant fleet who relaxed their severe discipline as the vessel neared its home port.

SHIPSHAPE AND BRISTOL FASHION   Everything neat and in its proper place.

SHORE SAINT AND SEA DEVIL   A common type of captain.

SHOOTING THE SUN   Taking its meridian altitude.

SHORT SEA A sea with the crests of waves close together—the opposite of a long sea.

SHOT Of the cable, a length of fifteen fathoms.

SHOT IN THE LOCKER, ANOTHER Originally this meant that there was still more chain to be let out. Later also slang for a reserve supply. When the sailor was financially embarrassed, his shot was low in the locker.

SHOW A LEG! Call used to awaken the new watch.

SHOW WILLING Said of a sailor who was ready for any task; the opposite of *hang back*.

SHOVE IN ONE'S OAR To interrupt a conversation.

SHOVE OFF To leave, to go away.

SHROUDS The set of ropes reaching from the mastheads to the vessel's sides, to support the masts. Standing rigging.

SINKAPORE Singapore.

SIX-WATER GROG A very thin drink, six parts water to one of rum.

SKIPPER The captain of a small vessel.

SKYSCRAPER A skysail when it is triangular in shape.

SKULL-JOE (SKULLY-JO, SCALJOS) (*f*) Dried codfish.

SLACK (SLACK AWAY) To pay out on a rope.

SLATCH A light passing wind, longer and stronger than a cat's-paw.

SLIP To let go a cable.

SLIP ROPE A rope bent to the cable just outside the hawsehole, and brought in on the weather counter, for slipping.

SLIPPING HIS WIND Said of a man who is dying.

SLOP CHEST The locker or chest containing sailor's clothes, tobacco, and other deepwater necessities, supplied to the crew, at a price, by the captain.

SLUM Slumgullion. Any stew served in the sailors' mess.

SLUE To turn anything around or over.

SLUNG HIS HAMMOCK IN THE BLOODY HOOKER Said of a sailor who has signed on.

**SMALL STUFF**   Spun yarn, marline, and the smallest kinds of rope.

**SMELL HELL, COULD**   A phrase used to describe a dangerous situation one has gone through.

**SMOKEJACK**   A steamship.

**SO!**   The order to 'vast heaving upon anything when it has come to the desired position.

**SOFTTACK**   White bread.

**SOFT-WATER MEN**   The professional seaman's term for yachtsmen and amateur sailors. "Any one who would go to sea for pleasure would go to hell for a vacation!"

**SOGER**   Soldier.   The worst term of reproach that could be applied to a sailor. It signified a shirker, a skulker, one who was always hanging back when heavy or dangerous duty was to be done.

**SOGER, MAHOUND**   A mahound was an Arab camel soldier, who slept with his mount, and was reputedly the world's laziest and dirtiest soldier.

**SOGER, PORT MAHON**   Port Mahon was originally an English fortified garrison on the Island of Minorca, and ceded to Spain in 1802. Later it became an American naval base and the Spanish soldiers practically lived by robbing drunken American sailors.

**SOLDIER'S WIND**   A wind that is equally fair for opposite courses, allowing a passage to be made without much nautical ability.

**SOOGY-MOOGY (SOUGEE)**   A mixture of soft soap, caustic soda, and water, used as a cleansing agent.

**SOUL AND BODY LASHINGS**   A temporary fastening, usually applied to the sailor's own clothing; a piece of yarn tied about the waist and between the legs to hold his oilskins in place while aloft in a gale.

**SOUL TO BE SAVED** (*n*)   " 'You have a soul to be saved, sir!' is a phrase which a man-of-war's man peculiarly applies to a humane and kind-hearted officer. It also implies that the majority of quarter-deck officers are regarded by them in such a light that they deny to them the possession of souls" (Melville).

**SOUND**   To measure the depth of water by lead and line.

SOUNDINGS   A ship is said to be in or on soundings when the bottom can be reached with the deep-sea lead. She is off soundings when the bottom cannot be reached.

SPEAK   To communicate with, as to speak another vessel.

SPELL   The term for the time given to any job. To spell a person is to relieve him at his work.

SPELL HO!   The call used to secure relief.

SPLICE   To join two rope-ends by interweaving their strands. When the splice is completed the ropes are said to be married.

SPLICE THE MAIN BRACE, ALL HANDS FORWARD TO   A summons to an extra ration of grog for work well done.

SPRING TIDE   The tides which occur at new moon and full moon, when the range between high and low tide is greatest.

SQUARE THE YARDS WITH THE BLOODY OLD ———, TO   To get even with someone, especially an officer who has imposed on you.

SQUEEGEE   Originally *squilgee*. A small board with a rubber edge used in drying the decks after flushing.

STASIA   St. Eustasius.

STAND BY   An old sea order to hold oneself ready for duty.

STANDING TO (or FROM)   The motion of a ship in sailing to or from an object at sea.

STANDING RIGGING   The part of the rigging used to support masts and spars and not altered in working the ship.

STARBOWLINS (STARBOLINS)   The men of the starboard watch.

STEADY, THE HELM!   To hold the ship as she goes.

STICK-AND-STRING SAILOR   An old-time sailing-ship sailor.

STIFF   Said of a vessel that can carry a great amount of sail without losing its stability. The opposite of *crank*.

STRETCH   The same as *tack*.

STRIKE   To lower sails or colors.

STRIKE A LIGHT, MEN!   An order to put some life into a task.

**STRONG BACKS AND WEAK HEADS**  A description of sailors.

**STRONG ENOUGH TO UNHAIR A DOG**  Blowing very hard.

**SUED**  To be left high and dry. If a vessel is left two feet above the water she is said to be sued by two feet.

**SUNDOWNER**  Sailors were supposed to be free when a ship moored at her home port, but some captains would not release the men until sundown, forcing them to do a full day's work. Also, slang for a man who will not take a drink until the day's work is done.

**SUN OVER THE FOREYARDS**  Time to have a drink.

**SUPERCARGO**  The business agent of the owner aboard a ship.

**SURGE**  A large wave. To surge a rope or cable is to slack off.

**SURGE HO!**  The order to slack it off.

**SVENSKER**  A Swedish sailor. Sometimes called *squarehead*.

**SWAB**  A cleaning mop made of old rope. A bucko's term for a sailor.

**SWABBER**  A man told off to work with a swab.

**SWABBER'S MATE**  A very ordinary seaman.

**SWALLOWED THE ANCHOR**  Said of a sailor who has left the sea.

**SWIG**  A very short haul on the halyards.

**SWIG AT THE HALYARDS**  A surreptitious drink taken when the officers are not looking.

**SWIVEL-EYED**  Cross-eyed or squint-eyed. Sometimes applied to a shore girl who has a roving eye.

**TACK**  The distance sailed with the wind on one side. Also, to put the vessel about so that from having the wind on one side, you bring it around on the other by way of her head. A vessel is on the starboard tack when she has the wind on her starboard side.

**TACKLE**  (Pronounced tay-kel.) A purchase formed by a rope rove through one or more blocks.

**TAKE A WALK UP LADDER LANE AND DOWN HAWSER STREET, TO**  To be executed by hanging.

TAFFRAIL The rail around the ship's stern.

TALL SHIP Originally a square-rigged vessel with topmasts, latterly any vessel with lofty masts. Also, a handsome ship.

TALL-WATER MAN A deep-sea sailor.

TARPAULIN MUSTER A collection taken up among sailors, usually to purchase liquor.

TAUNT High or tall.

TAUT Tight, firm. "He had a taut hand for his ship and his crew."

THIRD EYE, SAILOR'S The deep-sea lead.

THREE SHEETS TO THE WIND Drunk enough to find walking a little difficult. Sometimes *three sheets in the wind; three sheets to the wind and the fourth shaking.*

THROUGH THE CABIN WINDOW An officer who went directly to the quarter-deck without having served before the mast is said to have come in through the cabin window.

THROUGH THE HAWSEHOLE (HAWSEPIPE) Originally one who started to sea as a small boy was said to have come in through the hawsehole, but more generally the phrase was applied to one who had worked his way to command through all the grades.

TICKET An officer's certificate of rating.

TIMENOGUY "A rope carried taut between different parts of the vessel to prevent the sheet or tack of a course from getting foul, in working ship" (Dana). More commonly any labor- or time-saving device.

TIMONEER The helmsman.

TOM COX'S TRAVERSE Killing time; "two turns about the longboat and a pull at the scuttle butt."

TOM PEPPER A great liar. He was kicked out of hell because of his unbelievable yarns.

TOO MUCH OF THE MONKEY A little more harsh treatment than a sailor could stand.

TOWN HO! (w) "The ancient cry upon first sighting a whale from the masthead" (Melville).

TRICE  To haul up by means of a rope.

TRICK  A period of duty, usually at the wheel.

TRIM  The condition of a vessel's sails, cargo, or ballast, upon which her speed and seaworthiness depends.

TRIP  To raise (the anchor) clear of the bottom.

TUB OARSMAN (*w*)  The second oar from the steerer in a whaleboat. He tends the line as it leaves the tub.

TUMBLE HOME  Sometimes *fall home*. To slope inward from bottom to top; said of a ship's topsides. The opposite of *flare*.

UNBEND  To loosen, untie.

UNMOOR  To heave up one anchor so that the vessel rides at a single anchor.

UNDER THE LEE  Off the lee side.

UNSHIP  To detach or take away from its setting.

UP AND DOWN WIND  No wind at all.

UPHILL ROAD, THE  In packet-ship days, the westward passage. Owing to prevailing westerly winds, progress was slow.

UP ONE HATCHWAY AND DOWN THE OTHER  A form of soldiering or avoiding work.

'VAST  Avast; stop.

VEER  To shift; said of the wind. Also, to slack a rope or cable and let it run out.

VEER AND HAUL  To slack and haul alternately, as in warping.

WAIST  The part of the deck between the forecastle and the after deck.

WAISTERS  A general term for muscle men, green hands, and broken-down seamen who were used only on deck, for hauling ropes and cable. Sometimes called "sons of farmers," they were assigned to care for chicken coops, pig pens, potato lockers, etc. Also called *Jemmy Ducks, Jimmy Duxes*.

WARP   To move a vessel from one place to another by means of a rope made fast to some fixed object: also the rope used in the process.

WATCH   The period of time spent on duty. The anchor watch is the watch kept, usually by one or two men, while the vessel is at anchor or in port. On whaling ships a tryout watch was established when blubber was being tried out: the crew was divided into six-hour watches and continued working day and night until the work was completed.

WATCH AND WATCH   One watch on deck the other below; twelve hours' work each day.

WATCH HO! WATCH!   The cry of the man who heaves the deep-sea lead.

WATER BEWITCHED   A thin drink. From "water bewitched and rum begrudged."

WEAR   To turn a vessel around, so that, from having the wind on one side, you bring it upon the other, carrying her stern round by the wind. In tacking the same result is achieved by bringing the vessel's head round by the wind.

WEATHER   The direction from which the wind blows.

WESTERN OCEAN   The Atlantic north of the equator.

WET HER SALT (*f*)   A fisherman that has caught all she can carry and is homeward bound has wet her salt.

WET NURSE   More often *dry nurse*. A proficient mate who is shipped to check or balance an inefficient master.

WHERE AWAY?   What is the bearing?

WHISKERANDOES   An officer or passenger with a beard.

WHISTLING UP THE WIND   Talking wishfully or hopefully; from the practice of whistling for a fair wind during a calm.

WILD BOAT OF THE ATLANTIC   The American clipper *Dreadnought*, also known as *the* Liverpool Packet. See the chantey, "The Dreadnought."

WITHERSHINS (WIDDERSHINS)   Counterclockwise, against the sun.

WORKING UP   Hazing; assigning dirty, disagreeable, and dangerous tasks to a particular seaman—ostensibly a punitive measure but often a means of settling a grudge.

WORKING THEIR OLD IRON UP!   "Move smartly, you sogers, or I'll start working your old iron up," the threat of severe punishment by a driving mate.

YANKEE NEAT   The American equivalent for "all shipshape and Bristol fashion."

YARDARM TO YARDARM   The situation of two vessels lying alongside one another. Said of a sailor and a woman walking together.

YELLOW JACK   The flag "Q," quarantine. Also *yellow fever*.

YOU!   The only name some sailors ever had.

## Maxims

ANY fool can make sail but it needs a good sailor to take it in.

If he can brag without lying let him brag.

Come day, go day, God send Sunday.—A sailor's prayer for a day of rest.

The gallows and the sea refuse nothing.—A maxim expressing the seaman's contempt for his calling.

Growl you may, but go you must!—The sailor's philosophy, along with "You are allowed to think as you please, but you must not think aloud."

Horses at sea, asses ashore.—A sailor's description of the life he leads.

If it were not for sailors it would be a pleasure to go to sea.—The officers' opinion.

The more days the more dollars.—Simple arithmetic.

Never dance with the mate if you can dance with the captain. (f)—How to polish the apple.

Obey orders if you break owners.

One hand for yourself and one for the ship (the owners).—Caution.

He who shipped with the devil must sail with the devil.—A sailors' proverb.

A stern chase is a long one. (n)—A sailor's way of saying, "It's a long road that has no turning."

420

To work hard, to live hard, to die hard, and then to go to hell would
be hard indeed.—A sailor's belief.

What you can't carry you must drag.—Said of a vessel carrying
more canvas than necessary. Applied to one who has had too much
to drink.

Who wouldn't sell a farm and go to sea?—A sailor's cry when the
going gets difficult.

REELING'M OFF

# Index of Songs

## AMERICAN SEA SONGS AND CHANTEYS

# Bibliography
## A Sailor's Treasury

Adams, Robert C. *On Board the "Rocket."* Boston: 1879.

Albion, Robert Greenhalgh. *Square-Riggers on Schedule. The New York Sailing Packets to England, France and the Cotton Ports.* Princeton: 1938.

*American Neptune, The: A Quarterly Journal of Maritime History.* Vol. 1 to date. Salem, Mass: 1941–1950.

Ashley, Clifford W. *The Yankee Whaler.* Boston: 1938. Contains an excellent glossary of whaling terms.

Ayres, J. A. *Legends of Montauk.* New York: 1849.

Bishop, W. H. "Fish and Men in the Maine Islands," *Harper's Magazine,* September, 1880.

Baring-Gould, S. *Curious Myths of the Middle Ages.* New York: n.d.

Barker, H. M. *The Old Sailor's Jolly Boat. Tales and Yarns to Please All Hands.* London: n.d.

Bassett, Fletcher S. *Sea Phantoms, or Legends and Superstitions of the Sea and Sailors.* Chicago: 1885.

Bassett, Wilbur. *Wander-Ships, Folk Stories of the Sea.* Chicago: 1917.

Brady, William. *Kedge Anchor.* Many editions.

Bowen, Dana T. *Lore of the Lakes.* Daytona Beach, Fla.: 1940.

Bowen, Frank C. *Sea Slang.* London: n.d.

Bradford, Gershom. *A Glossary of Sea Terms.* New York: 1946.

Brewer, E. Cobham. *The Reader's Handbook.* London: 1923.

Bullen, Frank T. *The Cruise of the Cachalot.* New York: n.d.

Canfield, Geo., and Dalzell, Geo. W. *The Law of the Sea.* New York: 1921.

Cheever, Henry T. *The Whale and His Captors.* New York: 1849.

Clark, Arthur H. *The Clipper Ship Era, 1843–1869.* New York: 1920.

Clements, Rex. *A Gypsy of the Horn.* London: 1924.

Cleveland, Richard J. *Narrative of Voyages and Commercial Enterprises.* 2 vols. Cambridge: 1842.

Colcord, Joanna Carver. *Sea Language Comes Ashore.* New York: 1945.

Colton, Walter. *The Sea and the Sailor.* New York: 1860.

Cooper, James Fenimore. *The Red Rover.* Philadelphia: 1838.

Coxere, Edward. *Adventures at Sea.* Edited by E. H. W. Meterstein. New York: 1946.

*Cruise of the Bacchante, 1879–82, The.* London: n.d.

Dana, Richard Henry. *Two Years before the Mast.* Boston: 1840.

———. *The Seaman's Friend.* Boston: 1869.

de Lys, Claudia. *A Treasury of American Superstitions.* New York: 1948.

Drake, Samuel Adams. *New England Legends and Folklore.* Boston: 1883.

*Fisherman's Own Book, The.* Gloucester: 1881.

Gibbons, Thomas. *Boxing the Compass.* London: n.d.

Gould, R. T. *The Case of the Sea Serpent.* London: 1930.

Harlow, Frederick Pease. *The Making of a Sailor, or Sea Life aboard a Yankee Square-Rigger.* Salem: 1928.

Hart, J. C. *Miriam Coffin.* San Francisco: 1872.

Hawes, Charles Boardman. *Whaling.* New York: 1924.

Hazen, Jacob A. *Five Years before the Mast, or Life in the Forecastle aboard of a Whaler and Man-of-War.* Chicago and New York: 1886.

Higginson. T. W. *Tales of the Enchanted Islands of the Atlantic.* New York: 1898.

*History of the Mutiny at Spithead and the Nore.* Philadelphia: 1845.

Hone, William. *Table Book.* London: 1827–28.

Hudson, Henry. "A Second Voyage or Employment of Master Henry Hudson," in *Henry Hudson, the Navigator.* London: Hakluyt Society, 1860.

Inwards, Richard. *Weather Lore. A Collection of Proverbs, Sayings, and Rules concerning the Weather.* London: 1898.

Irving, Washington. *The Life and Voyages of Christopher Columbus.* 2 vols. New York: 1828.

———. *Bracebridge Hall.* New York: 1824.

———. *Chronicles of Wolfert's Roost.* New York: 1855.

Jal, A. *Scènes de la vie maritime.* Paris: 1830.

Jones, W. *Credulities, Past and Present.* London: 1880.

———. *Broad, Broad Ocean.* N.p.: n.d.

Leslie, Robert C. *Old Sea Wings, Ways, and Words, in the Days of Oak and Hemp.* London: 1890.

Livermore, Samuel T. *A History of Block Island.* Hartford: 1877.

Lovette, Leland P. *Naval Customs, Traditions and Usage.* Annapolis: 1939.

Lovette, Leland P. *School of the Sea: The Annapolis Tradition in American Life*. New York: 1941.

Macy, Obed. *History of Nantucket*. Boston: 1835.

Massachusetts Historical Society Collections.

McFee, William. *The Law of the Sea*. Philadelphia: 1950.

Meigs, John Forsyth. *The Story of the Seamen*. 2 vols. Philadelphia: 1924.

Melville, Herman. *Complete Works*. London: 1922.

Moore, John Hamilton. *The Practical Navigator and Seaman's New Daily Assistant*. Ninth Edition. London: 1791. Contains a glossary of eighteenth-century sea terms.

Morison, Samuel Eliot. *Maritime History of Massachusetts*. Boston: 1921.

———. *Admiral of the Ocean Sea. A Life of Christopher Columbus*. Boston: 1942.

Morris, Richard B. *Government and Labor in Early America*. New York: 1946.

Nordhoff, Charles. *Whaling and Fishing*. Cincinnati: 1856.

Olmsted, Francis A. *Incidents of a Whaling Voyage*. New York: 1841.

O'Reilly, J. B. *Songs from the Southern Seas*. Boston: 1873.

Pease, Zephaniah W. *History of New Bedford*. New Bedford: n.d.

———. *A Visit to the Museum of the Old Dartmouth Historical Society*. New Bedford: 1932.

Perley, M. H. *Reports on the Sea and River Fisheries of New Brunswick*. Fredericton: 1852.

Rappaport, Angelo S. *Superstitions of Sailors*. London: 1928.

Roads, Samuel. *The History and Traditions of Marblehead*. Boston: 1881.

Rowe, William Hutchinson. *The Maritime History of Maine*. New York: 1948.

Russell, William Clark. *A Voyage to the Cape*. London: n.d.

Samuels, Capt. S. *From the Forecastle to the Cabin*. New York: 1887.

Sanceau, Elaine. *Henry the Navigator: The Story of a Great Prince and His Times*. New York: 1947.

Scoresby, William. *Arctic Regions and the Northern Whale Industry*. 2 vols. London: 1820.

Scoresby, William, Jr. *The Whaleman's Adventures in the Southern Ocean*. London: 1859.

Scott, Michael. *Tom Cringle's Log*. 2 vols. Edinburgh: 1833.

Shay, Frank. *Here's Audacity! American Legendary Heroes*. New York: 1930.

Spears, John R. *The Story of the New England Whalers*. New York: 1910.

Starbuck, Alexander. *History of the American Whale Fishery*. Waltham: 1878.

Tripp, William Henry. *"There Go Flukes!"* New Bedford: 1938.

Winsor, Justin. *Narrative and Critical History of America*. 8 vols. Boston: 1889.